MADAGASCAR

Highlights

D0526270

Daniel Austin

Hilary Bradt

Edition 1

Bradt Travel Guides Ltd, UK
The Globe Pequot Press Inc, USA

Bradt

About this book

Since the 1980s, Bradt Travel Guides has been publishing the most widely respected travel guide to Madagascar – a book with extensive details of budget hotels and public transport targeted especially at backpackers and independent travellers. By contrast, this 'highlights' guidebook is more selective in the information it offers, and is written for the traveller on (or planning to go on) an organised tour. It has two main aims: first, to help those considering a vacation to decide what they would like to see and do, and therefore to construct their itinerary or liaise with tour operators in an informed way; and, second, to provide an entertaining, colourful and informative guide to carry on the trip itself. With that in mind, the book provides overviews of towns, parks and other attractions that rank as possible highlights, a quick summary of practicalities and a short list of recommended accommodation. The selections are made by Daniel Austin in collaboration with Hilary Bradt – two of the world's foremost experts on Madagascar. In addition, we have called upon the expertise of some of the leading tour operators – those who know best what Madagascar has to offer – to recommend their favourite lodges and itineraries. Those tour operators were carefully chosen by Bradt Travel Guides and invited to contribute on the basis of their reputations for excellence; they also made a payment towards the production costs of the book.

These pages are unique in bringing together the selections of top writers and top operators, ensuring this is the most useful guidebook available to those planning an organised tour to Madagascar.

Tour operator input

Accommodation in this guide has been carefully selected and reviewed by the following tour operators: Aardvark Safaris, Audley Travel, Extraordinary Expeditions, Imagine Africa and Rainbow Tours. These and the following operators have also contributed interviews with their opinions on Madagascar's best bits: ASISTEN Travel, Cortez Travel & Expeditions, Holidays Madagascar, Le Voyageur, Madagascar Airtours, Madagascar Rental Tour, Mora-Travel, Nomad Tours, Pulse Africa, RAMARTOUR Madagascar, Rova Travel Tours and Zà Tours. See pages 66–9 for more information on these operators, including details on how to book.

The authors

(SAG)

Daniel Austin

Daniel Austin aims to visit Madagascar
every year and has spent a combined total of 15 months exploring and
photographing the island since 2004. He is continually amazed by how
much is yet to be discovered in the country and, far from becoming
boring, each visit only makes him more eager to return. He founded
the Madagascar Library (® www. madagascar-library.com) and is a
committee member of the Anglo-Malagasy Society, which organises
Madagascar-themed events (® www.anglo-malagasysociety.co.uk).

Hilary Bradt

Hilary Bradt's career as an occupational therapist ended when potential
employers noticed that the time taken off for travel exceeded the periods
of employment. With her former husband George, she self-published
her first guidebook in 1974 during an extended journey through South
America. As well as running Bradt Travel Guides, Hilary worked for 25
years as a tour leader in Madagascar. Her in-depth knowledge of the
country has brought her lecture engagements at the Royal Geographical
Society, the Smithsonian Institution and on board expedition cruise
ships, as well as numerous commissions for travel articles. She now
lives in semi-retirement in Devon.

Daniel's story

I fell under the spell of Madagascar long before I had an opportunity to go there.
It was the island's bizarre flora and fauna that first attracted my interest, but
as I fed my curiosity with countless books I soon discovered that the people,
their culture and their language are equally intriguing. When I finally visited,
Madagascar exceeded all my expectations. I have since returned regularly
in various capacities: as a tourist, researcher, photographer, conservation
volunteer and trip lecturer. After my third three-month trip I had the good
fortune to meet Hilary Bradt who asked me to contribute to her guidebook,
which had by then become my travel bible. I soon became more and more
deeply involved with updating subsequent editions, as well as taking on the
role of editor of *Madagascar Wildlife: A visitor's guide*. Always keen to have
another excuse to explore Madagascar further, I am delighted to have been
asked to write this 'highlights' guide too.

Contents

Madagascar Highlights 103

List of maps

Feedback request

If you have any comments about this guidebook (good or bad), we would welcome your feedback. Please contact us via email on Ⓔ info@bradtguides.com. Alternatively you can add a review of the book to Ⓦ www.bradtguides.com or Amazon.

Introduction
Hilary Bradt

This picture below, stitched for me by the women at the Centre Fihavanana in Antananarivo, encapsulates everything that is special about Madagascar. Look at the detail: a beautiful white-sand beach, the Malagasy busy about their everyday lives, with children playing and their zebu cattle adorning the hills. Filling in all the spaces are baobabs, chameleons, tortoises and lemurs. Yes, it's Madagascar all right.

I first visited the island in 1976, fell in love with it, and returned in 1982 with a hardy group of tourists. Things were different then – to say that the infrastructure was unreliable is a lie; it was virtually non-existent. The roads were so potholed that at one point an entire car had disappeared into the chasm, the hotels were green with mildew and infested with cockroaches, planes were cancelled on a whim, and the food was dubious. But the wildlife was simply wonderful, and the people delightful. The most recent occasion that I accompanied a group of wildlife enthusiasts was in 2010; we ate superbly, slept in blissful comfort, and travelled on well-made roads. And the wildlife was simply wonderful. In fact these days I actually see more new species, and view the lemurs more closely, than I did 30 years ago. And that hardly seems fair – discomfort should be rewarded with exceptional sightings.

Why is it so much easier now to see the wildlife for which Madagascar is famed? Well, it's partly a question of habituation. The more that wild animals are exposed to harmless people, the sooner they lose their

fear. Today there are far more national parks and, on the whole, the wildlife is better protected than it was in the 1980s. Access is also so much easier and there is good accommodation near the best national parks and reserves, so visitors get the chance to see wildlife at the

Hilary Bradt (JB)

ideal time of day: early morning and evening. But Madagascar isn't just about wildlife. Someone once wrote to me saying 'The beauty of the land I had expected, but the gentle open-heartedness and hospitality of the people took me by storm.' And, yes, that is a surprise in one of the world's poorest countries. But as most of us know, wealth and happiness are not natural partners. That brings me to the Centre Fihavanana, where the Sisters of the Good Shepherd work with the poorest of the poor. They provide food and education for street children and

work for their mothers. The hardship these women and their children have had to face is sometimes horrendous, but visit the centre and you are enveloped in laughter and hope.

With so much going for it, it was inevitable that, in 1986, I would write and publish the first English-language guidebook to Madagascar. It was, after all, my favourite country. The booklet had 54 pages and just described the few places accessible to visitors. Every couple of years another edition would appear, and as my readers became more adventurous, the book became more and more comprehensive. By the ninth edition the guide had reached a chunky 468 pages. That was when I brought in Daniel Austin as co-author and we decided that a slimmer guide focusing on the places on most tour operators' itineraries should take its place alongside the 'fat guide' used by independent travellers.

This is it. We hope that every page will help you plan the best possible trip to match your interests, as well as providing information and entertainment while in the country. You will probably only visit Madagascar once, but we hope that you return to your home country not only euphoric from what you've seen and experienced, but determined to go again.

Hilary Bradt

Introducing Madagascar

1 History and People

By global standards, the history of human habitation in Madagascar is extremely short. There is a sharp contrast between mainland Africa - just across the other side of the Mozambique Channel - where mankind has been living for hundreds of thousands of years and Madagascar, which was peopled just a few centuries ago. But by no means does this make the Malagasy a less interesting people. Today's population has a complex mix of Malayo-Polynesian and African ancestry and the result is a fascinating genetic, cultural and linguistic melting pot. This unique Asia-meets-Africa experience is full of surprises. The Malagasy are proud of their island and always welcoming to visitors. Many a tourist has returned from a first trip to Madagascar expressing the sentiment that it was the wildlife for which they went, but the warmth and generosity of the people that touched them most and which will remain strongest in their memory.

Madagascar at a glance

Full name Republic of Madagascar (*Repoblikan'i Madagasikara*)
Motto *Tanindrazana, Fahafahana, Fandrosoana* (Fatherland, Liberty, Progress)
Location Off the coast of Mozambique in the Indian Ocean
Size 587,041km^2 (world's 4th largest island; 2$^1/_2$ times size of Britain/Minnesota)
Coastline 4,828km
Population 22$^1/_2$ million (2012 est); growing at 3% per year
Life expectancy Male 61 years; female 65 years
Age structure 0-14yrs 44% of population; 15-64 yrs 53%; 65yrs+ 3%
Poverty 68% live on less than US$1/day; 90% on less than US$2/day
Literacy 69% of over-15s can read and write
Capital city Antananarivo (Tana; Tananarive)
Major towns Fianarantsoa, Toliara (Tulear), Taolagnaro (Fort Dauphin),
Toamasina (Tamatave), Mahajanga (Majunga), Antsiranana (Diego Suarez)
Transport 7,617km paved roads; 854km railways; 432km navigable waterways
Main international airport Ivato Airport, Antananarivo (TNR)
Other main airports Antsiranana (DIE), Mahajanga (MJN), Morondava (MOQ),
Nosy Be (NOS), Toamasina (TMM), Taolagnaro (FTU), Toliara (TLE)
National airline Air Madagascar
Visa Required by all tourists; available on arrival; max 90 days; see page 79
Leader Andry Rajoelina (President of the High Transitional Authority)
GDP US$19bn (PPP); US$8.3bn (OER); US$860 (per capita PPP)
Main agriculture Rice, coffee, vanilla, sugarcane, cloves, cocoa, cassava
(tapioca), beans, bananas, peanuts, livestock products
Main exports Vanilla, prawns, coffee, sugarcane, cloves, cocoa, pepper, peanuts
Main import partners China (13%), Thailand (12%), Bahrain (7%), France (6%)
Official languages Malagasy, French
Religions Indigenous beliefs (52%), Christian (41%), Muslim (7%)
Time zone 3 hours ahead of GMT (no daylight savings time observed)
Electricity 220 volts, European-style round-pin sockets
Currency Ariary (Ar; MGA)
International dialling code +261 (followed by 20 for landlines)
Internet domain extension .mg
Driving side Right
Independence 26 June 1960 (from France)
Flag Horizontal bands of red and green alongside a vertical white band (the red
represents sovereignty, the green stands for hope, and the white for purity)
Public holidays 1 Jan, 29 Mar, Easter (movable), 1 May, Ascension Day (movable),
Whit Monday (movable), 26 Jun, 15 Aug, 1 Nov, 11 Dec, 25 Dec

History

The island is not thought to have been settled until around 1,500 years ago (see page 28) and much of the history prior to the 16th century has not been recorded in detail.

The first Europeans

The first Europeans to sight Madagascar were the Portuguese in 1500, although there is evidence of earlier Arab settlements on the coast. Attempts to establish French and British stations during the next couple of centuries failed due to disease and hostile locals. A remarkably homogeneous and united country was thus able to develop under its own rulers.

By the early 1700s, the island had become a haven for pirates and slave traders. These both traded with and fought the local kings who ruled the clans of the east and west coasts.

Rise of the Merina Kingdom

The powerful Merina Kingdom was forged by **Andrianampoinimerina**, who established the tiny kingdom of Ambohimanga in 1787. By 1808 he had united the various Merina kingdoms and conquered the other highland tribes. King Andrianampoinimerina was considered to have almost divine powers and his obedient subjects were well provided for: each was given enough land for his family's rice needs, with some left over to pay a rice tribute to the king, and community projects such as the building of irrigation canals were imposed through forced labour (though with bonuses for the most productive workers). The burning of forests was forbidden.

Conquest was always foremost in the monarch's mind, however, and it was his son, **King Radama I**, who fulfilled his father's command to 'Take the sea as frontier to your kingdom'. This king had a friendly relationship with Britain, which in 1817 and 1820 signed treaties under which Madagascar was recognised as an independent state. Britain supplied arms and advisers to help Radama conquer most of the rest of the island.

King Andrianampoinimerina as envisaged by a Malagasy artist. (ML)

A shipwrecked English slave boy

The most intriguing insight into 18th-century Madagascar was provided by the diary of Robert Drury, who was shipwrecked off the island in 1701 and spent over 16 years there, mainly as a slave to the Antandroy or Sakalava chiefs.

Drury was only 15 when his boat foundered off the southern tip of Madagascar (he had been permitted by his father back in Britain to go to India with trade goods). The survivors were treated well by the local king but kept prisoners for reasons of status. After a few days they made a bid for freedom by seizing the king and some of his courtiers as hostages and marching east. They were followed by hundreds of warriors who watched for any relaxation in the guard. They were without water for three days as they crossed the burning hot desert and just as they came into sight of the Mandrare River (having released the hostages) they were attacked and many were speared to death.

For ten years Drury was a slave of the Antandroy royal family. He worked with cattle and eventually was appointed royal butcher, the task of slaughtering a cow for ritual purposes being supposedly that of someone of royal blood – and lighter skin. Drury was a useful substitute. He also acquired a wife.

Wars with the neighbouring Mahafaly gave him the opportunity to escape north across the desert to St Augustine's Bay. Here he hoped to find a ship to England, but his luck turned and he again became a slave, this time to the Sakalava. When a ship did come in, his master refused to consider selling him to the captain, and Drury's desperate effort to get word to the ship through a message written on a leaf came to nothing when the messenger lost the leaf and substituted another less meaningful one. Two more years of relative freedom followed, and he finally got away in 1717. Ever quick to put his experience to good use, he later returned to Madagascar as a slave trader!

Some consider his diary, published in 1729, to be a work of fiction, although Robert Drury is known to have existed. The places and events described correlate so well with reality, however, that it is almost certainly a genuine, if embellished, account. A ghost-writer is thought to have been involved in preparing the diary for publication, and many scholars believe that to have been none other than Daniel Defoe.

Cover of the 1897 edition (ML)

London Missionary Society

To further strengthen ties between the two countries, Radama invited the London Missionary Society (LMS) to send teachers. In 1818 a small group of Welsh missionaries arrived in Tamatave (Toamasina). David Jones and Thomas Bevan brought their wives and children, but within a few weeks only Jones remained alive; the others had all died of fever. Jones retreated to Mauritius, but returned to Madagascar in 1820, along with equally dedicated missionary teachers and artisans, to devote the rest of his life to its people. The British influence was established and a written language using the Roman alphabet was introduced nationwide for the first time.

The 'Wicked Queen' and her successors

On his death in 1828, Radama's widow succeeded to the throne. Rejecting her late husband's pro-British politics, **Queen Ranavalona I** was determined to rid the land of Christianity and European influence, and reigned long enough largely to achieve her aim. These were repressive times for the Malagasy as well as foreigners. Suspected evildoers were made to swallow pieces of poisoned chicken skin; only those who regurgitated them all and survived the effects of the poison were declared innocent. The queen drove the missionaries out of Madagascar and many Malagasy Christians were martyred, often by being hurled over a cliff near her palace. (The tables turned shortly after the queen's death, however, when Christianity became the official religion of the Merina Kingdom.)

Ranavalona I is often cited as one of the most evil rulers in history. (ML)

After Ranavalona I came **King Radama II**, a peace-loving pro-European monarch who was assassinated after a two-year reign in 1863. His widow, **Rasoherina**, succeeded him, but the monarchy was now in decline and power shifted to the prime minister, who shrewdly married the queen. He was overthrown by his brother, who continued the tradition by marrying three successive queens and exercising all the power.

The two-man industrial revolution

Technology was largely introduced to Madagascar by two remarkable Europeans: James Cameron, a Scot, and Jean Laborde, a Frenchman.

James Cameron arrived in 1826 during the country's 'British phase' when the London Missionary Society had attempted to set up local craftsmen to produce goods in wood, metal, leather and cotton. He was only 26 but was already skilled as a carpenter and weaver, with a broad knowledge of other subjects. Cameron seemed able to turn his hand to almost anything mechanical. Among his achievements were Madagascar's first printing press, a reservoir, an aqueduct, and the production of bricks.

Cameron's success in making soap from local materials ensured his royal favour after the xenophobic Queen Ranavalona came to power. But when Christianity was forbidden in 1835, he left for South Africa. He returned in 1863, when the missionaries were once more welcome, to oversee the building of churches, a hospital, and the stone exterior to the queen's palace.

Jean Laborde (*below right*) was even more of a renaissance man. The son of a blacksmith, he was shipwrecked off the east coast in 1831. Ranavalona, no doubt pleased to find a less godly European, asked him to manufacture muskets and gunpowder. With incredible initiative, he produced munitions and arms, bricks and tiles, pottery, glass and porcelain, silk, soap, candles, cement, dyes, sugar, rum... in fact just about everything a thriving country in the 19th century needed. He ran a farm which experimented with suitable crops and animals, and a country estate for the aristocracy.

So successful was Laborde in making Madagascar self-sufficient that foreign trade was discontinued and foreigners – with the exception of Laborde – expelled. He remained in the queen's favour until 1857 when he too was expelled because of involvement in a plot to replace the queen by her son. The 1,200 workmen who had laboured without pay in the foundries of Mantasoa rose up and destroyed everything – tools, machinery and buildings. The factories were never rebuilt, and Madagascar's industrial revolution came to an abrupt end.

Laborde returned as French consul in 1861. A dispute over his inheritance was one of the pretexts used by the French as justification for the 1883-85 war.

(ML)

Colonial years

Even during the period of British influence, the French maintained a longstanding claim to Madagascar and in 1883 they attacked and occupied the main ports. The Franco-Malagasy War lasted 30 months, and was concluded by a harsh treaty declaring much of Madagascar a French protectorate. The prime minister, hoping for British support, managed to evade full acceptance of this status but the British government signed away its interest in the 1890 Convention of Zanzibar.

The French finally imposed their rule by invasion in 1895, forcing the queen to sign a treaty establishing the whole island as a protectorate of France. Within two years she had been exiled to Réunion, and then to Algeria, and the monarchy abolished.

The defeat of the Malagasy as depicted in an 1895 Paris newspaper. (ML)

The first French Governor-General of Madagascar, Joseph Simon Gallieni, was an able and relatively benign administrator. He set out to break the power of the Merina aristocracy and remove the British influence by banning the teaching of English and making French the official language.

The British in Madagascar

Britain has played an important part in the military history of Madagascar. Before colonisation British mercenaries trained the Malagasy army to fight the French. During World War I 46,000 Malagasy were recruited for the allies and over 2,000 killed. In 1942, when Madagascar was under the control of the Vichy French, the British invaded the island to forestall the possibility of the Japanese navy making use of the great natural harbour of Diego Suarez (Antsiranana).

In 1943 Madagascar was handed back to France under a Free French government. An uprising by the Malagasy against the French in 1947 was bloodily repressed (some 80,000 are said to have died) but the spirit of nationalism lived on and in 1960 the country achieved full independence.

(ML)

Independence

The first president, **Philibert Tsiranana** (*left*), was pro-France but in 1972 he stepped down in the face of increasing unrest and student demonstrations against French neo-colonialism. An interim government headed by General Ramanantsoa ended France's special position and introduced a more nationalistic foreign and economic policy.

In 1975, after a period of turmoil, a military directorate handed power to a naval officer, **Didier Ratsiraka**, who had served as Foreign Minister under Ramanantsoa. Ratsiraka established the Second Republic, changing the country's name from The Malagasy Republic to The Democratic Republic of Madagascar. He introduced his own brand of 'Christian-Marxism' and his manifesto, set out in a 'little red book' (*below right*), was approved by referendum. Socialist policies such as the nationalisation of banks followed.

Within a few years the economy had collapsed and has remained in severe difficulties ever since. Ratsiraka was nevertheless twice re-elected, though there were claims of widespread ballot rigging and intimidation.

(ML)

Political crisis of 2002

The official results of the elections showed the then mayor of Antananarivo (Tana), **Marc Ravalomanana**, leading with 46%, necessitating a second round. Results collected by independent observers indicating Ravalomanana was actually the outright winner with 52% were rejected by the incumbent president Ratsiraka. Both men declared victory. Ravalomanana installed his own ministers in government offices and Ratsiraka retreated with his government to his hometown of Toamasina.

The world looked on as the farcical situation of one country with two presidents and two capital cities descended into stalemate. In an attempt to gain the upper hand, Ratsiraka's supporters isolated Tana by dynamiting the bridges on the main transport routes into the city. The people of Tana faced a tenfold increase in the price of fuel, and basic staples such as rice, sugar and salt disappeared from the shops. Flights were grounded; tourism ceased. As the months passed, the blockade caused malnutrition and death to the vulnerable in Tana and hardship to all. Many businesses faced bankruptcy. Eventually the balance of power slowly shifted and Ratsiraka finally fled to France.

The international community soon recognised Ravalomanana as rightful president. He set about rebuilding the infrastructure, launching an ambitious road-building programme, and putting in motion a conservation plan to triple the protected areas. He is also credited with significant improvements in education, health and the reduction of corruption. As a successful businessman, Ravalomanana understood well the importance of promoting foreign trade and investment, but a blurring of his political role with his business interests was to be his eventual downfall.

The 2009 coup

Halfway through Ravalomanana's second term in office, the young mayor of Tana, **Andry Rajoelina** (*below right*), made an unexpected challenge to his presidency. Accusing Ravalomanana of undemocratic behaviour and abuse of his position, Rajoelina mustered sufficient military and popular support to stage a successful *coup d'état*. Ravalomanana fled to mainland Africa when the self-appointed High Transitional Authority vowed to capture and imprison him.

In the three years since, Rajoelina has acted with even less democratic decorum than the president he ousted and consequently he has failed to win international recognition as leader of Madagascar. This lack of legitimacy has helped to make impoverished Malagasy even poorer. Growth in economic output has declined to less than 1%, new foreign investment has slowed to a trickle, tourist income has fallen and most non-humanitarian aid has ground to a halt. Excuses are made as deadlines for organising democratic elections come and go. Meanwhile Rajoelina has been making constitutional and legal changes that will favour him if and when elections finally are held.

(HM)

People

Archaeologists believe that the first people arrived in Madagascar from Indonesian Borneo roughly 1,500 years ago. A journey in a reconstructed boat of those times has proved that a direct crossing of the Indian Ocean was possible, though most experts agree that it is much more likely that the immigrants came in their outrigger canoes via southern India and east Africa, establishing small colonies *en route*. The strong African element in the coastal populations of Madagascar probably derived from later migrations from these colonies since their language is also essentially Malayo-Polynesian with only slightly more Bantu-Swahili words.

Later arrivals, mainly on the east coast, from Arabia and elsewhere in the Indian Ocean, were also absorbed into the Malagasy-speaking population, while leaving their mark in certain local customs clearly derived from Islam. The two-continent origin of the Malagasy is easily observed, from the highland tribes who most resemble Indonesians, to the African type characterised by the Bara or Makoa in the south. In between are the elements of both races which make the Malagasy so varied and attractive in appearance. Thus there is racial diversity but relative uniformity of culture and language.

Ethnic groups and their customs

The different clans or tribes of Madagascar are based mainly upon old kingdoms. But traditions are changing and in today's more fluid society the groups are merging. Nevertheless, most Malagasy people

Peanut seller in Tana (SJB)

still consider themselves to belong to a particular ethnic group, of which there are traditionally considered to be 18.

The **Merina** are the people of the highlands around the capital city, with straight hair and typically Asian features. Most Merina houses are built of brick or mud; often these are two-storey dwellings where the people live mainly upstairs. Their villages generally have a church – probably two: Catholic and Protestant. There is much irrigated rice cultivation, and the Merina were the first tribe to become skilled in architecture and metallurgy. *Famadihana* (see opposite) is essentially a Merina custom.

To the east of the Merina are found the **Bezanozano**. The name means 'many small plaits' and refers to their traditional hairstyle. They are thought to be one of the first tribes to become established in Madagascar.

Further east still, the coast region between Nosy Varika and Antalaha is home to a large tribe called the **Betsimisaraka**. Their culture has been influenced by Europeans, particularly pirates. The Betsimisaraka cultivate rice, vanilla, coffee and lychees, and often wear clothes made from locally woven raffia. Traditional superstitious beliefs include ghosts, mermaids and rice-stealing goblins.

The turning of the bones

The core spiritual belief of the Malagasy is in the power of their ancestors. Recently passed-on generations are considered to exercise influence over all aspects of the lives of the living, so burial, exhumation and second burial are an important focus.

The reburial ceremony practiced by the Merina and Betsileo is known as the turning of the bones, or *famadihana*. This is a joyful occasion which occurs about every seven years after first burial, and provides the opportunity to communicate with and remember a loved one. The remains of the selected relative are taken from the tomb, rewrapped in a new burial shroud and carried around the tomb a few times (or even through the village) before being replaced. Meanwhile the corpse is informed of all the latest events. Generous quantities of alcohol are consumed amid a festive atmosphere with much dancing and music.

By law a *famadihana* may take place only in the dry season (June–September). It can last up to a week and involves considerable expense, as befits the most important celebration for any family. Variations of the ceremony are practised by several other tribes.

(FL)

13

Rice: a national obsession

The Malagasy have always had an almost mystical attachment to rice. King Andrianampoinimerina declared: 'Rice and I are one,' and loyalty to the Merina king was symbolised by industry in the rice paddies.

Today the Betsileo are masters of rice cultivation (they manage three harvests a year, rather than the normal two) and their neat terraces are a distinctive part of the scenery of the central highlands. However, rice is grown throughout most of the island, either in irrigated paddies or watered by the rain.

Rice production is labour-intensive. First the ground must be prepared for the seeds. Often this is done by chasing zebu cattle round and round to break and soften the clods – a muddy job, but evidently great fun for the boys who do it. Seeds are germinated in a small nursery plot and replanted in the irrigated paddies when half grown. In October and November you will see groups of women bent over in knee-deep water performing this arduous work.

The Malagasy eat rice three times a day, the average annual consumption being 135kg per capita – the highest of any nation in the world – although this is declining because of the availability of other foods and reduced productivity. Rice marketing was nationalised in 1976, but this resulted in such a dramatic drop in the amount of rice reaching the open market that restrictions were lifted in 1984. By that time it was too late to reverse the decline, which was mainly due to the decay of irrigation works. Despite a steady increase in acreage of paddy fields, frequently at the expense of the precious forest, production continues to fall.

Planting out the rice is backbreaking work. (SE)

Small farmers grow rice only for their own consumption but are forced to sell part of their crop for instant cash. Richer families in the community store this grain and sell it back at a profit later. To solve this small-scale exploitation, village co-operatives have been set up to buy rice and sell it back to the farmer at an agreed price, or at a profit to outsiders if any of the crop is left over.

(SE)

The southern highlands around Fianarantsoa are inhabited by the **Betsileo** people. Known for their agricultural prowess, they are energetic and expert rice producers. Their irrigated terraced rice fields are a prominent feature of the southern highland landscape. *Famadihana* was introduced to their culture by the Merina at the time of Queen Ranavalona I. The Betsileo traditionally lived in huts made from woven stems and leaves of plants, with wooden huts reserved for the nobles. These were often adorned with decorative motifs or even zebu horns. Nowadays dwellings in the Betsileo region are typically of a mud and brick construction, similar to those of the Merina.

A small clan of some 15,000 people distributed among a few dozen villages to the northwest of Fianarantsoa are known as the **Zafimaniry** – sometimes considered a subgroup of the Betsileo. The Zafimaniry are known for their woodcarvings and sculpture, and indeed the skills of these people area were declared a UNESCO Intangible Cultural Heritage in 2002 in an effort to protect the traditions. Houses are made from vegetable fibres, wood and bamboo and are constructed without nails so that they can be dismantled and moved.

The region of the **Tanala** (literally 'people of the forest') is to the east of the Betsileo. Traditionally they are rice and coffee growers who live in houses often built on stilts. Their burial customs include keeping the corpse for up to a month. Coffins are made from large trees to which sacrifices are sometimes offered when they are cut down. These may then be buried in the forest. Neighbouring the Tanala along the east coast are three very small tribal regions: those of the **Antambahoaka**, famous for their seven-yearly mass circumcision ceremonies, the **Antaifasy**, who fish in lakes and rivers, and the **Antaimoro** – among the most recent arrivals in Madagascar – whose culture shows a strong Arab influence.

Originally from the southwest near Toliara, the **Bara** are nomadic cattle raisers who now live further northeast in the south-central region. Among the Bara, zebu-stealing is regarded as proof of manhood and courage, without which a man cannot expect to get a wife. Nowadays the 'theft' is usually performed in a symbolic way with the consent of the animal's owner. The Bara are also sculptors, a unique feature of their carved wooden figures being eyelashes of real hair set into the wood. For burial of the deceased, they favour difficult-to-access caves in the mountains, the entrances of which are bricked up using rocks. Examples of this may be seen at Isalo.

To the south of the Bara region are found the **Antandroy** – or 'people of the thorns'. These dark-skinned people are also traditionally nomadic. Because their home is the inhospitably arid south, where there is insufficient water for growing rice, the Antandroy subsist predominantly on maize, cassava and sweet potatoes. Their villages are often protected by dense cactus hedges. Antandroy tombs are large rectangular constructions of uncut stone rising a metre above the ground and decorated with sculpted wooden posts and the horns of the zebu slain at the funeral feast.

In the extreme southeast of Madagascar around Taolagnaro (Fort Dauphin) are the **Antanosy**. The social structure within this tiny tribe is based on clans with a 'king' holding great authority over each one.

Men in the far south of Madagascar often carry spears. (MS)

Zebu cattle

The humpbacked zebu cattle, which number more than half the country's human population, produce a relatively low yield in milk and meat. These animals are near-sacred and are generally not eaten by the Malagasy outside of important ceremonies. Zebu are said to have originated from northeast India, eventually spreading as far as Egypt and then down into east Africa. It is not known how they were introduced to Madagascar but they are a link with the ancestors and a symbol of wealth and status as well as being used for burden.

In the south, zebu meat is always served at funerals, and among certain southern tribes the cattle are used as marriage settlements. Whenever

Chestnut-coloured zebu, *omby volavita*, are the most prized. (DA)

there is a traditional ritual or ceremony zebu are sacrificed, the heads being given to the highest-ranking members of the community. Blood is smeared on participants as it is believed to have purification properties, and the fat from the hump of the cattle is used as an ingredient for incense.

Zebu milk is an important part of the diet among the Antandroy; it is taboo for women to milk cows but it is they who sell the curdled milk in the market.

Tourists in the south will see large herds of zebu being driven to market, a journey that may take several days. All cattle crossing regional borders must wear a 'zebu passport' in the form of yellow ear tags. Cattle-rustling has become a major problem, with organised armed gangs snatching whole herds of zebu at night. In former times the punishment matched the crime: a fine of ten zebu would have to be paid by the thief, five for the family from whom the cattle were stolen and five for the king.

A herd of zebu is as symbolic of prosperity as a new car or a large house in Western culture. Government aid programmes must take this into account; for instance improved rice yields will indirectly lead to more environmental degradation by providing more money to buy more zebu. The French colonial government thought they had an answer: they introduced a tax on each animal. However, local politicians were quick to point out that since Malagasy women had always been exempt from taxation, the same rule should apply to cows!

Fady

The Malagasy word *fady* is usually translated as 'taboo', but this does not truly convey the meaning: these are beliefs related to certain behaviours considered 'dangerous'. Most *fady* are taken very seriously, but may be thought of as similar to Western superstitions (like the belief that seven years' bad luck will befall anyone who breaks a mirror, touching wood makes what you are saying come true and crossed cutlery foretells a quarrel). *Fady* may be universal or specific to a region, village, family or even an individual.

The Merina believe it is *fady* to sing while you are eating (violators will develop elongated teeth); it is also *fady* to hand an egg directly to another person (it must first be put on the ground); for the people of Andranoro it is *fady* to ask for salt directly, so one has to request 'that which flavours the food'. The spade used to dig a grave must have a loose handle since it is dangerous to have too firm a connection between the living and the dead.

Among the Betsimisaraka it may be *fady* for a brother to shake hands with his sister, or for a young man to wear shoes while his father is still alive. For some Antandroy children it is *fady* to say their father's name, or to refer by name to parts of their father's body. Instead the child may say 'what he moves with' for his feet or 'the top of him' for his head. It may be *fady* for a Betsileo family to eat until the father is present or for anyone to pick up his fork until the most honourable person present has started to eat. Social *fady* often involve the days of the week. It is *fady* to hold a Merina funeral on a Tuesday, or there will be another death. Among the Tsimihety it is *fady* to work the land on Tuesdays; Thursday is also a *fady* day for some people, both for funerals and for farming.

A *fady* is not intended to restrict the freedom of the Malagasy but to ensure happiness and an improved quality of life. That said, there are some cruel *fady*. One is the taboo against twins among the Antaisaka people of Mananjary. Historically twins were killed or abandoned in the forest after birth. Today this is against the law but still persists and twins may not be buried in a tomb. Catholic missionaries have established an orphanage in the area for the twins born to mothers torn between social tradition and maternal love. Many mothers who would otherwise have to suffer the murder or abandonment of their babies can give them to the care of the church.

Many *fady* benefit conservation. For instance the killing of certain animals is often prohibited in a particular region, and the area around a tomb must be left undisturbed. Within sacred forests it is strictly forbidden to cut trees or even to burn deadwood or leaf litter. In the southeast are similarly protected sacred forests along stretches of river where only women may bathe.

East of the Bara region is the stronghold of the **Antaisaka**, an off-shoot of the Sakalava tribe (see overleaf). They cultivate coffee, bananas and rice – but only the women harvest the rice. There are strong marriage taboos among them. Often the houses may have a second door on the east side which is only ever used for taking out a corpse. They use communal burial houses, bodies usually being dried out for two or three years before finally being put there.

The **Mahafaly** – or 'those who make taboos' (see box opposite) – inhabit the dry southwestern region to the south of Toliara (Tulear). They are farmers, with maize, sorghum and sweet potatoes as their chief crops; cattle-rearing occupies a secondary place. They kept their independence under their own local chiefs until the French occupation and still keep the bones of some of their old chiefs. Their villages usually have a special *hazomanga* post on the east side where sacrifices are made. Some of the blood is generally put on the foreheads of attendees. The tombs of the Mahafaly attract a great deal of interest. Their tombs are like those of the Antandroy and may bear many zebu horns. The tomb of the Mahafaly king Tsiampody is adorned with the horns of 700 zebu. Burial customs include waiting for the decomposition of the body before it is placed in the tomb, and giving a person a new name after death. The divorce rate among the Mahafaly is very high and it is not at all uncommon for a man to remarry six or seven times. It is often *fady* for children to sleep in the same house as their parents.

The **Mikea** subsist by foraging in the dry forests of the west and southwest. Various groups of people along the west coast are called Mikea, although their main area is the Mikea Forest between Morombe and Toliara. The Mikea are Malagasy of various origins, having adopted their particular lifestyle for various reasons, including fleeing from oppression and taxation imposed on them by the authorities.

(MS)

19

Living in the west between Toliara and Mahajanga are the **Sakalava**, a dark-skinned tribe with Polynesian features and short curly hair. They were at one time the largest and most powerful tribe, though disunited, and were ruled by their own kings and queens. Certain royal relics remain – typically being kept in the northeast corner of a house. The Sakalava are cattle raisers, and riches are reckoned by the number of zebu owned. There are records until as late as 1850 of human sacrifice among them on special occasions such

Sakalava girl wearing face paint (PYB/A)

as the death of a king. It is *fady* for pregnant women to eat fish or to sit in a doorway. Women hold a more important place among the Sakalava than in most other tribes.

In the same region but with a different way of life are the **Vezo**. They are a fishing people who use dugout canoes fitted with one outrigger pole and a small rectangular sail. In these frail but stable craft they go far out to sea, sometimes even undertaking seasonal migrations of hundreds of kilometres. The Vezo are also noted for their tombs, which are graves dug into the ground surrounded by wooden palisades, the main posts of which are often crowned by erotic wooden carved figures.

A typical Vezo outrigger canoe (DA)

Further north on the west coast are the **Makoa**. This group is descended from slaves taken from the Makua people of Mozambique, and although sometimes considered to be a subgroup of the Vezo, they maintain a separate identity. Typically of larger stature than most Malagasy, Makoa men were often employed by the French as policemen and soldiers, thus reinforcing their distinction from their fellow countrymen.

Tombs and ancestor worship

Death is the most important part of life, when a person abandons his mortal form to become a much more powerful ancestor. The ancestors, *razana*, hold a godly place in Malagasy belief: they may reward or punish the living by influencing the rice harvest, for example. One's tomb is seen as being for ever while one's house is only a temporary dwelling, so it follows that tombs should be more solidly constructed than houses. The Malagasy may invest many times more money in building a tomb than a house. Their style and structure varies widely from tribes to tribe, and also indicates the wealth and status of the family concerned.

Among the Merina, bodies used to be placed in a hollowed-out tree trunk and sunk into the mud at the bottom of a sacred marsh. Later they began constructing rectangular wooden tombs, then from the 19th century tombs were built with bricks and stone, and often painted with geometric designs. Sometimes the interior is lavishly decorated.

Early Sakalava tombs were simple piles of stones, later developing into cemented stone structures decorated with carved wooden stelae, facing east. Sakalava tombs are for individuals, not families, so they are not maintained – only when the wood decays will the soul be released.

The carefully maintained tombs of the Antandroy and Mahafaly are often decorated with paintings and carvings depicting scenes from the life of the deceased. This may even include a dramatic depiction of the manner in which they died.

A stone tomb near Antsirabe (NH)

The versatile *lamba*

The *lamba* is the most distinctive item of traditional Malagasy clothing, and among one of the island's most vibrant forms of artistic expression. There are many types of *lamba*, each with its own role in Malagasy culture. The Merina highlanders have a long tradition of handweaving; *lamba* are the fruit of this tradition. However, the variety most often encountered is not handwoven, but rather the machine manufactured *lamba hoany*.

This large decoratively printed rectangular cotton cloth is for everyday use. Some feature brilliantly hued patterns surrounding a central medallion; others, printed in two or three colours, depict a rural or coastal scene within an ornate border. You may also find some with images of Malagasy landmarks, the annual calendar, or historic events. A consistent feature of the various styles of *lamba hoany* is a Malagasy proverb or other words of wisdom.

As you travel the island you will discover that this seemingly simple wraparound cloth is adapted for many purposes. As clothing, it is worn in coastal regions as a sarong, while in the highlands *lamba* are draped around shoulders as shawls for added warmth in the evening chill. Everywhere the *lamba hoany* is employed as a sling to carry a child on a mother's back or rolled up to cushion the weight when carrying a large basket on one's head. You may also encounter it used as a light blanket, curtains in a window or door, and on occasion as a wall-hanging or tablecloth.

A selection of *lamba hoany* at the market (NH)

(SE)

North of the Bezanozano tribal region are found the **Sihanaka**, or 'people of the swamps'. They are fishermen, rice growers and poultry raisers with much in common with the Merina culturally. Swamps have been drained to make vast rice-fields cultivated with modern machinery and methods. They have a special rotation of *fady* days.

Further north are the **Tsimihety**, whose rulers originated from the Sakalava dynasty. Their name means 'those who do not cut their hair'. This stems from a time when they demonstrated their independence by refusing to cut their hair to show mourning on the death of a Sakalava king, as was the accepted custom. These energetic and vigorous people are still spreading west. The oldest maternal uncle occupies an important position in their society.

Living in the far north around Antsiranana (Diego Suarez) are the **Antakarana**, literally 'those of the rocks'. They are fishermen or cattle raisers, also with early Sakalava roots. Their houses are usually raised on stilts. Numerous *fady* exist among them governing relations between the sexes in the family; for example a girl may not wash her brother's clothes. At dinner, the legs of a fowl are the father's portion, whereas amongst the Merina, for instance, they are given to the children.

2 The Natural World

Madagascar is the world's top biodiversity hotspot, with the vast majority of its flora and fauna found nowhere else on earth. Most iconic are its adorable lemurs, which exist in almost a hundred different varieties, leaping through the trees in search of fruit and leaves. There is no doubt that the unique wildlife is the biggest draw for tourists coming here. This huge island contains a diverse array of habitats, from humid tropical rainforests and otherworldly mangrove swamps to arid spiny forest scrub and breathtaking expanses of razor-sharp limestone pinnacles known as *tsingy*. With a network of more than 40 national parks and special reserves (and at least as many private protected areas) there are opportunities to experience all of these different ecosystems, and the creatures that inhabit them, up close. Madagascar is also home to three designated UNESCO Biosphere Reserves and no fewer than seven sites declared Wetlands of International Importance under the Ramsar Convention.

The world's oldest island

To understand why Madagascar is so intriguingly different from anywhere else on our planet, we must peer back in time 200 million years to the early Jurassic period when the earth's continents were still fused into a single landmass known as Pangaea.

At the time of the early dinosaurs, Pangaea split into two supercontinents: Laurasia in the north and Gondwana in the south. Landlocked at the very heart of Gondwana was present-day Madagascar.

Tectonic forces began to rip Gondwana apart. Still fused to the India-Antarctica-Australia block, Madagascar soon broke away from Africa. Then, shortly after the time when the first ants and bees had appeared on earth, it broke free from India too. Since then – for the last 67 million years – Madagascar has been cast adrift in the Indian Ocean, making it the oldest island on earth.

The birth of Madagascar coincided with the last major extinction event. Widely supposed to have been caused by a massive asteroid impact, this global catastrophe famously wiped out the dinosaurs – along with 75% of all other species on earth.

There were still no grasses at this stage, no modern butterflies, no rodents, no bats, no bears, no cats, no dogs, no hoofed mammals. No lemurs, monkeys or apes had yet evolved either. Only in the aftermath of the mass extinction could mammals and birds finally begin to flourish.

It is the fact that the isolation of Madagascar predates all of this evolutionary development that sets it apart, quite literally, from the rest of the world.

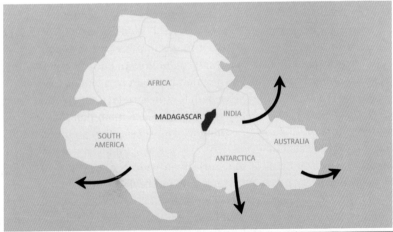

Gondwana started to break up into the present-day southern continents around 184 million years ago. (ML)

Evolution's playground

While much of the present-day plant life is descended from species that were marooned on Madagascar when it broke free – such as the ferns, cycads, palms and screw pines – the same cannot be said of the animals. In fact, all of the terrestrial mammals on the island today can be traced back to lineages that evolved in Africa after it became detached.

Against all the odds, a handful of creatures must have found their way across the 450km-wide Mozambique Channel separating Madagascar from the African mainland. Whether they were swept out to sea in a storm and crossed clinging to a raft of floating vegetation, or found their way by some other means (perhaps via a chain of islands long since lost beneath the waves), we will never know for sure. But cross they did, inadvertently adding themselves to the great evolutionary melting pot.

Having arrived, they would have been faced with very different conditions from those they had been used to. The different habitats, different food sources and different climate would have driven the evolutionary adaptations that eventually led to the rise of new species. Most importantly, there were few predators to hinder their progress.

The ancestral lemur was probably small like this mouse lemur. (DA)

Remarkable biodiversity

Eight whole plant families exist only on Madagascar, as do close to 1,000 orchid species, and many thousands of succulents. There are at least 350 species of frog, around 400 kinds of reptile, over 200 breeding species of bird – of which more than half are endemic – and approaching 200 different mammals, including an entire branch of the primate family tree, the order to which we ourselves belong.

This biodiversity is impressive both for the variety of species and their level of endemism. Overall 89% of plants, 93% of mammals, and 98% of reptiles and amphibians are endemic. The reason that so much of the flora and fauna is found nowhere else is clear: Madagascar has been insulated from the rest of the world by a wide oceanic barrier for an extraordinarily long time. But the reason for the sheer number of species is not so well understood. Evidently the climatic and geographical conditions were perfect to catalyse evolutionary development of new species in every corner of the island.

The arrival of man

Madagascar was one of the last places on earth to be colonised by humans. The consensus of the archaeological, genetic and linguistic evidence is that the first people turned up around 1,500 years ago. At that time many large native animals inhabited the land. There were giant tortoises, pygmy hippos, dozens of species of giant lemur (some as big as gorillas), and huge elephant birds that each weighed four times as much as an ostrich. But all were doomed.

If the entire history of the island – from its initial formation until now – were to be compressed into a single day, then humans didn't arrive on the scene until three seconds to midnight. Less than two seconds later, all of the large animals were dead. There seems little doubt that man was responsible, although it is not certain whether the extinctions resulted from direct hunting for food or sport, man's use of fire, the introduction of non-native animals and exotic diseases, or a combination of factors.

The biggest bird that ever lived

The **elephant birds** (*Aepyornis* and *Mullerornis*) were giant flightless birds endemic to Madagascar. They belong to the ratites – a Gondwanan group of which only the ostrich, emu, rhea, cassowary and kiwi survive today. The illustration shows their size in comparison to a man, ostrich and chicken.

The 13th-century traveller Marco Polo is believed to have been referring to these giants when he wrote, with some exaggeration, about a bird 'of enormous size, so big that its quills were twelve paces long and... so strong that it will seize an elephant in its talons and carry him high into the air and drop him so that he is smashed to pieces'.

Elephant bird eggs are estimated to have had a capacity equivalent to some 200 chicken eggs. Subfossil eggshell fragments are frequently found and may be seen for sale – often reconstructed into complete eggs – but you should avoid the temptation to buy as it is illegal to take them out of the country.

Geology

The rich diversity of mineral deposits in Madagascar rivals that of its flora and fauna. A wide range of gemstones, minerals and ores has been discovered, but there is relatively little commercial exploitation for reasons of infrastructure, politics and conservation. High quality coal and petroleum fields exist but with significant challenges for extraction.

The country has the world's largest reserves of sapphires. Most are blue, but pink, purple, orange, yellow, green and colourless ones have also been unearthed. They are extracted mainly from open pit mines, which are manually dug and may be 30m deep. Other precious gems that have been found include emeralds, rubies and garnets.

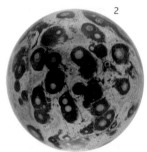

In addition to gold (not mined on a large scale for decades) there are also metal ores. These include chromite, which is exported for manufacture of metallic chromium, as well as notable deposits of aluminium (bauxite), iron, copper, lead and uranium. Controversial mining projects have recently been set up to extract ilmenite (for titanium) and laterite (for nickel and cobalt). Also mined for export are marble, mica and graphite.

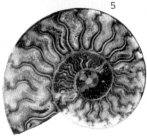

A number of attractive minerals are sold (often in polished form) as ornamental souvenirs. These include clear and rose quartz, amethyst, celestite, tourmaline, amazonite and labradorite (photo 4). There are several strikingly patterned colourful jaspers, including orbicular/ocean jasper (photo 1), polychrome jasper (photo 3) – a mineral entirely unknown to geology until its discovery in Madagascar in 2006 – and kambaba jasper (photo 2), which is two-billion-year-old fossilised blue-green algae. Other widely sold fossils include petrified wood, septaria (thought to be formed from dried mud around 60 million years ago) and ammonites (photo 5) of all sizes.

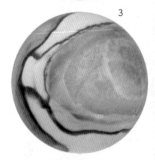

Habitats and conservation

A chain of mountains runs like a spine down the centre of Madagascar, splitting it into a wet eastern region and drier west. Rainforest habitats are found in the eastern zone, while the western plain supports deciduous forests, and savannah grassland. Spiny forest is found in the far south where the climate is hot and dry, and the shallow waters of the west coast are dotted with mangroves and coral reef ecosystems.

Rainforest

The rainforests are found from sea level to 1,800m, so there are examples of littoral, lowland and montane rainforest as well as high-

altitude cloudforest. These differ most notably in the height of the canopy, which can reach 35m above ground in low elevation rainforest but decreases to little more than 10m in the highest cloudforest. Where the canopy is low, there is a tangle of thick vegetation at ground level, but in rainforests at lower elevations the tall trees block so much sunlight from reaching the forest floor that the understory is much more open. Most visited are the national parks of Andasibe (see page 123), Ranomafana (page 142) and Montagne d'Ambre (page 188), all of which are primarily montane rainforest. The most important

Created in 1991, Ranomafana is an important wildlife site. (DA)

lowland rainforest is found in the northeast on the Masoala peninsula, where 230,000ha are protected.

Dry deciduous forest

The magnificent western dry forests once covered the vast lowland plain west of the highlands. Now only a few patches remain. Although biodiversity is lower in the deciduous forests than in the rainforests, they harbour some of Madagascar's most endangered species, many with very restricted ranges. Good examples are Kirindy (page 217) and Zombitse (page 157).

The deciduous trees are well adapted to the long dry season, losing their leaves for more than six months. Accordingly the wildlife is rather inactive until the return of the rains, so the wet season from December to March is the best time to visit. Heat, humidity and biting insects are also at their peak in this period, however, so October and November may be a more comfortable compromise.

Some dry forests, such as those at Ankarana (page 192) and Bemaraha (page 218), contain extraordinary limestone pinnacle formations known as *tsingy*. These virtually impenetrable 'stone forests' were formed by water erosion, and the ground beneath is typically riddled with networks of caves and underground rivers.

Spiny forest and gallery forest

Referred to variously as spiny desert, spiny bush, spiny thickets and spiny forest, the harsh environment of the far south is among the island's most surreal landscapes. It consists of deciduous shrubland dominated by tough succulent plants which protect their precious water reserves with extreme adaptations including sharp prickles and toxic sap. This habitat is unique to Madagascar, with 95% endemicity among plant species. Most notable are the cactus-like octopus trees, portly baobabs, 'elephant's foot' pachypodiums and numerous euphorbias.

Baobab and octopus trees (DA)

The easiest place to experience the spiny forest is Ifaty (page 162), where there is a protected parcel with well-maintained trails. Often within spiny forest regions, taller gallery forests have grown up in the fertile areas bordering major rivers. Superficially similar to the western deciduous forests, they contain different plant species and are dominated by tamarind trees. Gallery forest is well showcased at Berenty (page 176).

Wetlands and mangroves

Lakes, marshes and swamps are important ecosystems, especially for birds and the invertebrate life they feed upon. There is even a rare species of lemur that makes its home among the reed beds of Madagascar's largest lake, Lake Alaotra.

The country also has the largest expanse of mangrove forests in the western Indian Ocean region. Mangroves are coastal habitats flooded twice daily by the tide. The evergreen tree species that live there have evolved mechanisms of coping with the high salt levels and their specialised aerial roots are able to extract oxygen directly from the air, as the inundated mud is oxygen deficient.

Conservation challenges

Malagasy life depends on rice and zebu cattle. Neither can be raised in dense forest, so over the years the vast majority of the island's trees have been felled and the undergrowth burned. Meanwhile, the pressure on that which remains continues to mount; the country's population has more than quadrupled in the 50 years since independence, with the rate of growth showing no signs of abating. Remaining forest cover halved over the same period. Poverty is widespread – 90% live on less than US$2 per day – so most people rely on forest materials for building their homes and providing fuel for cooking.

Nevertheless, governments in recent decades have begun to recognise the importance of protecting Madagascar's unique flora and fauna, and a network of reserves has been set up. Countless NGOs, national and international, now run conservation projects, although many have been hindered by the protracted political crisis that began with a coup in 2009 and led to the cessation of most international aid.

Since the coup, illegal logging of precious rosewood, palissander and ebony has mushroomed, but those in power have shown little inclination to tackle the problem. Almost all of the wood is exported to China.

Protected areas

In 2003, then-president Marc Ravalomanana announced ambitious plans to triple Madagascar's protected areas. He managed to make significant advances with the project before his ousting six years later.

Today there are 20 national parks and 21 special reserves administered by Madagascar National Parks, a private organisation that operates under the supervision of the environment ministry. All of these are open to the public in theory, although only around half have infrastructure for ecotourism; many of the others are located in areas that are extremely difficult to access. In addition, there are five strict nature reserves operated by the parks service, which are only open to scientific researchers.

All visitors to parks and reserves must pay for an entry permit, from which half of the revenue goes towards management of the parks and the rest benefits local communities. It is obligatory for all tourists to be accompanied by an accredited local guide when inside protected areas, a requirement which not only ensures public safety and deters illicit behaviour, but also provides much-needed employment.

Many NGOs and a few hotels run publicly visitable private reserves as well. The map opposite shows those parks and reserves covered in this book.

Main protected areas

Plant life

Madagascar and its adjacent islands harbour some 13,000 species of flowering plant, of which a staggering 89% are endemic. Few other countries have levels of endemism above 50%.

Ferns and cycads

Ferns were in their heyday before Gondwana was even formed. Their best efforts were the impressive **tree ferns**, which formed vast forests in all warm, humid areas during the Carboniferous period. Although they eventually lost ground to seed-bearing plants, it is a credit to their design that they are still abundant and successful. Although some species are present in dry habitats, the vast majority of Madagascar's ferns are found on the branches and trunks of the eastern rainforests. One eye-catching species is the huge **bird's nest fern** (*Asplenium nidus*) which adorns many large trunks with luxuriant balconies of leaves.

Often mistaken for a tree fern, **cycads** are in fact one of the original seed-bearing plants. The evolution of seed propagation eventually led to the flowering plants that currently dominate all of the world's habitats. Resembling a tree fern with palm-like leaves, the single described Malagasy representative of the genus, *Cycas thouarsii*, is found only in the rainforests.

Orchids

The orchids of Madagascar number almost 1,000. They are extremely varied in form and 85% are endemic. Members of the family have adapted to every possible habitat, including the spiny forest and the cool highland mountain ranges, but their highest density is in the wet forests of the east. Although one or other can be seen in bloom at most times of the year, the best period for orchid flowers is the rainy season (Jan–Mar).

Among the most striking is the **comet orchid** (*Angraecum sesquipedale*), with flowers that may reach 26cm across (*left*). It was described by Charles Darwin who predicted that there would be a moth with an extremely long tongue that could reach down to the bottom of the nectary spur. This idea was ridiculed by his contemporaries, but in 1903 – more than two decades after his death – he was proved right: a hawk moth with a proboscis of over 30cm was discovered.

(DA)

Vanilla – Madagascar's biggest export

People are often surprised to learn that vanilla flavouring comes from an orchid. The *Vanilla* genus contains 110 species of which six are native to Madagascar, but the one grown commercially – *V. planifolia* – was actually introduced from Mexico.

(DA)

It is an ingredient used in everything from ice cream and confectionary to cakes and Coca-Cola, as well as perfume products. But most vanilla flavouring is artificial (made from wood tar or a by-product of papermaking). Synthetic vanilla is much cheaper to produce but vastly inferior; it contains only one of the aromatic components found in natural vanilla, of which at least 171 have been identified.

Real vanilla is expensive to produce because it is the most labour-intensive agricultural crop in the world. The plant grows as an evergreen vine that must be tutored along supporting trees. In its native Mexico it is pollinated by *Melipona* bees but in Madagascar there is no suitable insect, so in order for pods to develop every flower must be pollinated by hand using a needle. Harvesting is equally labour-intensive as the pods' development must be monitored to ensure they are picked on the right day.

They are killed by immersion in hot water for three minutes. This stops growth and initiates the enzymatic reactions responsible for the aroma. Next, these flavour-developing reactions are catalysed by 'sweating' the pods in hot, humid conditions for at least a week. To prevent rot and to lock in the aroma, they are then dried in the sun for some weeks until they have been reduced to a fifth of their original weight. The conditioning phase follows, in which the pods are stored for a few months in closed boxes while the fragrance intensifies. Finally the processed pods are graded into four quality categories and bundled for export. Some growers use a pin to brand the pods with a unique series of dots to insure against theft.

(AF)

Madagascar produces around 1,300 tonnes annually – more than half of the world's supply. One hectare of vanilla yields just 60kg of finished product. Prices peaked at €400/kg in 2005 but have since crashed to less than 10% of that.

Succulents

Succulents reign in areas of low rainfall. The entire southwest of Madagascar is dominated by their swollen forms. They also appear within the sparse dry forests of the west, among the stony chaos of the *tsingy*, and even venture onto the grasslands and into the rainforests.

Euphorbia have diversified into countless different forms, from bushes resembling strings of sausages, and trees sprouting smooth leafless green branches, to spiny stalks emerging from swollen underground tubers. The spiny crown of thorns is undoubtedly the most prominent, lining the streets of many towns and producing a blaze of red when in flower. All euphorbias have white milky sap which is toxic on skin contact and can cause temporary blindness.

Pachypodium rosulatum (DA)

Malagasy elephant's foot species, (*Pachypodium*) of which there are 20, range from towering tree-like species – such as *P. rutenbergianum* which may exceed 10m – to more compact forms like *P. rosulatum* (pictured) from Isalo.

The octopus trees of the Didiereaceae family in the arid southwest are the most intriguing plants in Madagascar. There are 11 species in four genera: *Alluaudia*, *Alluaudiopsis*, *Decaria*, and *Didierea*. Most resemble columnar cacti and some can reach a height of 20m.

Over 100 species of *Aloe* inhabit the island, many of which are very different from those found elsewhere. Some have stocky stems that raise their rosettes of foliage up to 3m off the ground. *A. suzannae* is unique among aloes worldwide in being a night-time bloomer.

Kalanchoe is represented by 63 species, many of which can reproduce by producing fully formed plantlets at their leaf margins. Most well-known are the panda plant (*K. tomentosa*) and the elephant's ear (*K. beharensis*), both of which have velvety leaves.

Senecio is a genus of leaf succulents, existing essentially as a collection of swollen leaves sprouting from the earth. The leaves are often ornamental, tinged with terracotta and bearing harsh spines.

Other succulents include the *Adenia* climbing vines, some *Cyphostemma*, the endemic genus *Uncarina* which comprises 13 shrubs and trees with substantial underground tubers and, most famous of all, the baobabs (*Adansonia*) – see opposite.

The upside-down tree

Baobab Avenue near Morondava was declared a Natural Monument in 2007. (DA)

When God first created the **baobab**, it kept walking off. Infuriated by this insolently untreelike behaviour, he ripped it from the ground and replanted it with roots skyward. This, so the legend goes, is why the short stubby branches of these swollen-trunked trees look so rootlike.

Botanists, who prefer more conventional evolutionary explanations for the origins of species, had long assumed baobabs to be an ancient Gondwanan group. One species is found in Australia and another across much of the African continent, so this was a logical conclusion – until the idea was blown out of the water by the discovery that baobabs only evolved around 12 million years ago, long after Gondwana's break-up. The current theory is that they first arose in Madagascar (where six endemic species are found) and that seed pods floated across the oceans to found the African and Australian species.

The velvety hard-shelled fruits (*right*) each contain a hundred or more seeds surrounded by sweet, dry pith. These nutritious fruits – often eaten by the Malagasy and used to make a drink like lemonade – have more vitamin C than oranges and a calcium content greater than that of milk. In 2008 the EU approved the use of baobab fruit pulp as a food ingredient and the US Food and Drug Administration followed suit in 2009, so perhaps we will start to see it appearing in Western products soon.

(DA)

37

Carnivorous plants

'The atrocious cannibal tree came to sudden savage life;' wrote a German traveller to Madagascar in 1878, 'the tendrils one after another, like great green serpents, with brutal energy and infernal rapidity, rose, retracted themselves, and wrapped her about in fold after fold, ever tightening with cruel swiftness and savage tenacity of anacondas fastening upon their prey.' He was describing a fatal encounter between a local woman and a man-eating tree that resembled 'a pineapple eight feet high'.

The story of this fearsome plant was perpetuated in the 1920s by an American explorer, who had heard many tales about it from natives across the island, although he admitted he had not seen one himself. Of course, the upas tree (as it was called) has never been seen by anyone else either; but Madagascar is home to a handful of more placid carnivorous plants.

There are two species of pitcher plant of the genus *Nepenthes*. Of the 130 or so other species in this genus, almost all live in Asia.

Madagascar pitcher (DA)

Nevertheless, the earliest known record of any *Nepenthes* is from Madagascar. In 1658, Etienne de Flacourt, governor of Madagascar for the French East India Company, recorded 'a plant growing about three feet high which carries at the end of its leaves, which are seven inches long, a hollow flower or fruit resembling a small vase, with its own lid; a wonderful sight.'

The pitcher's cup is in fact neither a flower nor a fruit, but a modified leaf with the purpose of trapping and digesting insects. Within each trap is a fluid of the plant's own production that recent research has found to contain not only digestive enzymes but also viscoelastic biopolymers, which increase the liquid's surface tension in response to an insect's movement, thus preventing it from escaping.

Flacourt further noted that 'the inhabitants of this country are reluctant to pick the flowers, saying that if somebody does pick them in passing, it will not fail to rain that day. As to that, I and all the other Frenchmen did pick them, but it did not rain.'

Pitchers are not Madagascar's only carnivorous plants. There are also sundews (*Drosera* species), which sport leaves covered in tiny tentacles topped with sticky secretions. These serve to attract, ensnare and digest insects in a manner that, seen through the eyes of a fly, might not be so far removed from the legendary upas tree.

Bismarck palms are common around Isalo, thanks to their fire-resistance. (NH)

Palms

The island has around 170 species of palm – three times more than in the rest of Africa put together – with 165 of those found nowhere else. Around a quarter have only been discovered in the last decade.

Madagascar is the world centre for **raffia palms** (indeed the word raffia comes from the Malagasy language). Fibres from the leaves of *Raphia ruffia* are woven into hats, baskets and mats. In the rainforest are **litter-trapping palms** with a crown of leaves arranged like an upturned shuttlecock so that it catches leaves falling from the canopy, perhaps to obtain trace minerals.

Looking like an untidy cross between a palm and a pine tree, **pandan palms** or screw pines (*Pandanus* spp) are common in both rainforests and dry forests. Of the 75 species, all but one is endemic.

Traveller's palm

The traveller's tree or traveller's palm (*Ravenala madagascariensis*) is one of Madagascar's most spectacular plants. Its elegant fronds are arranged in a dramatic vertical fan, which is decorative enough to have earned it a role as Air Madagascar's logo. It is not a true palm but rather a member of the bird-of-paradise family. It earns its common name from the relief it affords thirsty travellers: fresh water is stored in the base of its leaves and can be released with a swift blow from a machete.

(DA)

Wildlife

An unimaginably long period of isolated evolution has created a haven for a plethora of strange and unusual creatures. The seemingly random collection of animal groups that had the opportunity to prove themselves in the absence of large predators and herbivores are the chief reason Madagascar is becoming a tourist hotspot.

Lemurs

Lemurs belong to a group called the prosimians (literally 'before monkeys'), which also includes bushbabies, tarsiers and lorises. Their ancestors are the earliest primates, before monkeys and apes evolved.

Ringtails are most easily seen at Anja and Berenty. (DA)

It was just before the rise of the monkeys that an ancestral lemur ended up in Madagascar, founding a population on the island which soon spread out and exploded into dozens of different species.

Today there are close to a hundred species of lemur – all endemic to Madagascar. Incredibly, more than half of them have only been described in the last 20 years. They can be divided into about a dozen distinct groups, half of which are active during the night and the others in the day. The nocturnal lemurs tend to be small-bodied with large eyes and ears. They typically lead a solitary lifestyle, with insects a major part of their diet. Diurnal lemurs, on the other hand, are larger and more social, usually living in female-led groups of three to 12 individuals. They eat varied diets of fruit, seeds, buds and leaves, which they gather from a territory much larger than the home range of their nocturnal cousins.

The elegant **ring-tailed lemur** of the far south is the best known species. Ringtails form the largest troops (normally of about 14, but occasionally as many as 30) and spend more time on the ground than most lemurs. In the April breeding season, males engage in stink fights; after anointing their tails with secretions from their wrist glands, they waft them antagonistically at opponents.

Female black lemur (DA)

Similar in size and form to ringtails are the 12 species of **true lemur**. These include, in the northwest, the black lemur and the blue-eyed black lemur (the only blue-eyed primate besides humans) – in both cases the males look as their names suggest but the females are brown. This sexual dimorphism is common to all members of this genus to a greater or lesser extent. Others frequently encountered are the crowned lemur (far north), red-bellied lemur (east) and red-fronted lemur (south). Many true lemur species look rather similar, but their ranges do not overlap so locality is helpful in identification.

Bamboo lemurs (or gentle lemurs) are smaller, with short muzzles and round faces. Seven species are known, of which three may be seen at Ranomafana. They occur in small groups of up to four animals, cling to vertical branches, and feed mainly on bamboo. (It is not known how they are able to detoxify the dangerous levels of cyanide present in this diet.) The exception is the Alaotran bamboo lemur, which feeds instead on the papyrus reeds of Lake Alaotra.

In the same taxonomic family as the ring-tailed, true and bamboo lemurs are the two **ruffed lemurs**, both large species that spend their time eating fruit high in the rainforest canopy. Black-and-white ruffed lemurs are commonly found in captivity but often difficult to see in the eastern rainforest where they live in groups of three to 16. Restricted to the Masoala peninsula of the northeast, red ruffed lemurs may form even larger social communities.

Black-and-white ruffed lemur (DA)

In a separate family is the **indri**, the largest of the living lemurs, weighing 6–9kg. They live in small groups, comprising a monogamous pair and their offspring, throughout the northern half of the eastern rainforest belt. Indri are black and white with teddy-bear ears and are unique among lemurs in having virtually no tail. They have extremely long, powerful back legs, which they use to propel themselves up to 10m between trees. Their loud territorial vocalisations have been likened to whale song and may carry 2km across the forest. Like at least 25 other lemur species, indri are classed as endangered, but their susceptibility to habitat destruction is compounded by their need for large territories (up to 40ha) and the fact that they

Indri are most readily seen at Andasibe. (MS)

have never been successfully kept alive in captivity.

Sifakas belong to the same family as the indri, sharing the characteristic long back legs and spectacular jumping ability, but they are somewhat smaller, weighing in at 3½–6½kg. Species are easily distinguished by colouration. Most commonly encountered are Verreaux's sifaka in the south and southwest, Coquerel's sifaka (photo page 209) in the northwest, and the much darker-coloured Milne-Edwards' sifaka in the southern part of the eastern rainforest belt. The diademed sifaka has been described as the most beautiful of all lemurs. In the north are three endangered species: the all-white silky sifaka, the all-black Perrier's sifaka and the golden-crowned sifaka, which is mostly white with an orange skullcap. Fewer than 250 mature silky sifakas are thought to remain, making it one of the world's most critically endangered primates.

All of the lemurs described thus far are diurnal; the remaining six groups presented below are nocturnal. You may happen upon these during night walks and some can even be spotted in their sleeping holes during the day.

Woolly lemurs (avahis) are closely related to the indri and sifakas. They are considerably smaller (around 1kg) but adopt a similar vertical posture. Until 2005 there were only three species of woolly lemur, but recent research has led to a flurry of new descriptions bringing the total to nine. Only two species are at all widespread: the eastern woolly lemur in the northern rainforests and Peyrieras' woolly lemur in the southern ones; the rest are restricted to tiny ranges. One, from Bemaraha in the west, was named *Avahi cleesei* in honour of British comic actor John Cleese and his work to publicise the plight of lemurs.

The smallest of all primates are the **mouse lemurs**. Of the 18 species scattered across Madagascar, the most minuscule is Madame Berthe's mouse lemur, weighing just 30g fully grown. Mouse lemurs live in virtually all native forest types and can survive in smaller forest fragments than other lemurs. Easiest to see are the grey mouse lemur in the west, the brown mouse lemur in the east (photo page 27), and the grey-brown mouse lemur in the south.

Dwarf lemurs are mostly squirrel-sized and run along branches in a similar fashion. Some become dormant during the winter, sleeping in tree holes and surviving on reserves of fat stored in their tails. The widespread species are the greater dwarf lemur in the eastern rainforests and the fat-tailed dwarf lemur mainly found in the dry forests of the west.

Named for the distinctive dark markings on their heads, **fork-marked lemurs** prefer to live high in the canopy so can be rather difficult to see. They are, however, extremely vocal so are often heard on night walks. The best places to look for them are Kirindy, Zombitse and Montagne d'Ambre.

Grey-brown mouse lemur in its tree hole (DA)

The **sportive lemurs** (lepilemurs) mostly spend the day in tree holes from which they peer drowsily. Their name is something of a misnomer as they are rarely particularly energetic, even at night. They cling vertically to tree trunks and, after dark, their high-pitched calls are often a feature of the forests they

Hubbard's sportive lemur (DA)

inhabit. At the last count there were 26 species known, each restricted to a small pocket of the island and all rather similar in appearance.

Tips for a successful night walk

Night walks are an essential feature of forest visits in Madagascar. The official reserves managed by Madagascar National Parks do not permit entry at night time, but even so it is usually possible to have a rewarding night walk along a road at the park boundary. Private reserves often allow you to walk the forest trails after dark. Depending on the season, weather and even moon phase, night walks can be incredibly fruitful in terms of wildlife viewing.

The trick to seeking out lemurs is to watch for eyeshine. Nocturnal animals have a reflective area at the back of their eye which sends light directly back towards its source, but to be effective your torch must be held as close to your own eyes as possible. Ideally, wear a head torch that gives out a broad, even light. Lemurs have yellow or orange eyeshine. Red eyeshine is more likely to be a reptile or moth, while a pinpoint white twinkle often indicates a spider.

Chameleons are also much easier to spot in the dark – not because of

eyeshine (they sleep at night with their eyes closed) but because their bodies become much paler and are easily picked out in torchlight once you develop the eye for it. Look on foliage between knee and head height. On night walks you may also see nocturnal frogs and roosting birds.

The presence of a Pariente's fork-marked lemur is given away by its eyeshine. (DA)

Arguably the most specialised – and certainly the most bizarre – lemur of all is the **aye-aye**. It truly is unique, so much so that the first European scientists to receive a specimen from early explorers (see engraving below from 1858) scratched their heads in bemusement and eventually classified it as a type of squirrel. Only after much debate and several reclassifications was it finally agreed that the aye-aye is in fact a kind of lemur. It is the sole species not only of its genus, but in its entire family, meaning there is nothing else in existence remotely like it.

Aye-ayes are nocturnal cat-sized creatures with shaggy black coats, spending much of their lives high up in the canopy of both deciduous forests and rainforests. They have continually growing incisor teeth just like rodents (part of the reason they were first thought to be squirrels), huge satellite-dish ears that can be swivelled to locate the faintest sound with pinpoint accuracy, and a long, skeletally thin middle finger. These features collectively constitute a specialised toolkit for the aye-aye's favourite activity: grub hunting.

Tapping rapidly on the bark of a tree, an aye-aye listens for the echo that indicates a hollow chamber within. So sensitive are its ears that they can detect the movement of grubs beneath the bark. Once such a snack has been located, the sharp teeth are used to gnaw a small hole into which the slim bony finger can be inserted to winkle the grubs out into the aye-aye's waiting mouth.

(ML)

In this way, the species has evolved to fill the ecological niche typically occupied throughout the rest of the world by woodpeckers – a group of birds which has never found its way to Madagascar. It is little wonder that those early taxonomists had difficulty placing such an enigmatic creature in the system of biological classification!

Carnivores

Scientists have long argued over how Madagascar's ten carnivore species should be classified. Traditionally they were divided between the civets and mongooses, but recent evidence shows they are a separate family of their own: the euplerids.

Madagascar's largest predator is the fossa. (DA)

The largest, the **fossa**, is very cat-like with an extremely long tail which assists balance during canopy-based lemur hunts. This shy creature is quite widespread but almost never seen except in Kirindy where several have become rather tame. Almost as large – and almost as elusive – are the rainforest-dwelling **fanaloka** and **falanouc**, which feed on rodents and earthworms respectively. A century ago, explorer Chase Salmon Osborn reported that the fanaloka 'has a more pronounced odour than a civet cat and much more pleasant. The natives use it as a perfume and it is much more agreeable than much of the cheap scent with which the men and women in civilised lands offend the nostrils.'

The remainder of the carnivores are small and mongoose-like. They eat insects, eggs, frogs, reptiles, birds, fish, and sometimes even small lemurs and tenrecs.

Tenrecs and rodents

The **tenrecs** are a group of 34 species of insectivore similar in appearance and lifestyle to shrews, moles or hedgehogs. The tailless or common tenrec is a triple world record holder: weighing up to 2½kg, it is the biggest of all insectivores, the females give birth to the largest litters of any mammal (as many as 32 babies) and have a record-breaking 34 nipples with which to feed them.

The most appealing species are the lowland and highland streaked tenrecs

Highland streaked tenrec (DA)

with their mixture of fur and spines and their distinctive black and yellow stripes. One particularly shy tenrec, known as the web-footed tenrec, has diversified into living an aquatic life catching small fish and freshwater shrimps in fast-flowing highland streams.

Highly successful elsewhere, rodents have made little impression on Madagascar. There are 25 native species of **mice and rats**, most of which are nocturnal. The easiest to see is the red forest rat which is active during the day and sometimes spotted in Ranomafana.

Madagascar's most celebrated rodent is the giant jumping rat, whose name derives from its kangaroo-like method of locomotion. This charming creature is about the size of a rabbit and fills the same ecological niche, excavating an extensive burrow at the heart of its 4ha territory. Giant jumping rats are endangered, being restricted to a single forest less than 20km by 40km. They are also most unusual among rodents in being monogamous.

Bats

Around 60% of the bat species found in Madagascar are endemic. It is not surprising that this figure is lower than for the other mammals, given that they can fly. There are three large fruit bats (flying foxes) and around 30 much smaller insectivorous species. These tend to have shell-like ears and distorted noses as part of their echolocation apparatus, none more so than the Commerson's leaf-nosed bat.

Commerson's leaf-nosed bat is the largest of the insect-eating species. (DA)

Birds

Around 283 species of birds have been recorded in Madagascar, of which 209 regularly breed on the island. With five endemic families and 37 endemic genera, it is one of Africa's top birding hotspots. Those with a particular interest in birding should obtain a field guide for Malagasy birds (see page 255).

Madagascar fody (TJ)

Most commonly encountered throughout the country are the Madagascar white-eye, common newtonia, Madagascar paradise flycatcher, Madagascar magpie-robin, common jery, Madagascar bulbul, Madagascar fody, common mynah, Madagascar wagtail, Madagascar manikin, Madagascar bee-eater and Madagascar coucal. Easily seen larger birds include the cuckoo-roller, dimorphic and cattle egrets, hamerkop and pied crow.

Another frequent sighting is the crested drongo, an all-black bird which is a proficient mimic of other species' calls. There is an old Malagasy tale that tells of the time a remote village was invaded by slave traders. Seeing them approaching, the villagers escaped just in time and hid in a thicket close by. Angrily the attackers torched the empty houses but, as they were making to leave, a baby wailed. Cowering in the grass, the child's mother quickly hushed him, but the men had already heard and were heading towards the thicket. Just at that moment, a drongo flitted down from a nearby tree and repeated the baby's cry loudly. The slave traders saw that it must have been the bird that they had heard, so they returned to their boats and sailed away. To this day the drongo is celebrated as a good spirit.

To see a wide spectrum of the endemic birds, it is necessary to visit at least one site in each of the three

Crested drongo (FV)

chief habitat zones: rainforest, dry deciduous forest and spiny forest. The map shows important sites for avifauna in Madagascar and lists key species seen at each. Masoala, Andasibe and Ranomafana are rainforest areas; Ifaty and St Augustine's Bay are spiny forest sites; and Ankarafantsika is dry forest. The transition forest at Zombitse is also an essential port of call on any birding itinerary.

Nosy Be

Masoala
helmet vanga, Bernier's vanga,
red-breasted coua, brown mesite,
scaly ground-roller

Mozambique Channel

Ankarafantsika
Madagascar fish eagle, Madagascar crested ibis,
white-breasted mesite, Coquerel's coua, Schlegel's
asity, Van Dam's vanga, sickle-billed vanga

Île Ste Marie

ANTANANARIVO

Andasibe-Mantadia
red-fronted coua, blue coua,
blue vanga, Tylas vanga,
Madagascar long-eared owl,
scaly ground-roller

Ranomafana
pitta-like ground-roller, rufous-headed ground-roller,
yellow-browed oxylabes, Crossley's babbler,
Pollen's vanga, brown mesite, grey-crowned greenbul

INDIAN OCEAN

Ifaty
sub-desert mesite,
long-tailed ground-roller,
Lafresnaye's Vanga,
Archbold's newtonia,
running coua

Zombitse
Appert's greenbul, giant coua, crested coua,
Madagascar hoopoe, Madagascar partridge,
Madagascar buttonquail, Madagascar sandgrouse,
Thamnornis warbler

St Augustine's Bay
Verreaux's coua, littoral rock thrush,
red-shouldered vanga

Key birding sites

0 — 200km
0 — 100 miles

N

49

Crested coua (TJ)

Madagascar's most celebrated endemic bird family is that of the **vangas**. Beak variation in this group is remarkable: all 22 species have perfected the craft of capturing insects, frogs and reptiles in different ways, and have evolved appropriately shaped bills for the purpose. Most prominent are the sickle-billed vanga, the hook-billed vanga, and the helmet vanga with its large blue bill. Most vangas are predominantly black, brown or grey with white underparts. The brilliantly coloured blue vanga is notable as an exception.

The **couas** are another charismatic group of native birds, belonging to the cuckoo family. They are large birds with short wings, long tails, and a distinctive patch of bright blue around the eye. Six of the ten species are ground-dwellers including the giant coua, which is the largest at 62cm long. It is from the loud *koo-koo-koo* call of this southern and western species that the name coua derives.

Ducking out of extinction

One of the rarest birds on the island is the **Madagascar pochard**, a chestnut brown diving duck that had not been seen for so long that it was reclassified as possibly extinct. Thankfully a tiny population of around a dozen was discovered by The Peregrine Fund on a remote northern lake in 2006, but monitoring revealed three years later that their chicks were not surviving. A team of experts from Durrell Wildlife Conservation Trust and the Wildfowl and Wetlands Trust flew in to launch an emergency rescue plan.

A local hotel was commandeered as a temporary centre for the incubation and hatching of eggs gathered from the wild. They successfully reared 23 chicks and then in early 2012 the first 18 captive-bred ducks were hatched as part of an ambitious breeding programme.

(FV)

Wetland birds are present in large numbers, including nine heron species, ten ducks, two flamingos, three grebes, four egrets, three ibises, four rails, ten plovers, six sandpipers, yellow-billed storks and black-winged stilts, among others.

One of the two endemic **kingfishers** – the Madagascar malachite kingfisher – is also common in aquatic habitats. The other – the Madagascar pygmy kingfisher – is a forest-dweller. Both are found throughout the island, except for the pygmy kingfisher in the far south.

Madagascar pygmy kingfisher (FV)

There are two parrot species: the greater and lesser **vasa parrots**. Both are an unexciting drab blackish colour. But this modest exterior conceals a creature with an exhilarating sex life. It's the females that pursue their partners over a courtship of several weeks, ending up with as many as eight mates – rather licentious given that most other parrots are monogamous. Typically mating in birds lasts no more than a few seconds, but vasa parrots stay locked in passionate coitus for a full two hours. This is made possible by the fact that, unlike almost all other birds, the male has a penis, which is somewhat bigger than a golf ball when erect.

Madagascar's **birds of prey** include some of the world's rarest raptors. There are estimated to be just 40 to 100 breeding pairs remaining of the Madagascar fish eagle, a huge and majestic bird found near water (fresh or salt) in the west of the country. The Madagascar serpent eagle is thought to be even rarer. Sightings of the Madagascar red owl are also extremely infrequent.

Among the more common raptors are the Madagascar kestrel, yellow-billed kite, Madagascar harrier-hawk, Henst's goshawk, Frances's sparrow-hawk, Madagascar buzzard, Madagascar cuckoo-hawk, Madagascar long-eared owl and Madagascar scops owl.

Reptiles

Almost half of all **chameleons** in existence worldwide are native to this one island. Oustalet's and Parson's chameleons jointly hold the title of world's largest, measuring up to 70cm from nose to tail tip. One fiftieth of this size, the pygmy stump-tailed chameleons are the world's most minute. Considerably smaller even than some of the insects with which they share the forest floor, these miniature lizards are among the tiniest of all reptiles.

Chameleons famously possess the extraordinary ability to turn different colours – some much more strikingly than others – but, contrary to traditional wisdom, these changes reflect their mood rather than an effort to match their background. Some, on meeting a potential mate, or when faced with a rival trespassing on their territory, will puff themselves up and explode into an alarming kaleidoscopic display of polychromatic emotional expression.

A chameleon's armoured eyeballs swivel like gun turrets and operate independently from one another so that one can be used to look forwards while the other keeps watch for any danger from behind. On spotting potential prey – a juicy cricket, perhaps – the two roving eyes are coupled for binocular vision. Focusing on the target with both eyes allows distance to be judged, which is critical for the creature to utilise its deadly weapon accurately.

The highly elastic tongue can typically be extended by a full body length. It is unleashed with impressive accuracy and lightning speed, taking just three hundredths of a second to hit its prey – faster than

the perception of the human eye and, more importantly, faster than most insects' reactions. The tongue's tip is slightly sticky with mucus but actually grabs the prey by forming a suction cup. It is then swiftly reeled back in to be crunched up by strong jaws and a set of tiny sharp teeth.

There are more than 100 types of **gecko** in Madagascar. None is more visible than the day geckos, a group of

Male Parson's chameleon (DA)

medium-sized tree-dwelling lizards that are mostly bright green with red markings. They are found not only in forest habitats but also commonly amid human habitation. A bold day gecko may even visit your restaurant table in search of lunch scraps. Day geckos are unusual, however; most other geckos are nocturnal and inconspicuously coloured.

Madagascar giant day gecko, *Phelsuma madagascariensis grandis* (DA)

Hiding in plain sight

Leaf-tailed geckos (*Uroplatus*) are veritable masters of disguise. The 15 species are variously patterned and coloured to mimic closely the appearance of the bark, lichens and mosses found in their favoured resting places. Some of the smaller species pass themselves off as dry leaves in the effort to avoid detection by couas, vangas and other predators.

By night they hunt insects among the branches. During daylight hours they sleep out in the open, resting head-downwards on tree trunks. The largest ones may exceed 30cm in length, yet despite their size they are almost invisible; their camouflaged colouration allows them to blend in superbly with their background. Several species even have a frill of skin that breaks up their outline to ensure they have no shadow when at rest.

Leaf-tailed geckos tend to sleep at about human head height, almost as if mocking the tourists who pass by oblivious to their presence. Fortunately, most experienced forest guides will generally manage to find one.

Giant leaf-tailed gecko, camouflaged against a tree (DA)

Plated lizards range from 15cm to 70cm in length. (DA)

The **iguana** family is represented by seven endemic members living mainly in the drier areas. These include the three-eyed lizard of the south, which is very common in some spiny forest habitat. Its third 'eye' – a conspicuous black dot on the top of its head – is known as a parietal eye. Although this eye cannot see, it is sensitive to light and is thought to measure periods of sunlight to regulate daily rhythm.

Madagascar's 20 **plated lizards** occur throughout the island and are mostly handsome species with black and golden stripes, except for two arboreal types which are bright green.

The remaining 80 or so lizards all belong to the **skink** family and include representatives of the common skinks, Madagascar skinks, giant Madagascar skinks, stone skinks, shining skinks, short skinks, mabuya skinks and burrowing blind skinks. Over 30 of these are completely legless or have extremely reduced limbs.

The three-eyed lizard is Madagascar's smallest iguanid. (DA)

The Nile **crocodile** was once widespread throughout the island, but most have now been hunted. They remain mainly in areas where they are protected by spiritual beliefs. Crocodiles are farmed for their skins and meat near to Antananarivo.

There is good news for ophidiophobics (those with a fear of **snakes**): none of Madagascar's 100 or so species is dangerous to humans. The few that possess a mild venom are back-fanged, effectively making it impossible to inject through biting. Malagasy snakes are mostly quite small, but there are three boas that may exceptionally exceed 3m in length. These include the Madagascar ground boa and the Madagascar tree boa (which despite its name is also usually found on the ground).

The Madagascar banded tree snake is one of the most colourful species. (DA)

All five of Madagascar's endemic species of **tortoise** and **freshwater turtle** are classed as critically endangered. They are threatened by habitat loss, hunting for bushmeat and illegal collection for the international pet trade. There are a further four non-endemic species, which are not considered globally at risk.

The ploughshare tortoise – sometimes known by its local name of *angonoka* – gets its name from the spur projecting forward from the lower shell. Males joust with this when fighting and use it to roll females over during courtship. Just 300 individuals are thought to remain in the wild but a successful captive-breeding programme is under way.

The ploughshare tortoise is the rarest tortoise species in the world. (DA)

Green bright-eyed treefrogs, *Boophis viridis*, are easily seen at Andasibe. (DA)

Frogs

Madagascar is home to a staggering 290 frog species, with dozens more currently undergoing formal description. Frogs are the only amphibians in Madagascar – there are no toads, newts, salamanders or caecilians – and over 99% of them are endemic. They come in all colours and sizes: from the tiny *Stumpffia* measuring just 1cm to the giant Indian bullfrog reportedly reaching 17cm in length.

Frogs have a widely varied diet. They are well known to eat flies, ants, slugs and other small invertebrates, but some will even eat scorpions, young chameleons, tadpoles, other frogs, and – in the case of the largest species – even rodents, snakes and birds.

Each December, for just three or four days, *Aglyptodactylus* frogs gather in huge numbers to mate – a phenomenon known as explosive breeding. They turn from dull brown to bright canary yellow for the occasion. With many thousands of individuals gathered in a single marshy pool the noise of their excited croaking is remarkable. After this colourful orgy each female will produce a clutch of up to 4,000 eggs.

The **Malagasy reed frogs** (*Heterixalus*) are a group of small colourful tree frogs that usually spend the day sunning themselves on broad leaves near to pools or streams. They may be blue, green or orange, sometimes spotty and often with yellow stripes.

Madagascar reed frog (DA)

The frogs which most excite visitors to Madagascar are the 16 mantellas. Except for the golden mantella, which is uniformly bright orange, they are black with yellow, orange, green or blue patterns. Their dramatic colours warn predators that their skin contains alkaloid toxins, making them a rather unpleasant snack.

Another frog it would be wise to avoid eating is the aptly named **tomato frog.** When attacked these obese, bright red frogs gum up the predator's mouth with a thick gluey substance secreted from their skin. The unfortunate attacker is forced to release its prey and cannot eat for some days after.

New frog species are constantly being discovered in Madagascar, but for many it is a race against extinction. More than 65 of Madagascar's known frog species are considered vulnerable or endangered, yet fewer than 20 are protected by international laws against collection and trade.

Tomato frog, *Dyscophus antongilii* (DA)

Insects and other creepy-crawlies

There are thought to be at least 100,000 species of invertebrate in Madagascar, of which most are found nowhere else on earth. Every last one of the scarab beetles, snails, freshwater crayfish and scorpions so far identified on the island is endemic, and the same goes for the majority of the insects, millipedes, freshwater crabs, spiders and other invertebrate groups.

Undoubtedly the most famous native invertebrate is the **giraffe-necked weevil**, most easily found at Ranomafana. The male of this bright red beetle species has an extraordinarily long neck. This elongated appendage is used for fighting and in rolling leaves to make tubes that act as protected nurseries into which females can lay their eggs.

Giraffe-necked weevil (FV)

Madagascar has around 160 types of **millipede**, some of which can reach 25cm long and have 400 or more legs. Most are black or red, or may have stripes of both. Unlike centipedes, millipedes are not venomous and cannot bite. **Pill millipedes** have around 40 legs and are able to roll themselves into a perfect sphere when threatened. These dark balls are known in Malagasy as *tainkintana* – literally 'dung from the stars'.

Giant millipedes (DA)

In the wet season, **flatid leaf bugs** are often encountered in the western forests. The adults look like pinkish-red leaves or flowers but it is the white-coloured nymphs that are particularly fascinating. Each nymph excretes a waxy substance in feathery wisps from its back. If a bird makes a grab for one, it will come away with nothing more than a beakful of these waxy tufts

Flatid leaf bug nymphs (white) and adults (red), *Phromnia rosea* (DA)

while the insect leaps to safety. The nymphs gather on branches in large numbers, looking for all the world like a patch of lichen until you disturb them.

Often sighted in southern Madagascar, **rainbow milkweed locusts** are exquisitely colourful grasshoppers of around 10cm in length. Their bright colours indicate to potential predators that they contain toxins, a property obtained from their diet of poisonous milkweeds.

Rainbow milkweed locusts (DA)

The Madagascar emperor moth caterpillar is bigger than a human finger. (DA)

Some 4,200 **moth** species inhabit the island, along with about 310 **butterflies**, of which three-quarters are endemic.

Largest among the butterflies is the Madagascar giant swallowtail, which is black with red and white spots. There are several other large colourful swallowtails. These are mostly black and yellow (including the Madagascar emperor swallowtail, Grose-Smith's swallowtail and toothed citrus swallowtail) or black and blue (like the banded blue swallowtail and the rather similar mangoura swallowtail).

Contrary to widespread belief, moths are not necessarily small, drab and nocturnal. In fact one of Madagascar's most beautiful moths – the large, colourful, diurnal sunset moth – is frequently mistaken for a butterfly including by the entomologists who first described it.

Several of the silk moths are very beautiful. The comet moth (or Madagascar moon moth) has a pair of incredibly long tails – especially in the male. Madagascar emperor moths have pinkish lower wings with prominent eye spots. Both of these large species belong to a group of moths that never eat during their adult life; all of their food is consumed at the caterpillar stage.

Euchromia formosa day-flying moth (DA)

Spot the butterfly:
only one of those pictured
on this page is not a moth.
Above: Madagascar giant
swallowtail; wingspan 13cm (DA)
Above right: Madagascar sunset
moth (urania); wingspan 8cm (PB)
Below right: male comet moth;
wingspan 14cm (DA)
Below: Madagascar emperor moth
(also known as a suraka silk moth)
resting on a pachypodium at Isalo;
wingspan 13cm (KL)

3 Planning a Trip

This chapter is designed to help you easily map out the 'wheres', 'whens' and 'hows' of your trip without suffering from information overload. Throughout the following pages, there are recommendations from leading tour operators, guidance about the best time to go, advice on health issues to be addressed before you travel, and suggestions of what to pack. You cannot possibly hope to cover everywhere in Madagascar in a visit of a couple of weeks, so the *Top 20* section of this chapter will assist you in picking out what appeals to you most. Whether you opt for a group tour, a tailor-made trip or the semi-independent option of dealing direct with a tour operator in Madagascar, this section will allow you to choose or design the itinerary best suited to your interests while making the most efficient use of the time you have available. At the beginning of this chapter you will also find details of recommended tour operators, both international and locally based.

(DA)

When to visit

The driest months are April to August, but this is wintertime in Madagascar so wildlife is least active during this period. In winter it can get quite chilly in the highlands, but most coastal areas remain pleasantly warm. Starting from September it becomes warmer, making October and November perhaps the best all-round months for a visit, as there is plenty of wildlife to see but it is still fairly dry across most of the country. These are the optimum months for birders to see the widest range of species.

The hot rainy season begins in December or January and continues until March. This time is popular with the most serious naturalists and also those interested in plants, especially anyone keen to see orchids in flower. But note that several of the more remote areas without surfaced roads become inaccessible after the heavy rains have started. There is also a risk of cyclones during the rainy season so it would be unwise to head out to sea in a small vessel.

Late April is breeding season for ring-tailed lemurs (when you can witness their stink fights) and their young are born in September. Sifakas mate earlier in the year, so they have their babies in June or July. The indri give birth earlier still in May or June. The spectacle of mating fossas at Kirindy usually occurs in October but precisely when is unpredictable. Explosive breeder frogs mate *en masse* around December once the rains have arrived.

One advantage of dry weather: dinner on the beach at Anjajavy. (DA)

Public holidays

Most shops close on public holidays, as do banks, which also tend to finish at lunchtime on the preceding day. Where a public holiday falls on a Tuesday or Thursday, the connected Monday or Friday is sometimes – but not always – declared a bridge holiday. Where a holiday falls on a Sunday, the Monday is sometimes taken as a holiday in lieu – but again not consistently. In any case, tourist attractions such as national parks are typically open on most public holidays.

1 January	**New Year's Day**	15 August	**Assumption Day**
29 March	**Martyrs' Day**	1 November	**All Saints' Day**
1 May	**Labour Day**	11 December	**Fourth Republic Day**
26 June	**Independence Day**	25 December	**Christmas Day**

Movable dates: Easter Monday (March/April), **Ascension Day** (May), **Whit Monday** (May/June)

Booking a trip

An initial choice to be made is whether you want to join a group tour, arrange a tailor-made itinerary through a tour operator in your home country, book directly with a local operator in Madagascar, or arrange everything yourself. The independent option is the cheapest and most flexible, but requires considerably more effort and comes with the fewest guarantees. If you decide to organise your trip independently then you will find much more detailed information on direct booking of accommodation, transport and other services in the standard Bradt *Madagascar* guide, published separately. Group tours are often led by an expert who may give talks throughout the trip. Some of these have a special focus such as birding or photography.

Most people book through a tour operator in their own country. This option may cost more than doing so with a local ground operator, but comes with several benefits. It is more straightforward to pay an agent based in your home country and they are likely to have contracts with airlines for cheaper flights to Madagascar. They should be bonded (giving you much greater financial protection if anything was to go wrong) and are much more accessible either by phone or face-to-face during the itinerary planning stage. If you choose to book with a Malagasy operator then remember you may have to arrange your own flights. Tour prices are normally quoted all-inclusive, but it is always best to ask what is included if it's not stated explicitly. See page 85 for more on what is normally part of the package.

Aardvark Safaris

ⓣ +44 (0)1980 849160 ⓔ mail@aardvarksafaris.com

ⓦ www.aardvarksafaris.co.uk (UK); www.aardvarksafaris.com (US)

With offices in the UK and USA, Aardvark Safaris work with their clients to tailor-make their dream Madagascar holiday. With over 20 years' experience, they've slept in the beds, eaten the meals and walked with the guides. You can be confident that they have the knowledge and expertise to ensure all your holiday wishes are fulfilled. See page 242.

Audley Travel

ⓣ +44 (0)1993 838 585

ⓔ africa@audleytravel.com ⓦ www.audleytravel.com

Audley organise tailor-made journeys in Asia, Africa, Arabia, Latin America, Australasia, Canada, Alaska, Antarctica and the Arctic for discerning travellers who wish to travel according to their own, unique itinerary. Their country specialists use their unrivalled destination knowledge to create bespoke trips, using the best local guides and character accommodation.

Cortez Travel & Expeditions

ⓣ +1 858 755 5136 ⓔ info@cortez-usa.com

ⓦ www.cortez-usa.com

Designing and promoting travel to Madagascar in a sensitive way is the focus of Cortez, rated Top Travel Specialist by Condé Nast. With Monique Rodriguez in Madagascar and Susan Herbst in California, their in-depth and up-to-date knowledge of this challenging destination allows them to 'tell it like it is' so travellers come away with unforgettable memories. See page 227.

Extraordinary Expeditions

ⓣ +27 (0)11 706 5959 ⓔ conrad@ex-ex.co.za

ⓦ www.ex-ex.co.za

Extraordinary Expeditions is a small, specialist operator focusing on providing the ultimate in nature-centric and creative travel arrangements. Madagascar for the uninitiated can be a trying destination, but they ensure that a traveller's time is maximised in the various natural wonders that the Island Continent offers, and minimised in cities and travel. See page 232.

Imagine Africa

T +44 (0)20 7622 5114 E info@imagineafrica.co.uk
W www.imagineafrica.co.uk (UK); www.imagineafrica.com (US)

With offices in the US and UK, Imagine Africa pride themselves on giving expert advice. They visit the lodges, have strong relationships with the owners and can give you the low-down on the detail behind the glossy images. Add competitive prices, award-winning service and financial protection and you can be assured of an incredible holiday. See page 126.

Nomad Tours

T +27 (0)21 845 7400 E marketing@nomadtours.co.za
W www.nomadtours.co.za

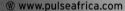

Since 1997, Nomad has run camping and accommodated experiential and adventure tours through southern and east Africa, as well as some exotic destinations. They respect every one of their travellers and want to show them the 'ultimate African experience'. This takes passion, experience and a deep understanding of this wonderful and unique continent. See page 177.

Pulse Africa

T +27 (0)11 325 2290 E info@pulseafrica.com
W www.pulseafrica.com

Pulse Africa specialises in tailor-made personalised holidays to southern Africa, east Africa and the Indian Ocean Islands. With over twenty years' experience, and thousands of miles under their belt, they are well equipped to turn your holiday dreams into a reality. They are based in South Africa with representation in UK, USA and Europe. See page 160.

Rainbow Tours

T +44 (0)20 7666 1252
E info@rainbowtours.co.uk W www.rainbowtours.co.uk

Rainbow's expertise earned them four *Best Tour Operator* awards in the last nine years. With honesty, enthusiasm and in-depth first-hand experience, they work closely with their Malagasy partners and support inspiring local initiatives. This local knowledge ensures a memorable, hassle-free holiday and a wonderful learning experience, with ATOL protection. See page 194.

Locally based tour operators

ASISTEN Travel

① +261 (0)20 22 577 55

Ⓔ info@asisten-travel.com Ⓦ www.asisten-travel.com

Founded and run by two young Malagasy entrepreneurs, ASISTEN Travel is a local inbound tour operator specialised in the conception of tailor-made trips in Madagascar. The company also offers some fixed-departure photography and luxury tours. Based in Antananarivo, the capital of Madagascar, it describes itself as 'the first 100% Malagasy tourism business'. See page 150.

Holidays Madagascar

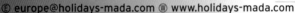

① +261 (0)20 24 365 37; +33 (0)680 220 249

Ⓔ europe@holidays-mada.com Ⓦ www.holidays-mada.com

Holidays Madagascar is a Malagasy tour operator, established in 1996 by Andria Raharinosy, specialised in tailor-made tours. Their main base is in Antananarivo but they also have a European office in France. They describe their company philosophy as 'highlighting the social with the biodiversity'. See page 118.

Le Voyageur

Le Voyageur

① +261 (0)20 22 435 21

Ⓔ voyageur@madagaskar.travel Ⓦ www.madagaskar.travel

Le Voyageur is a knowledgeable Madagascar tour operator with its offices in Antananarivo. Founded in 1998, under Swiss management with motivated Malagasy tour consultants and operations director, it has a firm focus on providing a reliable and efficient service for unforgettable tours at a reasonable price. See page 122.

Madagascar Airtours

① +261 (0)20 22 241 92

Ⓔ airtours@madagascar-airtours.com Ⓦ www.madagascar-airtours.com

Founded in 1968, Madagascar Airtours has been among the pioneers of travel agency and tour operators for over 40 years. Being representative of American Express in Madagascar, it ensures the security and safety of your stay and offers you an adventure of authenticity throughout Madagascar and its isles. See page 212.

Madagascar Rental Tour

ⓣ +261 (0)34 06 843 86 ⓔ contact@madagascar
-rental-tour.com ⓦ www.madagascar-rental-tour.com

Madagascar Rental Tour was founded by Dyna Michel Rasolomananarivo who has 12 years' experience as a driver-guide in Madagascar. He started the company with family and friends and it has now grown to a big team. They offer personalised journeys which will help you to discover the beauty and magnificence of the fauna and the flora of Madagascar. See page 133.

Mora-Travel

ⓣ +261 (0)20 22 020 12 ⓔ info@moratravel.com
ⓦ www.moratravel.com

Mora-Travel specialises in customised tours across Madagascar. Their highly flexible customer-choice approach combined with a twelve-year outstanding presence will give you a genuine and unforgettable experience of the Island, its people and all its riches. They are committed to delivering a good-value, quality service and make your trip really worth it. See page 114.

RAMARTOUR Madagascar

ⓣ +261 (0)32 02 133 68 ⓔinfo@ramartour.com
ⓦ www.ramartour.com

RAMARTOUR Madagascar is a family-run business with an emphasis on value for money and the human touch. The company, led by Jonah Ramampionona (Malagasy) and Wendy van Tilburg (Dutch), is a young and dynamic team offering an intimate customer experience and ready to make your trip unforgettable. See page 184.

Rova Travel Tours

ⓣ +261 (0)20 22 276 67 ⓔ rtt@moov.mg
ⓦ www.rova-travel-tours.mg

Rova Travel Tours caters essentially for individuals and groups seeking personal attention, and suggests planned itineraries for business trips as well as for incentive tours or theme-related trips. Their creative team relishes the challenge of designing totally personalised tours to bring you an unforgettable journey. See page 139.

Zà Tours

ⓣ +261 (0)20 22 424 22 ⓔ zatour@iris.mg
ⓦ www.zatours-madagascar.com

Named after the famous statuesque zà baobab, one of Madagascar's best-known treasures, Zà Tours is an Antananarivo-based tour operator. They specialise in customised itineraries for groups and individuals and cater for all interests. Their experienced staff are fluent in English and will take good care of your reservations, transfers and excursions. See page 220.

Your itinerary: 20 top attractions

The trickiest part of planning a trip to Madagascar is devising a workable itinerary that maximises the time spent seeing the places you want to see while minimising the time wasted travelling between them. It is a huge country with poor transport infrastructure, so it is worth giving this careful thought. Your tour operator is best placed to advise on the logistics (they will have access to information such as the latest domestic flight timetables, which change frequently) but a good starting point is to make a list of the places you cannot afford to miss. This section is designed to show you the best of Madagascar at a glance to help you put together a travel wish list that you can develop into a full itinerary in collaboration with your operator.

Nature

(DA)

1 Rainforest reserves

For those with an interest in wildlife, a visit to at least one rainforest site is essential. The most accessible is Andasibe, just a few hours' drive east of the capital – the only place you are likely to see the indri. Other top rainforest national parks include Ranomafana and Montagne d'Ambre.

2 Dry forest reserves

To see the widest range of wildlife, try to incorporate a variety of different habitats into your itinerary. The dry deciduous forests can be as rewarding as the rainforests. Particularly recommended are Ankarana, Kirindy and Ankarafantsika.

3 Spiny forest

The ethereal spiny thickets of the far south are a habitat unique to Madagascar. This ultra-dry region is inhabited by a host of bizarre botanical forms. A visit to Ifaty or Berenty is not to be missed for those interested in plants or birds especially.

(DA)

4 Night walks

Nocturnal wildlife viewing is an option at many parks and reserves, usually taking the form of an hour-long walk either just before or after dinner. Chameleons and nocturnal lemurs are much easier to find at night.

(DA)

5 Lemur encounters

For those who like to get close to the fluffy animals, Lemurs Park 25km west of Tana has a dozen species, mostly free-ranging. Similar experiences may be had at Ivoloina, Palmarium or at Vakona's Lemur Island, where two of the four species are tame enough to jump on tourists' shoulders.

(AP)

6 Botanical gardens

The extraordinary botanical wonders of Madagascar's dry south are showcased at Arboretum d'Antsokay, with some 900 species in its collection, and also at Reniala in Ifaty. Serious botanists might also like to visit the smaller arboretum featuring rainforest species at Ranomafana.

7 Whale-watching

Take a boat trip in search of these oceanic giants. The season for seeing migrating humpbacks is July to September and the best place to find them is around Ile Sainte Marie.

(JH)

Outdoors, scenery and adventure

8 Watersports

Swimming, snorkelling and scuba diving are best off the west coast. The southeast is the centre for surfing, while windsurfing and kitesurfing are on offer in the northeast. Head to the northwest for sport fishing, kayaking, water-skiing, parasailing and other watersports.

(CW)

9 Trekking

Hike through dramatic landscapes on a multi-day camping trek at Isalo or Andringitra. For a more cultural twist on the theme, you can trek round the Zafimaniry woodcarving region with overnight homestays in the villages.

(LE)

10 Train journey

Travelling by rail is a more relaxing way to see rural Madagascar. The FCE service takes one day to run between Fianarantsoa and Manakara on the east coast. Or for a truly unique experience take the vintage rubber-tyred Micheline railcar – the only one in the world still running a service. It goes from Tana to Andasibe or Antsirabe most weekends.

11 Tsingy

Vast areas of *tsingy* – sharp-pointed limestone pinnacles carved by erosion – form one of the country's strangest landscapes. Visit Bemaraha or Ankarana to see these bizarre impenetrable stone forests.

12 Baobabs

Perhaps Madagascar's most famous scene is the avenue of majestic Grandidier's baobabs near Morondava, popular among photographers at sunset. Other species of these elephantine trees can be found at sites mainly in the southwest and north of the island.

(DA)

Culture and history

13 Artisans

In the south highlands you can arrange to visit the workshops of craftsmen producing traditional Antaimoro paper, woodcarvings, silk scarves and various handicrafts. The area is also a centre for larger industry and it's possible to take factory tours of a winery, the Sahambavy Tea Estate and the brewery for Star's famous THB.

(DA)

14 Antananarivo

Although Tana has little by way of tourist attractions it is worth spending a couple of days absorbing its quaintly bustling atmosphere if you have time. Head up to the queen's palace to survey the whole city from this hilltop vantage point.

(OD)

(DA)

15 Craft markets

Wherever you go you will find local handicrafts for sale. Carvings, woven raffia, marquetry, polished stones, paintings, embroidery and jewellery are specialities of different regions, but all can be found in the artisanal markets in Tana.

16 Historical sites

The walled village on the royal hill of Ambohimanga some 25km from the capital is a site of cultural and historic importance, and is the burial site of several members of royalty. The *rova* (queen's palace) in Tana also merits a visit.

(HR)

Relaxation and inspiration

17 Beaches

If you're planning an adventure-packed trip then why not set aside a few days for relaxation at the end? Ile Sainte Marie has some splendid beaches, as do Anakao and Ifaty. Or for a really luxurious treat there are a number of exclusive resorts in the northwest.

(DA)

18 Pangalanes Canal

Take it easy with a gentle boat trip along the quiet waters of the Pangalanes, a canal built in colonial times to connect a series of lakes in the east. There are a couple of pleasant lakeside hotels along the route if you choose to take a few days over the journey.

(DA)

19 Charities

A visit to Akany Avoko, a heart-warming halfway house and orphanage, offers an insight into the tremendous work being put into helping the disadvantaged girls and women of Tana. Elsewhere around Madagascar, there are several other charitable organisations whose inspiring projects may be visited. You can even get hands-on and plant a tree as part of various reforestation programmes.

(CL)

20 Cruising and yachting

For the ultimate chill-out, how about some time aboard a catamaran? Typically lasting three to ten days, charters focus on the string of small islands running about 100km either side of Nosy Be and are ideal for family-sized groups. Alternatively, visit Madagascar on a cruise ship: expedition cruises use inflatable landing craft to access remote areas.

(DA)

Red tape

All visitors must have a passport with at least six months' validity beyond their intended dates of stay. On entry to Madagascar you are required to show your departure flight tickets (an e-ticket printout is fine). A visa is required by all foreign tourists and is easy to obtain at the airport on arrival. They are normally issued for the exact duration of your intended stay, up to a maximum of 90 days. At the time of writing visas for stays of up to 30 days are free. Longer-stay visas cost €45–65 (but check with your operator for the latest) and can be paid for in euros or dollars. If you prefer, you can get your visa in advance at the Malagasy embassy in your country. But UK residents should be aware that there is no longer a Malagasy embassy in London; advance visas have to be obtained from the embassy in Paris.

Getting there

Almost all international flights to Madagascar arrive into Antananarivo's Ivato Airport. There are no direct flights from the UK, but Kenya Airways (⑩ www.kenya-airways.com) flies from London via Nairobi twice a week; Air France (⑩ www.airfrance.com) goes via Paris most days; and South African Airways (⑩ www.flysaa.com) flies the rather longer route via Johannesburg. Air Madagascar (⑩ www.airmadagascar.com) flies direct between Paris and Antananarivo most days, taking 10½ hours. Air Mad is represented in the UK by Aviareps (⑩ www.aviareps.com). Corsairfly (⑩ www.corsairfly.com) connects Paris with Antananarivo four times a week and is usually cheaper than Air France, but they do not operate any connecting flights to the UK.

From other Indian Ocean islands you can fly with Air Madagascar from Mauritius, Réunion, and the Comoro Islands. Air Austral (⑩ www. air-austral.com) connects Madagascar with Mayotte and Réunion. Air Mauritius (⑩ www.airmauritius.com) also flies to Antananarivo from Mauritius. From Africa, Air Madagascar flies twice a week from Johannesburg and once a week from Nairobi. From South Africa, other options are South African Airways and Interair (⑩ www.interair.co.za). From the USA, Air France is probably the best carrier, or via United (⑩ www.united.com) or Delta (⑩ www.delta.com) to Paris to connect with an Air Madagascar flight. From California you can travel west via Bangkok – from where there are Air Madagascar flights. From Australia, flights are usually routed via Hong Kong or Bangkok. Alternatively you can go from Melbourne or Perth to Mauritius to connect with an Air Madagascar flight, or fly from Perth via Johannesburg.

Tourist information

Getting any sort of information out of the **National Tourism Board** is rather difficult and at the time of writing its website is seriously out of date (Ⓦ www.madagascar-tourisme.com) but it does publish a quarterly tourism magazine which has a slightly better website (Ⓦ www.info-tourisme-madagascar.com). About half of the 20 regional tourist offices also have their own websites, some of which are quite detailed but all are in French:

Ⓦ www.tourisme-antananarivo.com (Antananarivo)
Ⓦ www.tulear-tourisme.com (Toliara)
Ⓦ www.tamatave-tourisme.com (Toamasina)
Ⓦ www.majunga.org (Mahajanga)
Ⓦ www.office-tourisme-diego-suarez.com (Antsiranana)
Ⓦ www.antsirabe-tourisme.com (Antsirabe)
Ⓦ www.anosy.gov.mg (Taolagnaro)
Ⓦ www.baobab-madagascar.org (Mahajanga and Menabe)
Ⓦ www.ortalma.org (Alaotra Mangoro)
Ⓦ www.nosybe-tourisme.com (Nosy Be)
Ⓦ www.tourisme-sainte-marie.com (Ile Sainte Marie)

The **Madagascar National Parks** website (Ⓦ www.parcs-madagascar.com) has details of all the parks and reserves in four languages including English.

Health and safety
with Dr Felicity Nicholson

Deep-vein thrombosis (DVT)

Prolonged immobility on long-haul flights may result in DVT, which can be dangerous if the clot travels to the lungs. The risk increases with age, and is higher in obese, pregnant, tall or short travellers, heavy smokers, and anybody with a history of clots, recent major operation or varicose veins surgery, cancer, stroke or heart disease. If any of these criteria apply, consult a doctor before you travel. Ensuring that you are well hydrated and trying to move around during long periods of travel helps reduce the risk.

Malaria

There is a significant risk of malaria across the island, including the most dangerous *Plasmodium falciparum* strain. It is estimated that as many as 2,000 people in Madagascar die from the disease every year, so it is extremely important to take appropriate prophylaxis. Be warned that opting not to do so may invalidate your travel insurance policy.

There is widespread resistance to chloroquine and proguanil in the country, but Malarone, doxycycline and mefloquine (Lariam) are all considered effective. Of these, Malarone is associated with the fewest side effects, but you should discuss the most suitable malaria prophylaxis for you with your doctor or travel clinic. Do not leave this to the last minute, as some courses need to be started three weeks in advance of travel. Be sure to take sufficient tablets for your trip as you cannot rely on finding genuine antimalarials in-country.

Tablets do not give complete immunity, however, so where mosquitoes are present you should also apply DEET-based insect repellent, cover up with long trousers and sleeves, and always sleep under a mosquito net. Nets are usually provided in decent hotels. (These additional precautions will also help protect you against other serious mosquito-borne diseases, which include dengue fever, chikungunya, Rift Valley fever and elephantiasis.)

Inoculations

Proof of vaccination against yellow fever is required for travellers coming from endemic areas, but there is no risk from this disease in Madagascar itself. Before travelling, it is wise to check that you are up to date on tetanus, polio and diphtheria (given all-in-one as Revaxis), and hepatitis A. Few tourists bother to get immunised against rabies given the extreme unlikeliness of encountering it, but it is such a dangerous illness that some prefer to play safe.

Travel clinics and health information

A list of current travel clinic websites worldwide is available on Ⓦ www.istm. org. For other journey preparation information, consult Ⓦ www.nathnac.org. Information about various medications may be found on Ⓦ www.netdoctor. co.uk/travel. Other useful sites include Ⓦ www.fitfortravel.scot.nhs.uk (a useful source of general travel health information) and Ⓦ www.cdc.gov/ travel (includes updates on specific destinations and information for those with limited mobility and those travelling with children). Both the US State Department (Ⓦ www.travel.state.gov) and the British Department of Health (Ⓦ www.nhs.uk/nhsengland/Healthcareabroad) also provide dedicated travel health information.

Personal first aid kit

A minimal medical kit and other health-related items should include:

- A good drying antiseptic, eg: iodine or potassium permanganate
- Antihistamine tablets and cream
- Antifungal cream, eg: Canesten
- Aspirin or paracetamol
- Antibiotic eye drops
- Ciprofloxacin or norfloxacin for severe diarrhoea
- Oral rehydration salts
- A few small dressings (Band-Aids) and a pair of fine-pointed tweezers
- Alcohol-based hand rub or bar of soap in plastic box
- Insect repellent and suncream
- Travel sickness pills

Women travellers and family travel

Madagascar is not a dangerous place for **female travellers** by global standards. You are unlikely to be bothered by unwanted advances on an organised tour; if you are, then a firm refusal is usually sufficient. There are no special dress code requirements but note that topless bathing is not usual anywhere. Those **travelling with children** will find the Malagasy generally welcoming of youngsters, but special facilities such as highchairs and cots are found only in a few top-end establishments, mostly in Tana. Imported supplies such as baby food, nappies (diapers) and wipes are available in supermarkets in Tana, but don't rely on finding any of these goods elsewhere. Consider bringing a strap-on child carrier for when the little ones tire on long walks.

Disabled travellers

with Gordon Rattray ⑩ www.able-travel.com

Madagascar can be a physical challenge for any traveller, yet with some effort even those less fleet of foot can also appreciate much the country has to offer. No operator runs specialised trips for disabled people, but many travel companies will listen to your needs and try to create a suitable itinerary. It is rare to find 'accessible' accommodation or bathrooms with wheelchair access so, if necessary, be prepared to be lifted or do your ablutions in the bedroom. Most wildlife highlights are not disabled-friendly, but Anjajavy has an officially accessible villa and Berenty has broad, flat forest paths.

What to take

Clothing

There is quite some difference between summer and winter temperatures, particularly in the highlands and the south where it is distinctly cold at night between May and September. Even some of the hottest areas can be chilly first thing in the morning. A fibre-pile jacket or a body-warmer is useful in addition to a light sweater. In June and July a scarf can give much-needed extra warmth. At any time of the year it will be hot during the day in low-lying areas, and very hot between October and March. Don't bring jeans; lightweight trousers are more comfortable and dry quicker. In all months you will need a shower-proof jacket – some people find it useful to have a baggy one that can also protect their daysack and/or camera in a drippy rainforest. A light cotton jacket is always useful for breezy evenings by the coast. A sunhat and sunglasses are essential. For footwear, trainers and sandals are usually all you need. Sports sandals are better than flip-flops. Hiking boots are necessary only for trekking, especially in the wet season.

Photographic gear

One of the delights of wildlife viewing in Madagascar is that so much of it can be seen at close quarters. This means that even with a simple compact camera you can capture some reasonable shots. Keen photographers will want to take an SLR, but an expensive long lens (>200mm) is only really essential for birders. Serious enthusiasts might consider a lightweight tripod and separate flash – useful in the dim light of the rainforest and on night walks. Take all the memory cards (or film) and batteries you need from home; such items are hard to find and very expensive in Madagascar. It also pays to take a basic cleaning kit.

(DA)

Other essentials

A soft bag or backpack is more practical than a hard suitcase. Choose something strong and secure, especially if your itinerary involves travelling in a bus, as baggage is sometimes strapped to the roof and covered with a tarpaulin. If your luggage is indistinctive, consider making it stand out with a colourful strap, sticker or tag. This reduces the chance of someone inadvertently walking off with it at the airport and may make an opportunist think twice before doing so deliberately. When travelling as part of a group tour, the operator often supplies branded luggage labels. Use them; they help porters to see easily that your bags belong with the group's. You will also need a small daysack (which can double as your hand luggage). This should be big enough for your camera, binoculars, waterproof jacket and a bottle of water.

A travel alarm clock is useful (or equally a mobile phone with an alarm function). An inflatable travel pillow makes long road and air journeys more comfortable. Take a small hand torch and a head torch for night walks. It is easier to spot animals in the light of a head torch with a broad, dissipated beam rather than an intense, focused one. Some models can be switched between the two options. Many travellers find collapsible walking poles indispensable. Take binoculars if you're particularly interested in birds, and perhaps a field guide for the seriously keen. (Field guides also exist for Madagascar's mammals, reptiles and amphibians, but all are rather too hefty to be tucked into a pocket.)

Other items not to forget include a notebook and pens, reading material for downtime, spare glasses or contact lenses, and the medical items listed on page 82. There's no need to take towels as they are provided in all hotels, as are mosquito nets in upper-end hotels (except in areas where mozzies are rare).

Electricity

The voltage in Madagascar is 220V. Outlets take European-style plugs with two round pins. Travel adapters are hard to find in-country so take all you need from home. Power cuts occur fairly frequently in the towns. There is no mains electricity at all at most lodges sited in rural spots, such as near national parks, so these normally use generators. Typically they are only switched on for periods in the morning and evening, so take a note of the schedule if you have batteries to charge, and sleep with a torch by your bedside in case you need to get up in the night. Note that a few lodges use solar power and these may not have power outlets in the rooms but batteries can be charged at reception.

Organising your finances

Tours are usually quoted inclusive of all accommodation, meals, transport and activities. The elements of your holiday for which you will need to budget separately are: drinks (but bottled water may be included), tips (see page 97), laundry service, any optional excursions, travel insurance, visa (free for visits of up to 30 days at the time of writing), and spending money for souvenirs and snacks. Fees for pre-travel inoculations and antimalarial tablets can also be significant. Note that for solo travellers there is usually a 'single supplement' chargeable in addition to the quoted tour price.

Malagasy currency cannot be obtained abroad so you will need to exchange or withdraw cash on arrival. Euros and US dollars are convertible at banks across the country including in Tana's airport. Visa **credit and debit cards** may be used to withdraw cash from most ATMs and some also accept MasterCard. **Travellers' cheques** are somewhat less convenient but safer. Some banks can exchange them but generally only euro/dollar varieties. Some hotels will accept payment by Visa or hard cash in euros – but not always at a favourable rate.

Entrance fees for protected areas

Fees at national parks and special reserves will be included for those on an organised tour. These fees comprise an entry permit and a separate guide payment. At Isalo, Andasibe, Ranomafana, Montagne d'Ambre, Ankarana, Ankarafantsika and Bemaraha entry costs 25,000Ar (€9) per person for a day and at all other government-administered parks and reserves a one-day permit is 10,000Ar (€4) – with discounts for multi-day permits. Guides are obligatory. Their rates are set by each park and vary from 8,000Ar to 50,000Ar (€3–17) per guide per circuit, depending on length of walk. Each guide can usually take up to five visitors; larger groups must take additional guides. At private reserves (such as Kirindy and Mitsinjo's forest at Andasibe) pricing works differently but the overall rates are comparable. At some private sites the services of a guide are included in the entry charge.

N.7
AMBALAVAO
3
TOLIARY 462
467

4 On the Ground

Most day-to-day practicalities will be handled by the staff appointed by your tour operator for those on an organised trip. This includes all transport, checking in to your accommodation, arranging meals or packed lunches, obtaining park permits, appointing guides and paying any fees - leaving you free to relax and enjoy the food, activities and entertainment stress-free. Guides are generally very helpful and will assist you in matters requiring local understanding; nevertheless some advance knowledge will be useful. This chapter presents important health and safety advice, guidance on what to expect when wildlife-watching, and other useful information of how things work in Madagascar. This includes getting to grips with the local money, advice on tipping, haggling, shopping and exchanging currency, an introduction to the Malagasy cuisine, an overview of telecommunications facilities, and an introduction to the country's transport infrastructure.

Health and safety in Madagascar
with Dr Felicity Nicholson

Consideration of health and safety issues must be taken seriously wherever you travel, but this is particularly so in Madagascar. The reason is not that there are unusually many dangers on the island, but because of its poor infrastructure. If you fall ill in Madagascar, you may be several days' uncomfortable journey from proper medical care, and many drugs are not available at all. It is important therefore to be prepared for problems which could arise and be aware of the early symptoms of common illnesses.

Travellers' diarrhoea

Many visitors to unfamiliar destinations suffer a dose of travellers' diarrhoea and Madagascar is no exception. By taking precautions against travellers' diarrhoea you will also avoid more serious (albeit rare) sanitation-related diseases such as typhoid, cholera, hepatitis, dysentery and worms. The maxim to remind you what you can safely eat is: peel it, boil it, cook it or forget it.

This means that fruit you have washed and peeled yourself, and hot foods, should be safe, but raw foods, cold cooked foods, salads, fruit salads prepared by others, ice cream and ice are all risky. Decent hotels will take care to prepare such dishes from bottled or boiled water.

If you suffer a bout of diarrhoea, it is dehydration that makes you feel awful, so drink lots of clear fluids, ideally infused with sachets of oral rehydration salts. If the problem persists for more than five days or there is blood with the diarrhoea, seek medical attention.

Drinking water

To stay healthy, it is important to keep yourself hydrated. This means drinking a minimum of 2½ litres of fluids each day – more in very hot weather or if you are undertaking energetic activities. If you are suffering from diarrhoea or vomiting, then keeping up your water intake is even more vital.

Bottled water is available all over Madagascar. The most common brand is Eau Vive, which comes from the natural springs of Lohavohitra mountain, 40km northwest of Tana. The area is called Andranovelona, which means 'the place of the water of life' – hence the name Eau Vive. It comes in 500ml and 1½-litre bottles. The latter cost around 1,000Ar (€0.36) in the little roadside shops, but may cost as much as 10,000Ar (€3.60) in the most remote luxury hotels.

Sunburn and sunstroke

Overexposure to the sun can lead to short-term sunburn or sunstroke, and increases the long-term risk of skin cancer. Wear a T-shirt and waterproof sunscreen when swimming. When walking in the direct sun, cover up with long, loose clothes, wear a broad-brimmed hat and use sunscreen (at least factor 30). The glare and the dust can be hard on the eyes, so wear UV-protecting sunglasses. And remember that in the tropical heat you will need to drink more fluids than at home.

Bites and stings

Malagasy **snakes** are not likely to bite unless handled and in any case are not harmful to humans. Lizards such as **chameleons** may also bite if handled. Treat any such bites just as any other break in the skin: keep the wound clean and apply a drying antiseptic. **Crocodiles** are the only seriously dangerous reptile, but they are rare and you are unlikely to encounter them unexpectedly. Avoid swimming anywhere you are warned they may be present.

Large **centipedes** and one or two types of **spiders** can deliver very painful bites, but they are not fatal unless you suffer an anaphylactic reaction. Many Malagasy **wasps** have horribly painful stings, as do **scorpions**, which favour dark crevices as their hiding places and may inadvertently choose a rucksack pocket or unworn shoe, and then sting any hand or foot that suddenly invades their space. But they are rarely a problem for tourists.

Although you may find them revolting, **leech** bites are not dangerous. Leaches are small and hang around on bushes after rain to ambush a passing animal – or tourist. If you can stomach their presence, then the best course of action for a leech that has latched on is to wait till it has had its fill and drops off. Otherwise you can encourage it to let go with a pinch of salt or a lit match. They inject an anticoagulant when biting, so the wound may take some time to stop bleeding. Beware of strolling barefoot on damp, sandy areas, as you could pick up **jiggers**. These are maggotlike sand fleas that burrow into the soles of feet to incubate their eggs. Jiggers will eventually make it too painful to walk if not removed with a sterilised needle and the area disinfected.

In the ocean, avoid **sea urchins**. If spiked, use tweezers to ensure all broken spine tips are removed.

Scuba diving safety

There is no hyperbaric recompression chamber in Madagascar. Any diving casualty must be evacuated by air to Réunion, Mauritius or mainland Africa. Since such an evacuation would likely take some considerable time to organise (and in any case flying is very dangerous for a diver with the bends) it is advisable to dive within safety limits that keep the risks to a minimum.

Dive operators in Madagascar are not regulated, so consequently there are good ones and bad ones. Check the equipment provided and reject anything you feel is in an unsatisfactory condition. Be sure to report any safety concerns to your tour operator after your trip.

Divers should be wary of stings from rays, scorpionfish, stonefish, jellyfish, fire coral, cone shells and anemones, and potential bites from moray eels, sea snakes and sharks. But provided you avoid contact with the reef and refrain from interfering with any marine life when diving, the risk of being harmed by anything is very low.

Mosquitoes

Take all possible precautions to avoid being bitten by mosquitoes. They can transmit not only malaria but many other serious diseases. Apply insect repellent to exposed skin, keep your limbs covered especially in the evenings, and always use a mosquito net when it is provided.

It is essential to keep taking your malaria prophylaxis regularly, and to do so for the requisite number of weeks after your return home. Symptoms do not always manifest themselves right away: although it normally takes only a week or two, it is possible for malarial fever not to break out until a year after being bitten. If you experience fever symptoms including sweats and chills, muscle pains, headache, cough or diarrhoea, go to a doctor immediately.

Bilharzia

Also known as schistosomiasis, bilharzia is an unpleasant parasitic disease transmitted by freshwater snails in lakes and slow-moving rivers (but not hotel swimming pools or the ocean). If you do swim in a lake or river, you can test for bilharzia at specialist travel clinics, ideally six weeks or longer after exposure, and it is easy to treat. Avoid swimming in stagnant water, or at least avoid the reedy banks – bathing in the centre is safer. It takes several minutes for the tiny worm to work its way through your skin, so a quick wade across a river followed by vigorous towelling off should not put you at risk.

Rabies

Although extremely rare, rabies does exist and caution is warranted given that it is such a horrific disease. To be on the safe side, assume that any mammal might be carrying rabies. Stray cats and dogs, bats, and even – in theory – lemurs could be infected. So if you are bitten, scratched or licked over broken skin, scrub the wound with soap and running water for at least five minutes, flood the wound with antiseptic, dress it and seek medical help as soon as possible. If you have not been vaccinated against rabies, then the urgency of the need to seek medical help cannot be stressed too strongly.

Sexually transmitted infections

There are unusually high rates of sexually transmitted infection in Madagascar (a recent study in Tana found 78% of sex workers to be infected). And HIV/AIDS is on the increase too, albeit not as prevalent as in mainland Africa. So if you do decide to indulge, be sure to use condoms or Femidoms to reduce the risk of transmission.

Tips for avoiding theft

Violent crime is still relatively rare, and even in Tana you are probably safer than in a large American city. You are more likely to be robbed by subterfuge.

- Remember that most theft occurs in the street, not in hotels; leave your valuables in a safe at the hotel.
- Money kept in a safe at hotel reception should be in a sealed envelope that cannot be opened without detection.
- Do not leave money around, including in coat pockets hanging in your room or even in your hand while you are distracted.
- Carry your cash in a money belt, neck pouch or deep pocket.
- In busy areas (especially in Tana) be mindful of pickpockets and be aware that some may use blades to slash open backpacks.
- Pay particular attention to the security of your passport.
- Keep photocopies of important documents in your luggage, or keep scans of them in an email account that you can access from the web.
- In a restaurant never hang your bag on the back of your chair.
- In a vehicle never keep valuables within reach of an open window.
- Refrain from wearing showy jewellery and keep valuables out of sight.
- If you are robbed, you will need a police certificate for your insurance. Obtaining one may well take all day.

Getting around

Travel can be slow and distances far in Madagascar, so if you are short on time then **flying** is often the only practical option. Air Madagascar operates domestic routes to more than 25 towns across the island, but many places are only served once or twice a week (and not necessarily year-round) so up-to-date flight schedules are important when planning an itinerary. A typical domestic flight costs €185/US$250 one way inclusive of taxes in economy class – and often rather more at times of peak demand or at short notice.

For travel by road, a hired **4x4 or other car** is the choice for most tourists. Hire vehicles generally come with a driver, who may speak English and double as a guide. Except for private tour buses, the only buses are *taxi-brousses* – minibuses that operate between towns. They are much less comfortable and also less convenient because they tend not to serve tourist sites directly and there are no opportunities for photo stops. But they are economical (about €2 per 100km over long distances) so are favoured by budget travellers with plenty of time.

The passenger **railway** network is tiny, with only two operational stretches of track: Moramanga to Toamasina and Fianarantsoa to Manakara. In addition, a rubber-tyred Micheline railcar operates as a historical novelty between Tana and Andasibe/Antsirabe most weekends.

For local transport in most large towns you will find **taxis** (about €2 per journey within the town) and in some flatter places there are rickshaws called *pousse-pousses* (less than €1 per journey) and increasingly bicycle rickshaws called *cyclo-pousses* too.

There are 4x4s of all calibres and in all states of repair. Be sure to pick one that is up to the task. (DA)

Visiting protected areas

Unlike national parks in Europe and the US, the protected areas of rainforest and other habitat in Madagascar are not tracts of countryside where the public may come and go as they please. Rather they are carefully controlled natural zones. In most protected areas, including all national parks and special reserves administered by Madagascar National Parks, it is obligatory to be accompanied by an accredited guide, you must stick to the trails, and an entry permit must be purchased by all visitors (for prices see page 85).

Usually one guide is required per four or five tourists. This is to avoid visitors getting lost, to help keep them safe, and to deter irresponsible and illegal behaviour such as collecting wildlife. Respect the environment: do not litter, do not pick plants or flowers, and do not attempt to touch or feed any wild animals.

Spoiled by our exposure to action-packed nature documentaries nowadays, it is all too easy to embark on a forest walk with unrealistic expectations of teeming wildlife at every step. Remember that such TV programmes often take years to film. How much wildlife you will see on a walk depends on many factors, including the season, the weather, the guide's experience... and simple luck. For the most part, animals are not very active during rain – although a recent shower will encourage many creatures to emerge once it is over. Wildlife is most active between dawn and mid-morning, so a prompt start to the day will maximise your chances of good sightings. At many sites, night walks are also worthwhile (see page 44).

Keeping quiet and wearing drab colours will also help in making a closer approach to the shyest creatures. Keep your eyes open rather than relying solely on the guide; if he or she is scanning the canopy for lemurs and birds, then frogs and reptiles in the undergrowth may go unnoticed unless all members of the group stay alert.

Walking circuits typically last between one and five hours and cover the full range of difficulty from flat, well-maintained trails to hard-going, steep slopes that may be slippery after rain. If you have any difficulties with walking long distances over uneven terrain, make sure your tour operator and guide are made aware of your abilities in advance so that an appropriate trail may be selected. Consider taking a walking pole or poles to assist you over rugged terrain. Group tours may split into smaller walking parties according to fitness levels.

Take a small daysack with your water, suncream and hat if necessary, camera, and binoculars if you have them. Where there is any risk of rain, take a jacket (rainforest showers can start and stop quite unexpectedly).

Eating and drinking

Eating well is one of the delights of Madagascar, and even the fussiest tourists are usually happy with the food. International hotels serve international food, usually with a French bias, and often do special Malagasy dishes. Lodges and smaller hotels serve local food which is almost always excellent, particularly on the coast where crayfish and other seafood predominates. Meat lovers will enjoy the zebu steaks, although they are sometimes tougher than some may be used to (free-range meat usually is). In remoter areas, hotels tend to offer a three-course set menu.

The **national dish** in Madagascar is *romazava*, a meat and vegetable stew, spiced with ginger and containing *brèdes mafana* – tasty, tongue-tingling greens. Another good local dish is *ravitoto*, shredded manioc leaves with fried beef and coconut. Brochettes, or beef kebabs, are also a popular traditional meal, as is green peppercorn sauce served over chicken or beef.

The Malagasy eat a lot of rice, but most restaurants cater to foreign tastes by providing fries as an alternative. Rice sometimes comes with a bowl of stock to be spooned over it, or drunk as a soup.

Seafood is excellent in coastal areas. (DA)

Madagascar is gradually becoming more accustomed to **vegetarian** tourists, but meatless options are not always available at short notice. If you are vegetarian, or have other special dietary requirements, notify your tour operator in advance of your trip and make sure your trip guide or tour leader is also aware so that hotels and restaurants can be advised ahead of time.

There is a great variety of fruit and vegetables, even on the smallest market. A selection of fruit is often served in restaurants, along with raw vegetables or crudités. From June to August the fruit is mostly limited to bananas, but from September there are also strawberries, mangoes, lychees, pineapples and loquats.

Chocaholics should keep their eyes peeled for Chocolate Robert – available in several varieties. For those wishing to take some home, there is a Chocolaterie Robert shop in the international departure lounge of Tana's airport.

The most popular alcoholic drink, available absolutely everywhere, is **Three Horses Beer** – known universally as THB. The main variety is a 5.4% alcohol THB pilsener, available in 650ml bottles or 330ml bottles/cans. You may also find THB Special (6.2%), THB Bex (5%) and THB Lite (1%) – the last of these created to circumvent new laws restricting advertising of stronger alcoholic beverages. Another low-alcohol option is THB Fresh (<1%), a light shandy that's particularly refreshing on a hot afternoon.

Madagascar produces its own **wine** in the Fianarantsoa region of the southern highlands. Some of it is very good but unfortunately some is dreadful, and it is not always possible to be sure of the quality of what you are ordering. That said, it is inexpensive enough to be worth the gamble. The Lazan'i Betsileo label wines are normally pretty good and have won European wine awards. As well as white and red, Madagascar produces 'grey' wine – essentially a very pale rosé.

(DA)

Rhum arrangé – homemade flavoured rum – is found in most hotels. Often a dozen or more large bottles are proudly displayed behind the bar. There are endless varieties flavoured with different ingredients, including: vanilla, ginger, cinnamon, mango, lemon, lychee, and every other fruit imaginable. Adventurous bars may offer more unusual rums flavoured with such exotic ingredients as baobab seeds or even snakes!

The most popular mineral water is called Eau Vive, but other brands are available. Coca-Cola, Sprite and Fanta are also available. Bonbon Anglais is a very sweet drink purporting to be lemonade, but tasting rather more like a colourless version of the Irn-Bru of Scotland.

Most Malagasy **coffee** is of the Robusta variety, which suits some people but others find it has an odd aftertaste. In recent years Madagascar has also begun to grow some higher-grade Arabica coffee. Interestingly there are many native coffee species, including seven only discovered in 2009, but none is currently exploited for the drinks industry.

The locally grown **tea** is quite weak, the best quality being reserved for export. It is also available flavoured with vanilla.

Traditionally the Malagasy quench their thirst with *ranovola*, obtained by boiling water in the pan in which the rice was cooked. It has a slight flavour of burnt rice.

Banking and foreign exchange

The colonial currency, the Malagasy franc, was replaced in 2003 by the ariary (Ar). In major towns and tourist centres the new currency has now been fully adopted, so you are unlikely to encounter prices in francs, but in rural areas locals continue to use them. The two currencies are tied: one ariary is equal to five of the old francs.

Banknotes in circulation range from 100Ar to 10,000Ar. Smaller-denomination coins exist down to 1Ar, although they are not much used. The largest notes – the blue ones – are only worth about £3.00/€3.60/US$4.80, so if you are exchanging much foreign currency expect a large wad of notes in return – more than will comfortably fit in a wallet.

Almost all banks in Tana and the major towns now have ATMs. Those at branches of BFV bank accept only Visa, BOA only MasterCard, and BNI now takes both. BNI machines dispense a maximum of 385,000Ar per withdrawal; for BFV the limit is 300,000Ar. Remember that your home bank may charge a fixed fee for each withdrawal abroad.

When exchanging hard currency, it is best to bring €20/€50 or US$20/$50 denomination notes because some banks are suspicious of higher-value notes owing to the prevalence of counterfeits.

(ML)

Bargaining

Haggling is expected on markets and with street sellers, but not in shops. It can be a controversial subject for travellers in poor countries like Madagascar, where the typical tourist could easily be a hundred times richer than the locals. Hard bargaining over a few pennies that would bring little gain to wealthy buyers may make a world of difference to the sellers struggling to feed their families. On the other hand, it is not beneficial for the local economy in the long run if tourists routinely pay over the odds for goods, and such behaviour tends to change local attitudes to foreigners for the worse.

The answer is to strike a balance. Before beginning negotiations over the price of an item, try to establish what a sensible price would be (ask your tour guide or see what other stall holders are asking for similar wares). Haggling, when done with courtesy and good humour, is an enjoyable way of engaging with locals. Keep in mind that your goal is to reach a mutually agreeable price, not to eliminate their profit. And in the case of handicrafts remember that the best workmanship should be rewarded, otherwise you will only encourage production of cheap quality products in future.

Tipping

Tipping is normal for guides, drivers, porters, etc who have performed their duties impressively. On organised or group tours, gratuities may be handled by your tour guide, so check the arrangement. In restaurants, a tip of 5–10% is plenty. Baggage handlers at airports and some hotels are masters of the disappointment act. They may feign offence at the amount if they think you are new to Madagascar, but a tip of 100–500Ar is ample for carrying luggage. Taxi drivers do not expect a tip.

Forest guides should be tipped according to their service. There is no obligation to tip, but those enthusiastic guides who have done well in spotting animals, speak good English, and have shown themselves to be knowledgeable about the flora and fauna should be rewarded with a gratuity of 2,500–25,000Ar (€1–10) per day.

The hardest tipping question is how much to pay the guides and drivers who have spent several days with you and given excellent service. Keep in mind the cost of living in Madagascar and tip proportionately: teachers and doctors typically earn €85 per month (€4/day) while unskilled workers may earn less than €15 a month (€0.70/day).

Give tips in ariary rather than foreign currency and do try to ensure that the people who work behind the scenes, such as cooks and cleaners, also get rewarded if you feel they have worked well.

Shopping

A wide range of handicrafts is to be found in Madagascar. Most typical of the country are woodcarvings, raffia work (in amazing variety), carved zebu horn, Antaimoro paper (with embedded dried flowers), and marquetry. Each region has its specialities, but all are to be found in the craft markets of Tana.

In the south you can buy attractive heavy silver bracelets that are traditionally worn by men. In the east and north especially, you will be offered vanilla pods, peppercorns, cloves and other spices. Gemstones mainly come from the south. Tana is the best place to look for decorative rocks and minerals, usually sold as polished balls or sculpted into other shapes such as ashtrays. Carved wooden solitaire boards are produced where each marble is made from a different mineral. But if you would prefer a traditional Malagasy board game, ask for *fanorona*.

Almost anywhere you can find shops selling *lambas* (Malagasy sarongs – see page 22). Good quality cotton T-shirts bearing Malagasy designs and slogans are produced by the Baobab, Maki, Carambole and Fosa labels. Toamasina and Nosy Be are the best-known places for crocheted and embroidered tablecloths; and silk scarves coloured with natural dyes are produced in the southern highlands.

Delightful little toy cars and other vehicles constructed from scrap tin cans are among the most colourful wares on the craft markets.

Choosing vanilla pods

The quality of vanilla varies quite considerably, but with these tips you will be able to distinguish the good from the bad. Any pods will do for flavouring a jar of sugar but for cakes, puddings and other culinary uses it is worth seeking out some of reasonable quality.

Vanilla pods are traditionally graded according to length, the best class ('gourmet') being those over 15cm long. Try to find fattish pods with a slightly soft and moist feel. Reject brittle or split pods; they should be pliable enough to wrap around your finger without breaking. The best are dark – almost black – with an oily surface. You may even find some with a sparkly white frosting of fine vanillin crystals.

Be sure to smell them, as this is the most important indicator. Good vanilla should be strongly aromatic with a rich, almost creamy scent. Per kilo, you get about 240 gourmet pods, around 330 medium class, or 430+ low-grade ones. Each person may take up to 2kg of vanilla out of the country.

You may also see wooden toy trucks for sale by the roadside south of Tana. Musical instruments are represented by the djembe drum and the *valiha*, a tube zither unique to Madagascar.

Be sure to obtain receipts for wood and stone items and anything expensive. On departure you should take your receipts for any minerals or ammonites to the Ministry of Mines desk at the airport to obtain an export permit. There are also desks there for phytosanitary, forestry and veterinary export enquiries.

Each person may take out of Madagascar a maximum of 1kg of gemstones, 1kg of coffee and 1kg of pepper. Make sure that nothing you plan to take back contravenes your home country's import regulations (there are often restrictions on honey, for example, as well as alcohol).

Buying ethically

Not all handicrafts and souvenirs are to be encouraged. Many items made from animal products should be avoided for conservation reasons and you could even get into serious trouble for trying to take some out of Madagascar. Do not buy products from endangered species. These include tortoise shell, turtle shell, snake skin, sea shells, coral and, of course, live animals. The mounted bodies of butterflies and other insects are likely to come from wild-caught specimens too, so are best avoided unless you are sure of the source.

Other prohibited items include endemic plants without a permit and any genuine article of funerary art. Most bones or fossils cannot legally be taken out of the country, including subfossil elephant bird eggshell fragments (often on sale reconstructed into complete eggs) – however, ammonites and petrified wood are not a problem. Crocodiles are farmed commercially so their skins may be sold legally; products made from zebu horn are also fine.

The dilemma of wooden carvings is less clear cut. Most carved souvenirs are made from palissander, rosewood or ebony – all slow-growing precious woods that are being illegally logged from Madagascar's forests at an alarming rate. But these carvings provide employment and income for many poor families, and the quantity of wood used for making souvenirs is minuscule compared to the hundreds of tonnes of timber being illegally exported to China to make furniture. You may therefore feel that, on balance, small carved items are not unethical.

(ML)

Media, communications and business

Internet

Cybercafés exist in most towns, although the computers tend to be slow – with the French-layout keyboards an added frustration for anglophone users. Temperamental web connections and frequent power cuts mean that internet access should never be relied upon. Hotels and some restaurants in the main towns increasingly have Wi-Fi available, but those in more remote, scenic spots typically do not. Since 2008, the use of BlackBerry mobile devices has been supported.

Telephone

Nowadays, the mobile phone network is quite extensive; you will find a signal in most populated places, even quite small villages. If you plan to use your phone on international roaming while on your trip, you should check prices with your network operator before you go because Madagascar is usually in the most expensive price band. In fact, if you expect to use your phone much at all, you would be best advised to buy a Malagasy SIM card at the airport on arrival. They cost very little.

There are three operators: Orange (numbers starting with 032), Airtel (033) and Telma (034). Top-up cards are available in shops everywhere, but for high-value recharge cards (over 20,000Ar) you will have to go to an Orange/Zain/Telma boutique.

Domestic mobile numbers are seven digits starting with 03. Landline numbers are five digits and must be prefixed by 020 (or +261 20 when calling from abroad). To make an international call from within Madagascar, dial 00 followed by the relevant country code.

Mail

Usually postcards and letters take about two weeks to reach Europe and a little longer to North America. But the mail service is unpredictable, with international mail sometimes taking months to reach its destination. Stamps are quite expensive. There are post offices even in small towns, with some 220 branches around the country.

If you splash out on any particularly large souvenirs, it may be best to ship them home by courier. The domestic parcel service, Colis Express (ⓦ www.colis-express.net), has some 70 branches around Madagascar. Internationally it hooks up with DHL, which also has its own offices in major towns (ⓦ www.dhl.com.mg), and there is a FedEx office in Tana too (ⓦ www.fedex.com/mg).

Media

There are a number of daily and weekly newspapers, mostly published in a mixture of French and Malagasy. These include *L'Express de Madagascar* (Ⓦ www.lexpressmada.com), *La Gazette de la Grande Ile* (Ⓦ www.lagazette-dgi.com), *Madagascar Tribune* (Ⓦ www.madagascar-tribune.com) and *Midi Madagasikara* (Ⓦ www.midi-madagasikara.mg).

Malagasy TV channels are similarly bilingual, but mostly carry music videos for much of the day. Hotels with satellite TV usually offer an English-language channel – normally CNN, or sometimes BBC World – but the majority of channels are French.

Malagasy language

As evidenced by grammatical and vocabulary similarities, the Malagasy language can be shown to be of Malayo-Polynesian origin. Indeed, it was first demonstrated from detailed linguistic analysis that Madagascar was settled by people from the Malay Archipelago who had passed through the Barito River area of southern Borneo.

Across Madagascar there is significant variation in the language. Some authorities consider the regional dialects to be sufficiently distinct to warrant separate language status, with most linguists now treating Malagasy as a group comprising around ten languages. That said, *malgache officiel* (essentially the Merina dialect) is universally understood as the language of administration and the press.

Since 1823, when British missionaries began translating the Bible into Malagasy, the language has been written using the Latin alphabet, or rather a subset of it: Malagasy uses the 26 English letters except C, Q, U, W and X. Just as the word 'alphabet' derives from the first letters of the Greek alphabet, the Malagasy call their alphabet the *abidy*, after its first three letters.

Approximately 70% of Malagasy words have Malayo-Polynesian roots. Unsurprisingly, given the colonial history, many of the others come from French – for example: *labiera* is beer, *bisikilety* is bicycle, and *sofera* is driver (from the French *'chauffeur'*). There are a handful of words from English too, including *sekoly* (school) and *boky* (book). Names of the days and months come from the Arabic, and many animal names are of Swahili origin, such as *amboa* (dog, from *mbwa*), *angisy* (squid, from *ngisi*) and *lolo* (butterfly, from *mlulu*, insect).

People warm instantly to any attempts to speak their language and learning a few words is easy. Hello, goodbye, please and thank you are all you need to have your first short exchanges in Malagasy. Turn to the language appendix on page 250 for these and other useful words and phrases.

Business hours

Most businesses open from 08.00 until 17.30 or 18.00 on weekdays, usually closing down for lunch between 12.00 and 14.00. In the hottest areas of the country, the midday closure may last three hours. Banks and post offices are normally open from 08.00 to 16.00 and closed at weekends, although the largest towns generally have a bank that opens on Saturday mornings. One bank in Tana, the BFV on Avenue de l'Indépendance, stays open until 17.00 on Saturdays.

Time zone

Madagascar is three hours ahead of GMT. The country operates on this time zone year-round, as daylight savings time (summer time) is not observed. This time zone applies across the whole island – except for Anjajavy, a luxury hotel resort in the northwest, which has chosen to operate in its own local time zone bubble an hour ahead of the rest of the country!

Madagascar Highlights

5 Antananarivo and Surrounds

The bustling capital city, which often goes by the informal moniker of 'Tana', is situated in the highlands at the heart of Madagascar. As the hub of almost all international and domestic flights, and the starting point of most of the island's major roads, it is virtually impossible to visit the country without passing through this region at least a couple of times - yet few travellers linger to appreciate the city. What it lacks in designated tourist attractions, it makes up for with an allure unique among the world's capitals. This chapter gives an overview of places to stay, eat and visit if you can afford to spend a little time in Tana. A handful of places can be reached as a day trip or overnight trip from Tana, and these are also covered in this chapter. Most notable (and certainly not to be missed) is the rainforest at Andasibe. Here is the only place in the world that you can witness the largest of all lemurs - the lovable teddy-bear-shaped indri - singing his haunting song.

NTANANARIVO

Antananarivo

Looking down from the plane window as you approach Tana you can see how excitingly different this country is. Clusters of red clay houses and steepled churches stand isolated on the hilltops overlooking a mosaic of paddy fields. Old defence ditches, *tamboho*, form circles around villages or estates, and dotted in the empty countryside are the white concrete Merina tombs from where the dead will be exhumed in *famadihana* ceremonies.

Built on a cluster of a dozen hills, the capital city itself is a higgledy-piggledy nest of narrow winding streets and hidden flights of steps best appreciated on foot. At its centre, a grand colonial railway station stands proudly at one end of Avenue de l'Indépendence, where street sellers spread out their wares on the pavement as columns of uniformly beige Renault 4 taxis rattle past.

History

At the end of the 16th century the Merina king Andrianjaka conquered a Vazimba town called Analamanga, built on a great rock thrusting above the surrounding plains. He renamed it Antananarivo (which means 'city of the thousand', supposedly because a thousand warriors protected it) and ordered his palace to be built on its highest point. With its surrounding marshland ideal for rice production, and the security afforded by its position, this was the perfect site for a Merina capital.

In the 18th century there were two centres for this kingdom: Antananarivo and the nearby Ambohimanga. The great king Andrianampoinimerina began to expand his empire from the latter, but moved his base to Antananarivo, whereupon his son Radama succeeded him and continued his father's mission to conquer the rest of Madagascar. The country's history centred around the royal palace or *rova* until the 1890s, when the French colonised the island. There was no reason for them to move the capital elsewhere: its pleasant climate made it an agreeable place to live, and plenty of French money and planning went into the city we see today.

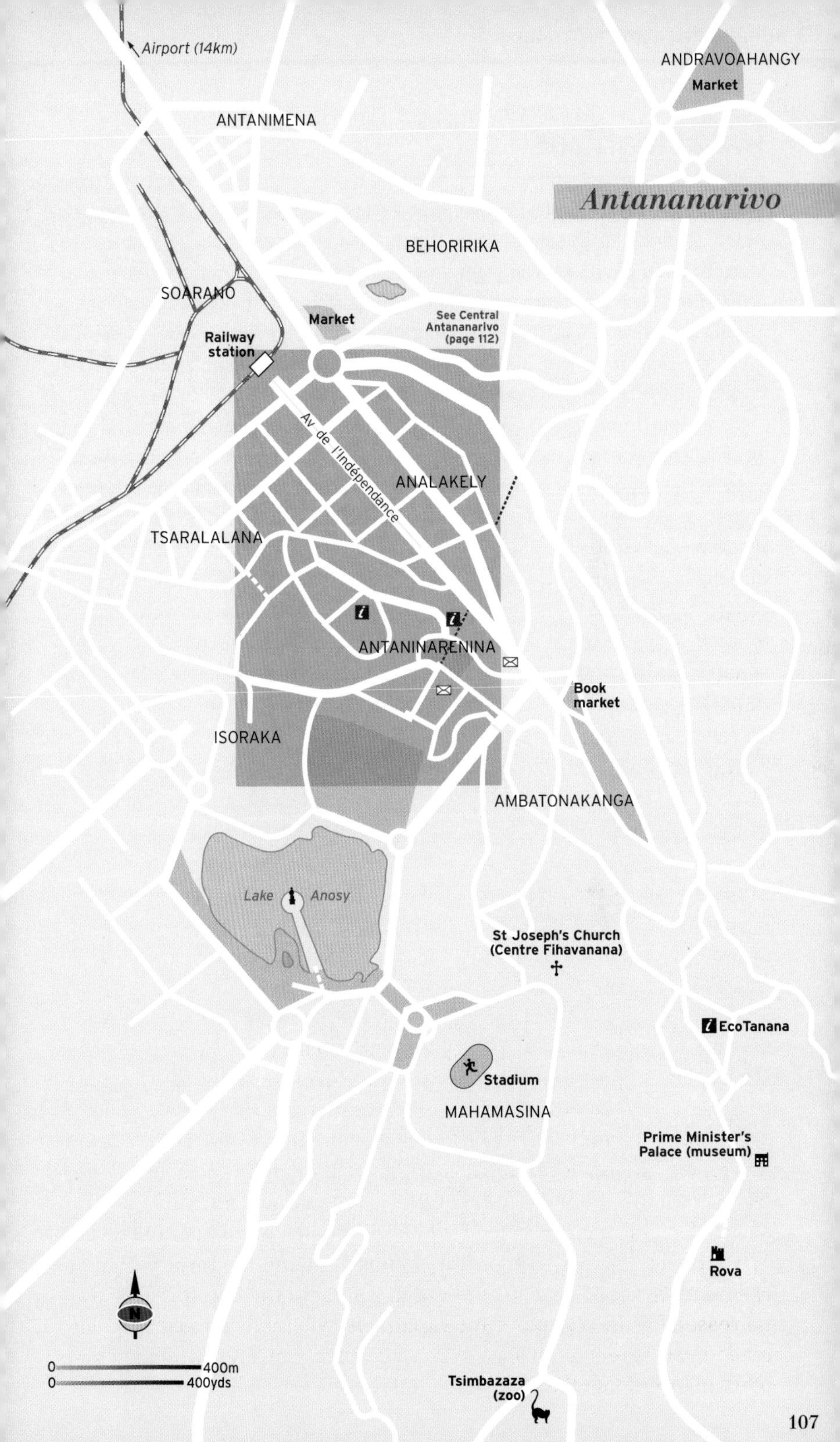

Airport (14km)

ANTANIMENA

ANDRAVOAHANGY
Market

Antananarivo

BEHORIRIKA

SOARANO

Market

See Central
Antananarivo
(page 112)

**Railway
station**

Av de l'indépendance

ANALAKELY

TSARALALANA

ANTANINARENINA

**Book
market**

ISORAKA

AMBATONAKANGA

Lake Anosy

St Joseph's Church
(Centre Fihavanana)

i EcoTanana

Stadium

MAHAMASINA

Prime Minister's
Palace (museum)

Rova

0 —————— 400m
0 —————— 400yds

N

**Tsimbazaza
(zoo)**

Practicalities

Most international **flights** to Madagascar come in to land at Ivato Airport, which is on the north side of Tana. It may take anywhere from 20 minutes to more than an hour to travel from here to the city centre by road, depending on traffic. Those on an organised tour are usually met at the airport by their ground operator. If not, then some hotels offer a transfer service, otherwise there are taxis for about 30,000Ar (€11) to the centre and an airport shuttle bus for 10,000Ar (€3.60) per person.

On **arrival** from abroad, you must first pass through immigration. If you already have your visa, then join the 'with visa' queue on the left. Otherwise head to the 'stamps for visa' kiosk to pay in euros or US dollars (skip this step if your visa is free – see page 79) then join the 'no visa' queue on the right. At the desk you will need to show the border official your completed landing card (usually handed out on the plane), your return flight ticket/e-ticket, and your passport. Check your visa has been issued for the correct number of days, proceed to the baggage carousel to collect bags, then through the baggage and passport inspection and into the arrivals area. Here you may be mobbed by porters; be firm in refusing their help if you don't require it.

Accommodation near the centre

Upmarket
Carlton ⓦ www.carlton-madagascar.com
Colbert ⓦ www.hotel-colbert-tananarive.com
Pavillon de l'Emyrne ⓦ www.pavillondelemyrne.com
Royal Palissandre ⓦ www.hotel-palissandre.com
Tamboho ⓦ www.hoteltamboho.com
Tana Plaza ⓦ www.hotel-tanaplazza.com

Moderate
Louvre ⓦ www.hotel-du-louvre.com
Radama ⓦ www.radama-hotel.com
Sakamanga ⓦ www.sakamanga.com
Varangue ⓦ www.tana-hotel.com

Budget
Isoraka ⓣ 22 355 81
Tana-Jacaranda ⓦ www.tana-jacaranda.com

Before leaving the airport, you will probably want to **exchange currency**. There is a SOCIMAD bureau de change at the far end of the main hall and in the middle is a BNI bank with an ATM that takes both Visa and MasterCard. If you are on an organised tour, it may be many days before your next opportunity to get cash, so check with your operator before deciding how much to change.

When **leaving Madagascar**, you need to be aware that local currency is not accepted in the departure lounge shops; make sure you have spent or exchanged any unwanted ariary *before* passing through security.

If you don't have your own transport, then the most convenient way of getting around in the city is by taxi. These are mostly decrepit beige-coloured Renault 4s and 2CVs. They do not run on meters so agree the price before the journey; a typical trip (10-15 minutes) within the city should cost around 5,000Ar (€1.80). Taxis are independent – there are no minicab firms – so there is no central number to call if you need one. However, most hotel receptions keep a list of reputable drivers and will make arrangements for you.

Some hotels have **internet** access for their guests, but often only in the form of a Wi-Fi connection for which you need your own laptop. The best internet café in the city centre is Teknet on Avenue Ramanantsoa in Isoraka. Many of Tana's restaurants (see pages 110-1) also have Wi-Fi internet.

Accommodation near the airport

Upmarket
Orchid Ⓦ www.orchidhotelantananarivo.com
Relais des Plateaux Ⓦ www.relais-des-plateaux.com

Moderate
Au Bois Vert Ⓦ www.auboisvert.com
Combava Ⓦ www.hotel-combava.com
Flots Bleus Ⓦ www.lesflotsbleustana.com
Hautes Terres Ⓦ www.leshautesterres-hotel.com
IC Hotel Ⓦ www.ichotel.mg
Mahavelo Ⓦ hotel-antananarivo.com
Manoir Rouge Ⓦ www.manoirrouge.com

Budget
Raphia Ivato Ⓦ www.hotelsraphia.com
Tonga Soa Ⓔ tongasoahotel@moov.mg
Transit Motel Ⓣ 033 11 338 31

Antananarivo highlights

Central Antananarivo

From the right place, in the right light, Tana is one of the most attractive capitals in the developing world. In the evening sunshine it has the quality of a child's picture book: colourful houses stacked up the hillsides with mauve jacarandas and purple bougainvillea against the dark blue of the winter sky. The central area of the city is divided into a Lower Town and Upper Town, with a steep climb between the two.

The Lower Town (districts Analakely and Tsaralalana) centres on the Avenue de l'Indépendance, a broad, grass-centred boulevard lined with shops, snack bars and hotels. But keep an eye out for pickpockets if you stroll around here. At one end is the imposing Soarano **railway station**, a recently renovated colonial edifice now housing a small upmarket shopping plaza. Halfway along the Avenue is the new (in 2010) **city hall**. Heading to the other end of the avenue and climbing the long staircase

Eating out

Most of Tana's best restaurants are found in the upper town districts, with more cafés and snack bars being in the lower town. Eating out is very affordable; a typical three-course meal costs about €10 per head excluding drinks. If you want foreign wine, this will add to the bill substantially.

Central

Anjary (Indian with Bollywood ambience) 89 Rue de Liège, Tsaralalana ① 22 279 58 Ⓦ www.anjary-hotel.com

La Boussole (French bar and restaurant; a little pricey, but pleasant outdoor seating area) 21 Rue du Docteur Villette, Isoraka ① 22 358 10

Café de la Gare (top location, great décor, sometimes live music; food mediocre, but worth going for a drink; Wi-Fi) alongside railway station, Avenue de l'Indépendance, Soarano ① 22 611 12 Ⓦ www.cafetana.com

Chez Sucett's (simple, unpretentious venue serving some splendid Malagasy dishes) 23 Rue Raveloary, Isoraka ① 22 261 00

Colbert (hotel with three restaurants, bar and patisserie) Rue Ratsimamanga, Antaninarenina ① 22 202 02 Ⓦ www.hotel-colbert-tananarive.com

Cookie Shop (a Starbucks-style coffee shop with snacks) 14 Rue Rainizanabololona, Antanimena ① 032 07 142 99

Honey (café with wide selection of ice creams and pastries) 13 Avenue de l'Indépendance, Soarano ① 22 621 67

on the right will take you to the smarter Upper Town (districts Antaninarenina and Isoraka). From the top of the steps, beneath the jacarandas of Jardin Antaninarenina, cross over and walk down the road opposite to reach the **presidential palace**. Turn right, past the Malagasy National Bank, and then left into Isoraka. Here is the quarter where you will find the art shops and craft boutiques, the

Soarano railway station (HZR)

atmospheric hotels, a number of pleasant restaurants (see box below) and a small **museum of art and archaeology** (17 Rue Dr Villette ⊕ Tuesday–Friday 12.00–17.00).

KuDeTa (French cuisine with some exotic dishes, but pricey; Wi-Fi) 15 Rue de la Reunion, Isoraka ① 22 281 54 ⑩ www.kudeta.mg

Ozone (Thai restaurant with extensive menu) Rue Rasoamanarivo, Isoraka ① 24 749 73

Petit Verdot (good varied menu; popular with expats) 27 Rue Rahamefy, Ambatonakanga ① 22 392 34

La Varangue (inventive menu and charming atmosphere) 17 Rue Ratsimamanga, Antaninarenina ① 22 273 97

Villa Vanille (in a charming old house; famous for its soufflé) 24 Rue Radama Place, Antanimena ① 22 205 15

Zebu Original Bistrot (a new place rapidly getting a name as one of the best eateries in town; Wi-Fi) 28 Rue du Docteur Villette, Isoraka ① 22 299 97

Airport area

Akany Avoko (support this charity by lunching at its café) see page 117

Au Bois Vert (inside and outside dining in tranquil forested surroundings) Ivato ① 22 447 25 ⑩ www.auboisvert.com

Combava (stylish restaurant with traditional and European menu) Ambohimanarina ① 23 252 49 ⑩ www.hotel-combava.com

Ivato Airport (eatery upstairs in airport terminal; nothing special, but convenient if awaiting a flight)

Orchid (reliable food less than 5 minutes from the airport; Wi-Fi) Mandrosoa ① 22 442 03 ⑩ www.orchidhotelantananarivo.com

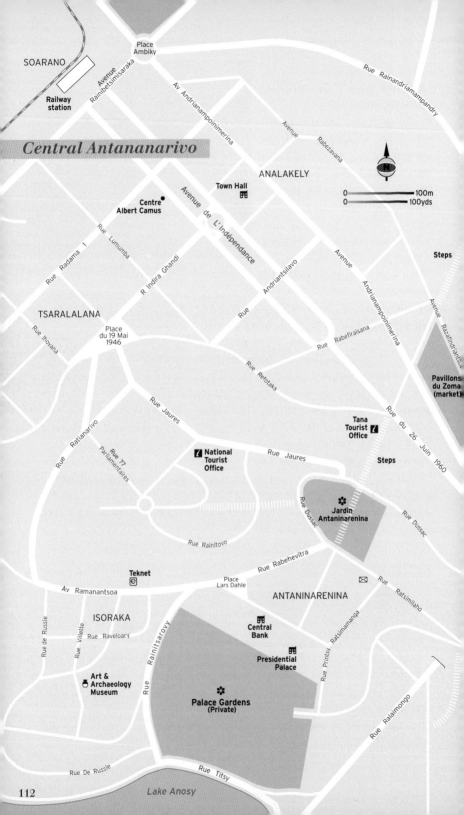

Central Antananarivo

SOARANO

Railway station

Place Ambiky

Avenue Rainibetsimisaraka

Av Andrianampoinimerina

Rue Rainandriamampandry

Avenue

Rabezavana

ANALAKELY

Town Hall

Centre Albert Camus

Avenue de L'Indépendance

Rue Lumumba

Rue Radama 1

R Indira Ghandi

Andriantsilavo

Avenue

Andrianampoinimerina

Steps

Avenue Razafindrianitse

TSARALALANA

Rue Ihovana

Place du 19 Mai 1946

Rue

Rabefiraisana

Rue Rabefiralsana

Rue Refotaka

Pavillons du Zoma (market)

Rue Jaures

Rue du 26 Juin 1960

Rue Ratianarivo

Rue 77 Parliamentaires

Tana Tourist Office

National Tourist Office

Rue Jaures

Steps

Rue Dussac

Jardin Antaninarenina

Rue Dussac

Rue Rainitovo

Rue Rabehevitra

Teknet

Place Lars Dahle

ANTANINARENINA

Rue Ratsimilaho

Av Ramanantsoa

ISORAKA

Rue de Russie

Rue Villette

Rue Raveloary

Rainitsarovy

Rue

Central Bank

Presidential Palace

Rue Printsy Ratsimamanga

Art & Archaeology Museum

Palace Gardens (Private)

Rue Ralaimongo

Rue De Russie

Rue Titsy

Lake Anosy

0 ———— 100m
0 ———— 100yds

Handicraft markets

While traditional Malagasy handicrafts (see pages 98–9) are available at boutiques across the city, you will find a wider selection of souvenirs at better prices on the artisan markets. The most centrally located handicrafts market is at **Marché Pochart** near Soarano railway station. A second one, accessible from Rue Ramananarivo in the **Andravoahangy** district, has a particularly good selection of carved games. And another extensive one is the **Digue market**, conveniently sited on the road from the city to the airport.

The *rova* (queen's palace)

The *rova*, the spiritual centre of the Merina people, dominates the skyline of Tana. Only its stone shell remained after a serious fire in 1995 – rumoured to be an act of politically motivated arson. Around 5,000 historical treasures were destroyed in the disaster, but some 1,500 artefacts were rescued by quick-thinking bystanders and are currently on display in the nearby **prime minister's palace** (🕒 10.00–17.00

The *rova* in 1894 (ML)

daily, except Friday 10.00–12.00). The *rova* itself has been closed since 2005 for a ten-million-euro reconstruction programme, which has been hampered by lack of funds since the 2009 coup but will hopefully be completed soon. In any case, it is worth the walk up to the palace for the splendid views over the city and to browse the items on display at the prime minister's palace, an 1872 building designed by British architect William Pool. Note that once the palace reopens, it is expected that the collection of artefacts will be transferred back into a museum there.

The *rova* complex contains several buildings of historical importance. (HZR)

What can make travelling to Madagascar really special?

Madagascar is best known for its wildlife, but there's much more than that. It is in itself a mini continent characterised by an awesome mix of Africa and Asia seen through the people, the culture and the landscape. We will connect you, on your journey, as closely as possible to its natural world – lemurs, baobabs, chameleons etc – but also, if desired, to the lives of the Malagasy themselves to make your trip really special.

How would you advise travellers to get the best out of their holidays?

Madagascar is a huge island with so much diversity that requires an infinite amount of time to discover and appreciate to the full. We therefore suggest that travellers read about and pick one or two choice destinations, especially if time is an issue, specifying their main interests and travel style – we provide the framework to make it possible!

In what way can travellers contribute to local development and wellbeing?

We value responsible and sustainable tourism that benefits the locals. Thus, we work closely with local professionals, organisations and communities in different regions. Our staff, drivers and guides are all Malagasy who know the country very well. We support training and offer volunteer, photo and grassroots tours for a genuine experience and understanding of the local ways.

Mora-Travel SARL specialises in customised tours across Madagascar. Their highly flexible customer-choice approach combined with a 12-year outstanding presence will give you a genuine and unforgettable experience of the Island, its people and all its riches. They are committed to delivering a good-value, quality service and making your trip really worth it. We spoke to general manager Monique van der Heijden.

☏ +261 (0)20 22 020 12; +261 (0)32 07 115 11
Ⓔ info@moratravel.com Ⓦ www.moratravel.com

Ambohimanga

🕐 09.00–17.00 daily

Lying 21km (around 30 minutes' drive) northeast of Tana, the **sacred historical site** of Ambohimanga – for a long time forbidden to Europeans – makes an easy day trip. From here began the line of kings and queens who were to unite Madagascar into one country, and it was here that they returned for rest and relaxation among the forested slopes of this hill-top village. These days tourists find the same tranquillity and spirit of reverence at this UNESCO World Heritage Site.

Some of Ambohimanga's seven gates have enormous stone discs that would have been rolled across the gateway each night. On the slope to the left of the main entrance to the compound is a sacrificial stone, still often used for sacrifices today. The centrepiece is the wooden house of King Andrianampoinimerina, a simple one-room building with a display of cooking utensils, weapons, and two beds – the upper one for the king and the lower for one of his 12 wives. The roof is supported by a 10m rosewood pole.

The king's successors built themselves elegant summerhouses at the complex. These have been renovated and provide a fascinating glimpse of the strong British influence during those times, with very European décor and gifts sent to the monarchs by Queen Victoria. French influence is evident too: there are two cannons forged in Jean Laborde's iron foundry. Here also is the small summerhouse of Prime Minister Rainilaiarivony who, cautious about being overheard, chose an open design with glazed windows so that spies could be spied first.

Croc Farm

☏ 22 030 71/007 15 ⏰ 09.00–17.00 daily

Just ten minutes from the airport, this French-owned site is a working farm, raising crocodiles for leather, meat and other products. But the 3ha park is also a zoo, home to some 80 animal species. Crocs of every size are top of the bill with many hundreds in residence. You will also learn about the threats faced by the few wild crocs left in Madagascar and local superstitions surrounding them. For an unusual culinary experience, try crocodile – perhaps grilled in vanilla sauce – at the restaurant overlooking the main lake (non-croc dishes also available). Other animals on display include lemurs, fossa, chameleons, tortoises and parrots – but sadly not all kept in the best of conditions.

(DA)

Lemurs Park

☏ 22 234 36 or 033 11 728 90 ⓦ www.lemurspark.com ⏰ 09.00–16.30

This free-range 'zoo' makes a good day trip, particularly for those on a quick visit who are not able to see lemurs in the wild. Bordered by the dramatic Katsaoka River, the 5ha park is divided into areas planted with endemic flora of Madagascar's different climate zones. Nine species of lemur live free; many are confiscated pets, and this is the first step towards rehabilitation. A few nocturnal species are kept in rather small cages. The park is 22km west of Tana on RN1. If you don't have your own transport, their minibus can collect you from central Tana (☏ 033 03 991 77 or 033 11 025 25).

Charities

A visit to the heart-warming halfway house and orphanage of **Akany Avoko** (⊛ www.akanyavoko.com) offers an insight into the tremendous work being put into helping the disadvantaged girls and women of Tana. It is near the airport, so why not schedule a visit on your last day to donate your leftover ariary, clothes or medical supplies? Various handicrafts are produced and sold here and you can support them by having a meal at the café. Allow up to an hour for a tour as well as time for lunch and shopping, but do contact them ahead of your visit.

An inspiring project with a similar mission is the **Centre Fihavanana** (© bpfihavanana@moov.mg) run by the Sisters of the Good Shepherd near Mahamasina stadium. Some 300 young children are taught, undernourished babies are fed and their destitute mothers given training in childcare. The women here work to a very high standard, producing beautiful embroidery and greeting cards for sale.

Anjozorobe

This is a **private reserve** to the northeast of Tana, established in 2005 to protect 2,500ha of dense primary forest. The park is home to a rich diversity of wildlife and at least 550 species of plant. The reserve itself has a variety of hiking trails and, being situated 90km from the city, it is best to stay at least one night.

Tried & Tested

Mananara Lodge
⊛ www.mananaralodge-madagascar.com

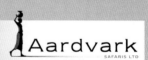

Few people have heard of this five-tent lodge, built as a joint venture between a Malagasy tour operator and a conservation NGO. Offering access to Anjozorobe, Mananara Lodge is set in an unspoilt area of primary rainforest, home to 11 species of lemur, 82 species of birds and teeming with endemic reptiles and plants. The simple tents offer comforts such as baths and open fires for chilly evenings, and the food is hearty. Wildlife walks are the main activity here but visits to the local school and village (supported by the lodge) are very worthwhile.

In Conversation with...

How are you different from other tour operators offering ecotourism in the parks and reserves of this 'megabiodiversity hotspot'?

We try to go where the others do not. Thus 'Pangalanes Canal' means Holidays Madagascar, for example, as we are the greatest specialist of this eastern part of the island. We offer a large variety of tours, mostly with a good balance between biodiversity, culture and landscape. We propose also tailor-made trips or highly specialised tours like birding or lemur-watching. Most visitors to Madagascar just leave one park for another. But for us, a trip is not just a series of park visits and photography; we give a very good

understanding during our journeys so that our travellers will be richer in the mind by the end of the tour. Interpretation is a great element in the success of a tour.

What kind of opportunities do you offer for an adventurous approach?

A 4x4 trip in the west from Morondava to the southwest, Toliara and to the south, Taolagnaro, is a good example. This area is the most exotic and the wildest part of the island. Hotels are scarce and tarmac road is to be forgotten. The vegetation is dry thorny shrub with cactus-like plants such as the members of the Didieracea family, succulents like the elephant's foot *Pachypodium* and 'upside-down' baobab trees. Meeting a group of lemurs or a terrestrial coua suddenly crossing the dirt road are usual highlights. The temperature might be rather high but the feeling is really extraterrestrial! This is just one example; we can also arrange a 4x4 journey along the east coast, which is as wild as the west but with evergreen vegetation and many large river-mouth ferry-crossings, and driving on sandy or muddy roads.

Ecotourism is good for conservation if local communities benefit. How do you involve local people?

We do not stick solely to national parks. Wherever it is possible, we propose community parks and other attractions run by locals. We keep close to local communities by walking through villages and letting travellers buy goods – like handmade traditional hats or other handicraft products – directly from them.

How would you arrange a tour for a first-time visitor to Madagascar?

A journey encompassing parts of the east, the highlands and the southwest should give the necessary desire to return to see more the island in more detail. This trip allows a visit to two national parks with evergreen rainforest, highlighted by the indri (largest extant lemur) and some others like the

greater bamboo lemur (one of the world's most threatened primates). To the east, the wooden stilt huts of the Pangalanes area give an Indonesian coast atmosphere. The drive through the highlands is an unforgettable social experience. Then comes Isalo National Park with its ruiniform landscape and extraordinary rocky vegetation. Down to the southwest coast, at Ifaty, the landscape is totally different again, with cactus-like vegetation and true baobabs, which are small and fat here. Ifaty is also home to two local endemic bird species: the long-tailed ground-roller and the subdesert mesite.

Holidays Madagascar is a Malagasy tour operator, established in 1996, specialised in tailor-made tours. Their main base is in Antananarivo but there is also an office in France. 'Highlighting the social with the biodiversity' is the philosophy of the company. We spoke to Andria Raharinosy, the founder of Holidays Madagascar.

① +261 (0)20 24 365 37 (Madagascar); +33 680 220 249 (France)
Ⓔ europe@holidays-mada.com Ⓦ www.holidays-mada.com

Andasibe area

Some 140km (three hours' drive) east of Tana is the long-established reserve of Analamazaotra Forest. Sometimes still known by its colonial name of Périnet, it was combined in the late 1990s with Mantadia (20km to the north) to form Andasibe-Mantadia National Park. Because of its proximity to Tana, its exceptional fauna, and expert guides, this is now one of Madagascar's most popular reserves. A further tract of Analamazaotra Forest is protected by an excellent local NGO called Mitsinjo, which is well worth supporting.

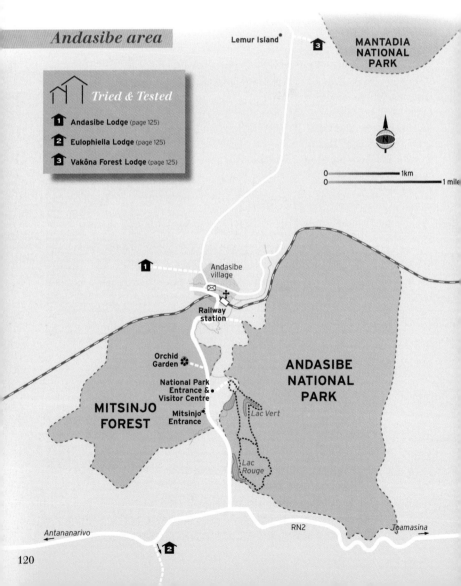

Andasibe area

Lemur Island

MANTADIA NATIONAL PARK

Tried & Tested

1 **Andasibe Lodge** (page 125)

2 **Eulophiella Lodge** (page 125)

3 **Vakôna Forest Lodge** (page 125)

N

0 ——————— 1km
0 ——————— 1 mile

Andasibe village

Railway station

Orchid Garden

National Park Entrance & Visitor Centre

Mitsinjo Entrance

Lac Vert

MITSINJO FOREST

ANDASIBE NATIONAL PARK

Lac Rouge

Antananarivo

RN2

Toamasina

Practicalities

The majority of visitors spend one or two nights in the Andasibe area. It is just about possible to visit the forest as a day trip from Tana, though not really advisable as you need to make a very early start to arrive in time to see and hear the indri. For those heading eastwards to Toamasina or the Pangalanes Canal, Andasibe makes a convenient stop along the route. For a truly unique experience, you can do an overnight visit from Tana in a vintage Micheline railcar (see page 135).

Andasibe is most famed for its indri. (DA)

The guides here are among the best in Madagascar and an example to the rest of the country for knowledge, enthusiasm and an awareness of what tourists want. They all know where to find indri and other lemurs, but if you have another specialism, such as birds, reptiles or plants, ask your operator or the park office to assign you a guide knowledgeable in that field. Night walks are not permitted in the national park, but they are allowed in the Mitsinjo-managed reserve. There is a visitor centre and shop at the entrances to both the Andasibe national park and the Mitsinjo forest. They are only 200 metres apart so you can easily visit both to browse the handicrafts, even if you only plan to visit one protected area.

Accommodation

For full details of tour operator-recommended accommodation, see page 125.

Moderate
Feon'ny Ala Ⓣ 56 832 02
Grace Lodge Ⓔ gracelodge@blueline.mg
Mikalo Ⓣ 56 832 08

Budget and camping
Orchidée Ⓔ hotelorchideeandasibe@yahoo.fr
Camping – enquire at Mitsinjo or national park offices

You have been a Madagascar tour operator for more than 14 years; what is the secret of your success?

Our philosophy is to provide reliable and efficient service for a reasonable price. We have eight strongly motivated staff in our office and a team of very competent freelance drivers and guides with whom we have strong, longstanding relationships. We know the country very well, and frequently revisit our destinations and hotels.

What is so special about Madagascar and what tour would you recommend most?

Madagascar is an absolutely amazing country! It has not only a unique flora and fauna with more than 80% endemism, but also fantastic and very varied landscapes. It is a melting pot of Asia and Africa, with its 18 tribes living in harmony. My favourite tour is from Antananarivo to Toliara in 7-10 days, with ever-changing landscapes *en route*, and great national parks and reserves. Madagascar still has the flavour of the adventure – wild and untouched.

What more has Madagascar to offer?

One can do so much in Madagascar: for the sporty, there's hiking, cycling, trekking, diving, swimming, motor- and quad-biking, sailing etc; for the culturally interested, there are many fascinating sites; for nature lovers, there are national parks and reserves, and bird- and whale-watching too; there are worthwhile projects for those keen to get involved with community-based tourism; and then there are endless beaches for those who just want to relax.

Le Voyageur is a Madagascar tour operator with its offices in Antananarivo. Founded in 1998, under Swiss management with motivated Malagasy tour consultants and operations director, it has a firm focus on providing reliable service for unforgettable tours. We spoke to managing director Michael Horn.

Ⓣ +261 (0)20 22 435 21   Ⓕ +261 (0)20 23 309 28
Ⓔ voyageur@madagaskar.travel   Ⓦ www.madagaskar.travel

Andasibe area highlights

Andasibe National Park

This 810ha reserve of montane rainforest most famously protects several families of indri, the largest of all lemurs. Their long back legs are immensely powerful, and they can propel themselves 10m, executing a mid-air turn, to hug a new tree and gaze down benevolently at their observers. And you will be an observer: everyone now sees indris here, and most also hear them. For it is the voice that makes this lemur extra special: while other lemurs grunt, mew or bark, the indri sings. It is an eerie, wailing sound that carries for up to 3km as troops call to each other across the forest. They generally call at dawn, mid-morning, and sometimes shortly before dusk. During the middle of the day they take a long siesta in the canopy. There are ten other species of lemur here too, as well as tenrecs, beautiful and varied insects, spiders, frogs and reptiles – especially chameleons and boas. Birders will want to look out for the velvet asity, blue coua and nuthatch vanga.

Mitsinjo's forest reserve

Ⓦ www.mitsinjo.org Ⓣ 56 832 33 or 033 14 474 89 Ⓔ info@mitsinjo.org

This local NGO offers broadly the same attractions as the national park in its 700ha reserve, while leading the way in an ambitious reforestation programme as well as various community projects. In addition to seeing indri and other wildlife, you can visit some of the nurseries where each year half a million seedlings of 151 endemic species are being raised to help establish 'corridors' connecting blocks of isolated forest. A night walk here is highly recommended.

Young Parson's chameleon (DA)

Lemur Islands's diademed sifaka (DA)

Lemur Island

Owned by Vakôna Forest Lodge, this 1½ha forested river island a few minutes' drive north of Andasibe has been turned into a sanctuary for former pet lemurs. Four different species have the freedom of the island, some of which have become so used to humans that they will obligingly jump onto your shoulder for a photo. The star of the show is a beautiful diademed sifaka – a species you are unlikely to see up close anywhere else, for they are almost impossible to keep alive in captivity.

Mantadia National Park

Despite being almost 20 times the size of the Andasibe park, Mantadia is much less visited. While Andasibe is for almost everyone, Mantadia is for the enthusiast. There are fewer trails here, and the terrain is more rugged, but the rewards are exceptional. With a broader altitude range (800–1,260m) Mantadia harbours many different species, so it is worth visiting both areas if you have the time. What makes it so special is that, in contrast to Andasibe, it comprises virtually untouched primary forest. You may see diademed sifaka and indri, among other lemurs. Birding specials include the scaly ground-roller, pitta-like ground-roller and red-breasted coua. There is a two-hour circuit, but to do justice to Mantadia you should start early and spend the whole day. Permits and guides are obtained from the park office at Andasibe.

Andasibe Hotel
Ⓦ www.andasibehotel.com

This splendid new hotel is conveniently located just 800m outside Andasibe village, from where it is only 1.6km to the national park entrance and Orchid Garden. The smartly furnished semi-detached chalets have TV, fridge and spacious bathrooms. Rooms are spotlessly clean and have heaters for the cooler winter nights. There is a sparkling pool in an attractive garden, and the main building has a bar and restaurant. The staff are attentive and always ready to respond to requests in order to ensure guests have an enjoyable stay.

Eulophiella Lodge
Ⓦ www.eulophiella.com

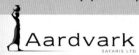

Most people coming to Madagascar will visit Andasibe National Park and Eulophiella Lodge is one of the newer properties offering somewhere nearby to stay. A little further from the park itself than some competitors, this 17-roomed lodge – separate bungalows spread through the property – has the advantage of being set on a hillside with spacious grounds as well as its own area of forest in which daytime and nocturnal walks can be taken and where a number of varieties of lemur and countless birds may be spotted.

Vakôna Forest Lodge
Ⓦ www.hotelvakona.com

One of Madagascar's most popular, this lodge is praised by all. Perfectly located for exploring the Andasibe region, it is wonderfully designed with 25 comfortable en-suite rooms set amongst gorgeous gardens. Food in the central restaurant is excellent. It almost feels like a private reserve and, despite the mostly exotic vegetation, birdlife and night walks here are very good! Vakôna also has a small zoological park with two fossas as well as the must-visit Lemur Island, where orphaned lemurs live freely and sit on guests' shoulders to feed.

In Conversation with...

You offer tailor-made private holidays to Madagascar; what would you include in a holiday designed for a first-time visitor?

We try to tailor each holiday to our clients. A first-time holiday will depend on what clients are most interested in, the budget, length of travel, any children that will be coming along, and also whether it's a honeymoon. Having said that, one of my favourite trips that I recommend for first-time visitors looking for a mix of wildlife and beach would be three to four days in Andasibe National Park just east of Antananarivo, which is fantastic for wildlife with 11 species of lemur and 112 bird species as well as reptiles. I'd then head north and to the beautiful palm-fringed beaches of Ile Sainte Marie on the coast.

For a bit more of a wildlife fix but without too much extra travel time, I would add in a trip to Montagne d'Ambre National Park offering fantastic wildlife-viewing with a backdrop of waterfalls and crater lakes. I would also add in a couple of days at Ankarana, known for its limestone karst pinnacles called *tsingy* along with its extensive cave system and network of underground rivers.

Another fantastic option that allows you to get an idea of the variety of the exotic flora and fauna in Madagascar would be to head south to Berenty Private Reserve and Ifotaka. Here you get fantastic sightings of ring-tailed lemurs and sifakas and instead of the rainforests of the north you are in a drier landscape with spiny forest creating surreal landscapes.

Where are your favourite places to spot lemurs?

Like most of our clients, I love the indri, the largest jumping lemur. They provide great entertainment when you're lucky enough to see one. Andasibe, world-famous for its indri population, offers the best opportunity for this to happen. Montagne d'Ambre is great for spotting the crowned lemur and Sanford's brown lemur. For the more rare lemurs, I like Ranomafana with its rainforested hills and three species of bamboo lemur including the golden bamboo lemur, or the unique landscape of eroded sandstone formations at Isalo for spotting the ring-tailed lemur and brown lemur.

How does your experience as a company make your trips to Madagascar special?

We love Madagascar and we love sharing our knowledge of all it can offer with people who want to visit. All of our Madagascar consultants have travelled to the country and experienced different areas, lodges and guides. We have travelled with our families as well as with work. All in all, we have a thorough knowledge of the destination and have great relationships on the ground to ensure we know the best places to include in a Madagascar holiday.

What are your top tips for visitors to Madagascar?

Ensure you have a good English-speaking guide to give you the lowdown on the wildlife, the different areas of the country and the general culture, which can vary quite significantly from region to region. Go with an open mind and relaxed attitude. Try new things and don't worry if travel arrangements change or things take longer than expected. This is all part of the experience of a country like Madagascar.

With offices in the US and UK, Imagine Africa pride themselves on giving expert advice. They visit the lodges and hotels, have strong relationships with the owners and can give you the lowdown on the detail behind the glossy images. Add competitive prices, award-winning service and financial protection and you can be assured of the most incredible holiday to Madagascar. We spoke to Jo Shuttleworth, Commercial Director of the company.

⊤ +44 (0)20 7622 5114 (UK); +1 888 882 7121 (US)
Ⓔ info@imagineafrica.co.uk (UK); info@imagineafrica.com (US)
Ⓦ www.imagineafrica.co.uk (UK); www.imagineafrica.com (US)

6 RN7: The Route South

The Route Nationale 7 runs from the capital city of Antananarivo down to Toliara (Tulear) in the far southwest. Many visitors drive its full length, often with a hired car and driver. Indeed this is deservedly the most popular route in Madagascar, with almost two-thirds of tourists incorporating at least some of it into their itinerary. Part of the RN7's appeal is that it is one of the few good roads in the country and passes through several different types of scenery and habitat, allowing the traveller to pack a great diversity of experiences into a relatively short time. This delightful journey begins in the Merina highlands, then passes through the regions of the Zafimaniry and Betsileo peoples, famed for their woodcarving and rice-growing respectively. There are opportunities to visit rainforest here before heading for the spectacular scenery of the Andringitra and Isalo massifs, and on to the coast where you can explore the dry spiny forest or relax on the beach.

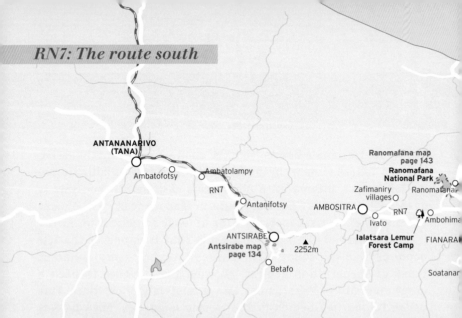

Practicalities

Do not be fooled by the map into thinking that the RN7 is a small undertaking. Although it is one of the best surfaced roads in Madagascar, it is more than 950km in length. Driving non-stop between Tana and Toliara takes at least 16 hours. Given that there is so much to see and do along the route, typical tour itineraries budget between seven and 14 days for this trip – although if your time is not constrained then it would not be unreasonable to set aside even three weeks.

Most visitors drive down the RN7 then fly back to Tana from Toliara (or do the same route in reverse) but you could equally drive to Toliara and back again, visiting some sites on the way down and the rest on the return leg. This option will add half a day or so to your itinerary but is cheaper because, regardless of whether you fly one way or not, you will be footing the bill for the driver and vehicle to make the round trip. And it is more flexible as you are not reliant on flight schedules.

A extension of the RN7 itinerary involves combining it with the southeast region (*Chapter 7*). After driving from Tana to Toliara, you fly to Taolagnaro (Fort Dauphin), the base for exploring the southeast. From there you can fly directly back to Tana.

The main road is good enough for any type of vehicle, but you will need a 4x4 to access some of the sites along the route, such as Andringitra. Budget travellers may be tempted to travel by *taxi-brousse*, but this can be a false economy; *taxi-brousses* travel between the main towns, meaning you often have to hire a local vehicle to take you to the national parks and other sites.

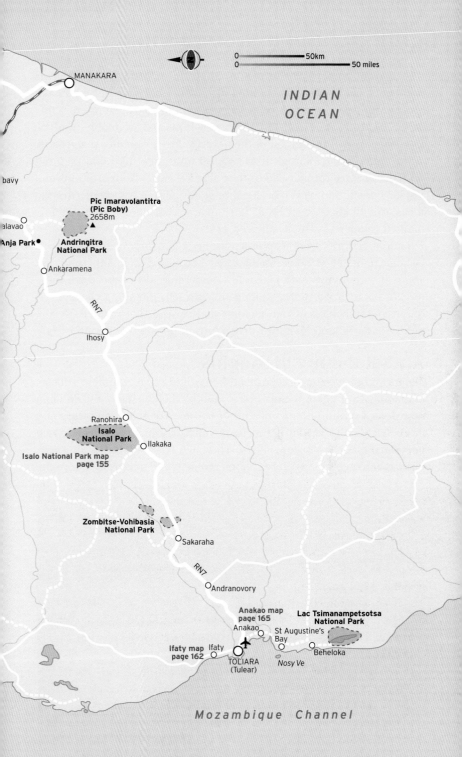

MANAKARA

INDIAN
OCEAN

bavy

Pic Imaravolantitra
(Pic Boby)
2658m ▲

alavao

Anja Park ●
Andringitra
National Park

○ Ankaramena

RN7

○ Ihosy

Ranohira ○
Isalo
National Park

○ Ilakaka

Isalo National Park map
page 155

Zombitse-Vohibasia
National Park

○ Sakaraha

RN7

○ Andranovory

Anakao map
page 165

Lac Tsimanampetsotsa
National Park

Anakao ○

St Augustine's
Bay

Ifaty map   Ifaty
page 162   ○   ✈

○ Beheloka

TOLIARA
(Tulear)

Nosy Ve

Mozambique   Channel

Antananarivo to Ambositra

The journey begins with a gentle climb through the scenic Merina highlands, peaking at an elevation of 1,725m after some 140km. Each village you pass through has its speciality, often displayed prominently at the roadside to attract passing trade. Fruit and vegetable produce is seasonal, of course, but other wares are available year-round: 30km from Tana (marked by the PK 30 milestone, like that pictured on page 86) are animals and other articles make from sisal; around PK 36 you will find woven baskets; religious garden ornaments are the focus around PK 48; near PK 93 it is musical instruments; then brightly painted wooden toy trucks after PK 110.

Soon afterwards, you drop down to the colourful town of Antsirabe. Driving non-stop it takes about three hours to reach Antsirabe, but you will no doubt want to take a few camera breaks as there are some terrific photo opportunities along this stretch, including the labour-intensive cultivation of rice paddies and several fine painted Merina tombs. Some 90km (1¾ hours' drive) further on you reach Ambositra.

Ambatolampy highlights

Some two hours from Tana, Ambatolampy and its surrounding villages are famous for their metalwork – mainly cooking pots and kitchen utensils. Cast aluminium souvenirs are often for sale along the main road outside the restaurant Rendez-vous des Pêcheurs, which is a popular lunch stop for tour buses. The town has a colourful Thursday market and on Sundays there is horseracing at the nearby hippodrome.

The sight of zebu working the rice fields is common in the highlands. (SF)

Madagascar Rental Tour

Who is behind Madagascar Rental Tour?

My name is Dyna, I am 39 years old, I am married and I have three kids. I live in Ivato village near to the airport in Tana. I worked in different tour companies for nine years as a driver-guide, organising trips all around Madagascar. This means I have 12 years of experience in this job. As a driver-guide, I gained a lot of experience in tourism, especially in the field and organising trips. I have driven and guided many clients, mostly coming from English-speaking countries, and on whose advice I started my own tour company with family and friends. Now we have grown to a big team, but I am still guiding clients to ensure the quality of services we provide.

What are the Madagascar Rental Tour 'highlights tours'?

In general, we organise trips all around Madagascar. But we have our highlights tours, such as the south tour with Mangoky River, and the north and west tour including the national parks and reserves of Baly Bay, Tsingy de Namoroka, Daraina, Marojejy and Anjanaharibe-Sud.

How do you organise your Madagascar trips?

Madagascar is a new destination for tourists. There are several tour operators and one of them is Madagascar Rental Tour, who can help you to organise your trip the best way. We will arrange your stay in the country so that you can meet both the wildlife and the local people. We have an experienced team who will be very helpful during your visit.

Madagascar Rental Tour offers you personalised journeys which will help you to discover the beauty and magnificence of the fauna and the flora of Madagascar. We spoke to manager Dyna Michel Rasolomananarivo.

ⓣ +261 (0)34 06 843 86
ⓔ contact@madagascar-rental-tour.com
ⓦ www.madagascar-rental-tour.com

Antsirabe highlights

Antsirabe was founded in 1872 by Norwegian missionaries attracted by the cool climate and the healing properties of the thermal springs. It is an elegant city with a broad avenue linking the handsome railway station with Hôtel des Thermes, an amazing building in both size and architectural style. Fleets of brightly coloured *pousse-pousses* (*right*) fill its streets.

(DA)

This area is the agricultural and industrial centre of Madagascar. It is also the centre for beer; you can smell the Star Brewery as you enter the town. The cool climate allows it to produce apples, pears, plums and other temperate fruit. Indeed, it can get so cold that you will need a sweater in the evening if you are travelling between May and September.

Antsirabe

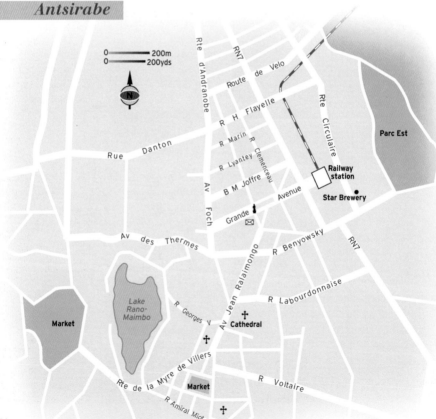

Is it a bus? Is it a train? No, it's the Micheline!

In the 1930s, the Michelin tyre company designed a rubber-tyred railcar which could give a smoother ride. Only a few countries adopted this new form of transport, but Madagascar once had three of them. Now the refurbished Micheline 'Viko-Viko' is the only one still in service anywhere in the world – a true working museum piece. More reminiscent of a bus, the vehicle averages just 50kph, giving you plenty of time to enjoy the view.

Weighing in at almost seven tonnes and measuring over 13m in length, Viko-Viko is furnished with 19 comfortable wicker armchairs, a bar and a toilet. Punctures are a frequent hazard, and when this happens the train is jacked up where it stops so that one of the six spare wheels can be fitted.

Most weekends it runs from Tana either to Antsirabe or to Andasibe, departing Saturday morning and returning Sunday afternoon for the return price of 130,000Ar (€47). The schedule can be found at Ⓦ www.madarail.mg. But be warned: this unique rail experience is becoming popular and runs such a limited service that it can be fully booked almost a year in advance.

(DA)

(MJ)

Antsirabe's artisans

Tourism in Antsirabe centres around its industry. Numerous workshops open their doors so that visitors can come and admire the skill and ingenuity of the craftsmen. Local handicrafts and products include jewellery made from zebu horn, toys crafted from recycled tin cans, wooden carvings, billiard tables, polished minerals and gemstones, embroidered tablecloths and clothing. The demonstrations are generally free but you are expected to buy something after.

Kololandy (Ⓦ www.kololandy.com) does traditional weaving of silk, cotton, sisal and raffia. It is also possible to visit local producers to see wine, beer, honey, cheese and sweets being made.

In addition to the many cottage industry workshops and handicraft boutiques around town, you may also like to explore the local markets. The Petit Marché at the southern end of town is always bustling, while the much larger Asabotsy Marché to the west of Lake Rano-Maimbo is most active on Saturdays.

And if you are interested in larger-scale industry, be sure to visit Star Brewery to see the famous Three Horses Beer in production. Guided tours of the factory are only possible Tuesday to Thursday at 09.00 and 14.00 and it is necessary to book in advance (Ⓔ a.razafindrabe@star.mg).

Accommodation in Antsirabe

Upmarket
Couleur Café ⓦ www.couleurcafeantsirabe.com
Vatolahy ⓦ www.vatolahyhotel.e-monsite.com

Moderate
Arotel Ⓔ arotel.inn@moov.mg
Green Park Ⓔ greenparktsara@yahoo.fr
Guesthouse Madalief (7km south of town) ⓦ www.madalief.nl
Hôtel des Thermes ⓦ www.sofitrans-sa.com/remake/Thermes.htm
Résidence Camélia ⓦ www.laresidencecamelia.com

Budget
Au Geranium Ⓔ geranium@moov.mg

The Lakes: Andraikiba and Tritriva

Just 7km west of Antsirabe, Lake Andraikiba is a large volcanic lake often overlooked in favour of the more spectacular Lake Tritriva – an emerald-green crater lake surrounded by vertical gneiss cliffs. The scenery here is picturesque and the area very peaceful. It is reached by continuing past Lake Andraikiba for 12km on a rough 4x4 track through small villages of waving kids. You will notice that these villages look relatively prosperous; they grow the barley for the Star Brewery.

Lake Tritriva (LH)

Ambositra highlights

Ambositra town and woodcarvings

The compact and friendly town of Ambositra is the centre of Madagascar's woodcarving industry. Even the houses have ornately carved wooden balconies and shutters. In the two dozen or more handicrafts shops you will find an abundance of choice of carved figures and marquetry. If you have time for more than a brief shopping stop, then Ambositra's Benedictine convent is worth a visit, and there is a beautiful 1½-hour walk to a royal palace.

Zafimaniry villages

The area to the southeast of Ambositra occupied by the Zafimaniry people is protected by UNESCO as a Masterpiece of the Oral and Intangible Heritage of Humanity in recognition of the locals' traditional woodcarving skills. Some two dozen Zafimaniry villages are connected by a network of footpaths. The starting point for the walks is the village of Antoetra, two hours beyond Ambositra (14½km on RN7 then 25km on a dirt track) where you pick up your guide and permit for visiting the region.

The nearest villages to Antoetra are Ifasina (2hrs on foot) and Sakaivo Nord (3½hrs in a different direction). None of the others is close enough for a day trip, but you can arrange multi-village treks of two to six days, overnighting in very simple accommodation. Visits to the Zafimaniry villages are interesting mainly from a cultural perspective; the area is largely deforested and there is relatively little diversity of wildlife.

Accommodation in Ambositra

Moderate
Artisan Hotel Ⓔ artisan_hotel@yahoo.fr
Hôtel Mania Ⓔ toursmania@moov.mg
Relais des Tropiques ① 47 711 26

Budget
Grand Hotel ① 47 712 62
Prestige ① 47 711 35

What is your favourite itinerary?

Madagascar, *the* wildlife destination, legendary for the diversity of its flora and fauna which cannot be found anywhere else on earth.

Excluding itineraries customised for private groups, we can tailor-make any itinerary for you – trips to suit all tastes and budgets. To get the most out of magical Madagascar, we would suggest the western dry forest at Kirindy and the *tsingy* limestone forest, one of the country's World Heritage Sites. *En route* you will see the famed Baobab Avenue. Then tour the south. Eighteen tribes constitute the Malagasy population, speaking the same language. During this trip, you witness the dazzling diversity of the country from the skills of Zafimaniry wood carvers to the ancient traditions of Antaimoro papermaking.

What are your top tips for visiting and travelling in Madagascar?

It would be to choose the right company! Make sure you don't end up going to the wrong place, ask the right questions before you go, and make sure you're comfortable with your itinerary. Then, adopt the flexible *mora mora* attitude of Malagasy and go with an open mind. You might be set on spotting a specific animal, but the magic of Madagascar will really hit you when you least expect it.

Take time to talk to your guides one-on-one whenever you get the chance. You may have questions that were not answered on a trek or that occurred to you afterwards, and if there's time to chat with your guide then you may be rewarded with some incredible insights.

Rova Travel Tours caters essentially for individuals and groups seeking personal attention, and suggests planned itineraries for business trips as well as for incentive tours or theme-related trips. Their creative team relishes the challenge of designing totally personalised tours to bring you an unforgettable journey. We spoke to managing director Mishou Randimbiarisoa.

① +261 (0)20 22 276 67
Ⓔ rtt@moov.mg Ⓦ www.rova-travel-tours.mg

Around Fianarantsoa

On the next section of the RN7, running from Ambositra to Ihosy, the scenery becomes increasingly spectacular as you pass remnants of the western limit of the rainforest. The road climbs up and down steep hills, past neat rice paddies interspersed with eucalyptus and pine groves. And there are more roadside stalls along the way: carved kitchenware is in abundance around PK 302; then come the eucalyptus honey sellers after PK 338.

Some way to the east of the road are the rainforest of Ranomafana National Park and Madagascar's only tea plantation, before you begin the approach into the administrative capital of Betsileo: Fianarantsoa. This has long been an important academic centre, a fact reflected in its name which literally means 'good education'. In 2008, the old town district of the city was placed on the World Monuments Fund Watch List of the 100 Most Endangered Sites because many of the beautiful buildings there are at serious risk of irreparable damage if urgent investment in their maintenance is not made.

Beyond Fianarantsoa, you pass by a landscape of countless pretty villages of two-storey mud huts. Terraced rice fields continue to predominate, with the occasional vineyard cloaking a distant hilltop. Then the road twists and turns tightly as you drop 300 metres in less than 10km and suddenly you are in the pretty highland town of Ambalavao. Most people schedule a stop here to watch the famous Antaimoro paper being handmade in the workshop.

The scenery becomes more mountainous as you continue south into the Andringitra Massif. Huge domes of granite dominate the grassy plains. The most striking are the twin pillars of Varavarana Ny Atsimo – 'The Gateway to the South'. This is best viewed from around PK 493, just before the road embarks on another sharp 300m drop in elevation. Thereafter the rice paddies and agriculture begin to peter out, giving way to grassy hills. As you continue further into the dry region, villages become more widely spaced and you will notice the mud huts are all single storey. One of the last dramatic granite monoliths goes by the name of Bishop's Cap (optimum vantage points are near Mahasoa at PK 529 and PK 538). Part of this imposing mountain can be seen in the background of the photograph on the page opposite.

The landscape is much less hilly now and soon your arrival at the medium-sized town of Ihosy (pronounced 'ee-oosh'), capital of the Bara tribe, indicates that you have reached point 600km from Tana, with 350km remaining until your destination of Toliara.

Girls by the RN7 at Mahasoa (DA)

Highlights north of Fianarantsoa

Ialatsara Lemur Forest Camp
Ⓦ www.madagascar-lemuriens.com

Created in 2002, this private reserve is on RN7, 65km from Fianarantsoa and 84km south of Ambositra. It has 2,500ha of forest to the south of the road, comprising 1,000ha of natural forest and 1,500ha of managed pine and eucalyptus, and a separate 600ha on the north side. Several species of lemur can be seen here, including Milne-Edwards' sifaka. Chameleons, snakes, tenrecs, frogs, geckos and birds may also be found. Seven wood-frame canvas chalets have been built on stilts in the forest.

Ranomafana National Park

The name Ranomafana means 'hot water' and it was the waters, not the lemurs, that drew visitors in the colonial days and financed the building of the once-elegant Hôtel Station Thermale de Ranomafana. These days the baths are often ignored by visitors anxious to visit Ranomafana National Park, which was created in 1991. This hitherto unprotected fragment of mid-altitude rainforest first came to the world's

HerpetoGasy BioBlitz

There are over 600 known species of reptiles and amphibians in Madagascar and several new ones are being discovered every year. Incredibly, many of these come from the most studied and most visited forests, so there is every chance you could encounter a new species during your trip. The difficulty is in recognising that it is undescribed, of course, since many can be very difficult to distinguish even for the experts.

The HerpetoGasy BioBlitz Project is a citizen science effort which has been set up online to harness amateur observations of frogs and reptiles in Madagascar. You can upload your photos so that specialists can identify them for you. The data gathered will be used by herpetologists to understand better the distribution and conservation status of these creatures (and you retain full copyright to all your photos).

The more information you can contribute the better. Adding the date and location with multiple detailed photos will increase the chance of an accurate identification being possible. And if you are able to provide accurate GPS co-ordinates of the sighting then that is even better still. To get involved, register at Ⓦ www.inaturalist.org/projects/herpetogasy-bioblitz.

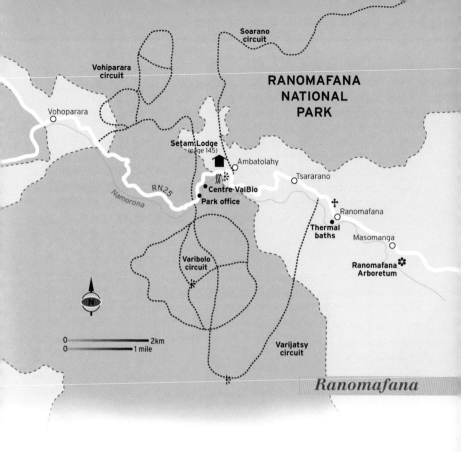

Ranomafana

attention with the discovery of the golden bamboo lemur in 1986 and is particularly rich in wildlife.

Hidden among the trees are 12 species of lemur: Milne-Edwards' sifaka, red-fronted brown lemur, red-bellied lemur, black-and-white ruffed lemur and three species of bamboo lemur. At night you can add mouse lemur, woolly lemur, sportive lemur, greater dwarf lemur and aye-aye. Then there are the birds: more than 100 species with 36 endemic. And the reptiles. And the butterflies and other insects... Even if you saw no wildlife, there is enough variety in the vegetation and scenery, and enough pleasure in walking the well-constructed trails, to make a visit worthwhile. And in the warm summer months you can swim in the cold, clear water of the Namorona while a Madagascar malachite kingfisher darts overhead.

On the downside, the trails are steep and arduous and it often rains. So you do need to be physically fit, even for the shorter walks here. Most of the standard routes take a couple of hours or so but there are longer ones taking six or eight hours. You are most likely to see red-fronted brown lemurs, grey bamboo lemurs and the rarer red-bellied lemur; and star attractions such as greater bamboo lemur and golden

Female red-bellied lemur (DA)

bamboo lemur are now fairly frequently seen too.

A world-class research station has recently been built near the park entrance. The research scientists of **Centre ValBio** has recently begun to give lectures to tourists on a wide range of wildlife and conservation subjects every evening except Sundays. If you book in advance you can even request a particular topic. See ⓦ www.centrevalbio.org.

Ranomafana Arboretum
🕐 07.30-16.30

This small community-run arboretum situated 8km past the national park entrance displays more than 100 native trees in a 2ha plot. The trail is less than 1km but allow an hour to see everything. The specimens are labelled not just with their names, but with descriptions explaining the social roles of each species in Malagasy life, including the main purposes each type of tree is traditionally put to by the locals. You will discover why one type of wood is best for roof supports, another for door frames, and another for zebu carts; which tree is used for making rope; how the sap of another can be used for catching birds; the one considered the optimum firewood locally (despite an ability to survive forest fires); and the tree whose leaves are regarded as a better alternative to toilet paper!

Most of the specimens were planted around 20 years ago but one palm is labelled as having been present on the site at the arboretum's inception and bears the following description: 'no one who has seen the tree knows its local name or knows of other palms like it'.

Accommodation in Fianarantsoa

Upmarket
Tsara Guest House Ⓦ www.tsaraguest.com

Moderate
Peniela Ⓔ peniela.house@yahoo.fr
Tombontsoa Ⓦ www.hotel-tombontsoa.com
Zomatel Ⓦ www.zomatel-madagascar.com

Budget
Mini-Croq Ⓔ mini.croq@yahoo.fr

Accommodation in Ranomafana

Moderate
Centre-Est Sejour Ⓔ centrestsejour@gmail.com
Domaine Nature Ⓦ domainenaturemada.com
Forêt Australe Ⓦ www.groupeaustralhotel.com

Camping/dormitory
Enquire at the office at the entrance to the national park.

Tried & Tested

Setam Lodge
Ⓦ www.setam-madagascar.com

Definitely the best accommodation in the area, Setam Lodge is located close to the entrance of Ranomafana National Park, arguably the best Malagasy rainforest for birdwatching, with brown mesites, Henst's goshawks and rufous-headed ground-rollers among the species in residence. It is also a key destination for viewing rare, endemic species such as the golden bamboo lemur, which the park was specifically set up to protect. The comfortable rooms are housed in ten single-storey bungalows on a steep hillside overlooking the forested valley.

Fianarantsoa highlights

While most of Fianarantsoa's hotels are in the lower or upper town areas, the part of the city most worth exploring is the old town, perched high on the hilltop where once a royal palace stood. Some 500 late-19th-century homes line picturesque cobblestone streets in the only site in Madagascar where buildings from this era form a coherent architectural ensemble.

Sahambavy Tea Estate

Ⓔ sidexam@yahoo.fr ⊕ 07.30-15.30

The tea estate, 23km from Fianarantsoa, has been manufacturing black tea for over forty years and green tea since 2004. The 335ha plantation produces some 550 tonnes of tea each year, of which more than half is exported to Kenya. Guided tours of the factory, which employs 120 workers, take about an hour and end with a tasting.

It is set in a pretty valley with a lake, on the shores of which is a resort-style hotel (Ⓦ www.lachotel.com) – a peaceful and romantic spot, where you can swim, ride, boat, cycle or hike as the mood takes you. If you don't have your own vehicle, the easiest way to get here is by train.

Vineyards

The famous Lazan'i Betsileo vineyard (Ⓔ lazan_i_betsileo@yahoo.fr) produces red, white, rosé, and 'grey' wines, as well as some liqueurs and aperitifs. It is located some 12km south of Fianarantsoa and it is best to book ahead for a visit. Alternatively, you can witness the wine-making process at the Cistercian-Trappist Monastery of Maromby (also near Fianarantsoa) or at the Soavita Winery (just north of Ambalavao).

Highlights south of Fianarantsoa

Ambalavao

The **Antaimoro paper factory** is the main attraction in the town of Ambalavao. This papyrus-type paper impregnated with dried flowers is sold throughout the island, made into such items as wall-hangings and lampshades. The people in this area are Betsileo, but paper-making here copies the

(DA)

coastal Antaimoro tradition which goes back to the Muslim immigrants who used it for writing verses from the Koran. At the open-air workshop you get a good tour of the whole step-by-step process. A shop sells the finished product in dozens of forms: from bookmarks and greeting cards to photo albums and picture frames.

At nearby Soalandy you can take a similar tour of a **silk production workshop**. The whole process from silkworm to silk scarf – including picking, drying, boiling, spinning, dying and weaving – is explained by a guide. And just as at the paper factory, the finished products are available to buy in a shop after the visit.

Accommodation in Ambalavao

Moderate
Aux Bougainvillées Ⓦ www.auxbougainvillees.sitew.com
Résidence du Betsileo Ⓔ sorafahotel@moov.mg
Tsienim-Parihy Ⓔ tsienimpari@moov.mg

Budget
Samoina Ⓣ 75 341 48

Accommodation at Andringitra

For full details of tour operator-recommended accommodation, see page 149.

Moderate
Camp Catta Ⓦ www.campcatta.com
Tranogasy Ⓦ www.tranogasy.com

Andringitra National Park

This park was created in 1999 to protect the flora and fauna around Madagascar's second highest peak: Pic d'Imarivolanitra (2,658m), meaning 'close to the sky'. Andringitra has some wildlife, but landscape, vegetation and trekking are the chief attractions. Against a dramatic backdrop of granite peaks and gneiss formations you can see endemic succulent plants, distant ring-tailed lemurs, forest and waterfalls. In the wet season the meadows are carpeted with flowers, including 30 species of orchid. Great care has been taken in creating the trails which are beautifully engineered through difficult terrain. Although the trail system covers a variety of ecosystems, the park also protects an area of montane rainforest in the east (closed to visitors) which provides a sanctuary for such rare species as golden and greater bamboo lemurs.

If you don't have your own transport, then visits can be arranged from Ambalavao. Even if you only plan to hike one of the shorter circuits, come equipped for serious walking: bring boots or tough trainers, hiking poles, daysack and raingear.

Tsara Camp
Ⓦ www.tsaracamp-madagascar.com

You know you're off the beaten track when you turn off what passes for a main road and head along the bumpy track to Tsara Camp and its 15 tents sitting close to the head of the Tsaranoro Valley. The scenery here is amazing, with an 800m vertical face to one side of you and the mountains of the Andringitra National Park on the other. The facilities are simple but the camp is a perfect base from which to experience remote walking through villages cut off from 21st-century life, a sacred forest, or proper mountain hiking.

Anja Park

This community-run park, 13km south from Ambalavao on RN7, offers superb scenery, intriguing plants adapted to the dry southern climate, some interesting Betsileo history and several troops of cheeky ring-tailed lemurs. The forest is sacred to the Betsileo; their ancestors are buried here and so it has always been forbidden to hunt the lemurs, around 300 of which make their home in this 8ha reserve. The well-maintained short trail winds past some impressive rocks to a sacred cliff where there is an apparently inaccessible tomb high in the rock face. The tour takes one to two hours.

Ringtails are easily seen up close at Anja. (DA)

149

In Conversation with...

If they had only ten days, what would you recommend for a first-time visitor to Madagascar?

Madagascar is known for its unique flora and fauna, and the diversity of cultures and landscapes. So we advise visitors to opt for a tour which will showcase all these aspects. Our tour called 'Madagascar Essentials' would be a good fit: in less than ten days, the traveller will cross no fewer than four microclimates and experience their unique biodiversity. Starting from the colourful capital in the highlands, they will learn about the rich history and culture of the country, explore Madagascar's endangered rainforest, see lemurs, dry bush and canyons, before finishing on the beautiful beaches of the Mozambique Channel. The landscape will change every day. This itinerary is highly customisable and many extensions in other regions can be added. This is just one suggestion among many possibilities.

If you had time to spare at the beginning or end of your tour, what would you recommend to do?

Although it's a big island, with a little organisation it is fairly easy to discover other regions of Madagascar. Some of the popular options we propose are to spend some time in Nosy Boraha (Ile Sainte Marie), which is an excellent place for whale-watching in season. Or head to the western part of our country and watch the sun set over Baobab Avenue; it's an amazing show. If you feel like going north, the landscapes and possible activities in the region around the second largest bay in the world will surprise you.

What makes your tours and services unique?

We like to work hand-in-hand with customers to design their itineraries based on their specific needs and interests. The more out of the ordinary, the better! Don't hesitate to contact us if you are short on ideas, though. The fact that we are a local tour operator helps us to be very flexible.

ASISTEN Travel

How do your tours manage the impact of visitors when visiting Madagascar?

We understand that tourism is one of our chances to have a positive impact and help our fragile economy. ASISTEN Travel establishes partnerships with locally owned, very small businesses to mutually develop our know-how and capacities. Most importantly, we would like our travellers to be in touch with the local population, so we only employ Malagasy guides who are able to interpret and share the wealth of tradition and cultural heritage in our country. We have a very proactive approach to make sure our activities and our customers preserve the environment, the fauna, the flora and the habitats.

What tips would you give for travellers wanting a more adventurous approach to exploring Madagascar?

The basics: a very good travel guide book, a dose of patience and flexibility, a tour operator who will help with some logistics, and finally once in Madagascar learn the concept of *mora mora*, which characterises the country's lifestyle and is undoubtedly the way to discover and appreciate its immense richness. Please remember that tourism infrastructure is still being developed, so you cannot expect four or five star accommodation at every location. Nevertheless, we have plenty of charming hotels and lodges.

Founded and run by two young Malagasy entrepreneurs, ASISTEN Travel is a local inbound tour operator specialised in the conception of tailor-made trips in Madagascar. The company also offers some fixed-departure photography and luxury tours. Based in Antananarivo, the capital of Madagascar, it describes itself as 'the first 100% Malagasy tourism business'. We spoke to founders Njaka Ramandimbiarison and Haja Rasambainarivo.

☏ +261 (0)20 22 577 55   Ⓔ info@asisten-travel.com
Ⓦ www.asisten-travel.com

RN7 passing Zombitse (DA)

Ihosy to Toliara

Once you pass Ihosy, you are truly in the south – the most famous part of Madagascar, home to the spiny forest where weird cactus-like trees wave their thorny fingers in the sky, where fragments of elephant bird eggshells may still be found, and where the Mahafaly tribe erect their intriguing and often entertaining carved *aloalo* stelae above the graves. Here also is the country's most-visited national park, as well as beaches and coral reefs.

For the first 15km after leaving Ihosy, the road rapidly climbs some 400m to the Horombe Plateau where the landscape is utterly transformed: the rocky outcrops of Andringitra have been left far behind and a vast open grassland spreads into the distance with barely a tree in sight. During the next 70km it is difficult to avoid reflecting on the scale of deforestation suffered by Madagascar as you pass through this rather desolate savannah. But thankfully the road is flat and straight all the way, so you will quickly reach Ranohira. This small town at PK 690 is the base for visiting Isalo National Park. Around here the grassland is dotted with handsome Bismarck palms (see photo on page 39) but the most spectacular features of the landscape are the imposing sandstone escarpments rising all around, their strange eroded shapes silhouetted against the horizon.

The final section of the RN7 from Isalo to Toliara has just been resurfaced in 2012 so this 243km stretch takes about four hours. Shortly after Ranohira, the rugged mountains of the Isalo Massif give way to grasslands once again and you will pass through Ilakaka – a curious sapphire town that has grown up from nothing in the last decade or so. But the sapphire rush is moving south and the next town of Sakaraha is already being taken over by gem-seekers. A little further and Zombitse National Park comes into view, straddling the road. This protected transition forest is especially worth a visit for birders.

The coastal town of Toliara marks the end of your 952km journey down the RN7, and here you have a choice: you can turn south and head down the coast to Anakao, or go north up the coast to Ifaty. Both destinations offer spiny forest, beach and watersports. Alternatively, from Toliara's airport you can take a flight to back to Tana or across to Taolagnaro on the opposite coast.

Ranohira highlights

Isalo National Park

The combination of sandstone rocks cut by deep canyons, rare endemic plants and dry weather (between June and August rain is almost unknown) makes this park particularly rewarding. For botanists there are pachypodiums and a locally endemic aloe; and for lemur-lovers there are sifakas, brown lemurs and ringtails. Isalo is also sacred to the

Sandstone formations viewed from hotel Relais de la Reine (DA)

Accommodation near Isalo

For full details of tour operator-recommended accommodation, see page 157.

Upmarket
Relais de la Reine ⓦ www.lerelaisdelareine.com
Satrana Lodge ⓦ www.hotel-isalo-lodge.com

Moderate
Isalo Ranch ⓦ www.isalo-ranch.com
Palme de l'Isalo ⓦ www.groupeaustralhotel.com

Budget
Berny ⓦ http://hotel-ranohira-ihosy-isalo.lagrandeile.com
Momo Trek ⓔ momo_trek@yahoo.fr
Motel de l'Isalo ⓦ www.motelisalo.com
Orchidée d'Isalo ⓦ www.orchidee-isalo.com

Bara tribe; for hundreds of years they have used caves in the canyon walls as burial sites.

Hiking should not be undertaken lightly at Isalo. It can get very hot and many trails offer little shade. There are several options. **Circuit Namaza** has you following a stream up a leafy canyon to the Cascade des Nymphes. The walk takes 30–45 minutes and you are rewarded at the end with a refreshing dip in the surprisingly cold water of a deep pool. The trail to the **natural swimming pool** is justifiably the most popular option. The palm-fringed pool, constantly filled by a waterfall, is both stunningly beautiful and wonderful for swimming. At the **Canyon des Makis** a path goes over rocks and along the edge of the tumbling river; there are pools into which you can fling yourself at intervals and, at the top, a small waterfall under which to have a shower. The sheer rocks hung with luxuriant ferns broaden out to provide views of the bare mountain behind, and trees and palms provide shade for a picnic. A visit may be combined with the neighbouring **Canyon des Rats** for a full-day trip. Multi-day treks with camping are also possible, allowing the most adventurous to penetrate deeper into the park.

The **Maison de l'Isalo Interpretation Centre** (⊙ 06.30–18.00) 10km south of Ranohira is a tremendous museum in a beautiful building, well worth a visit to learn more about the wildlife of the park and the people who live locally. The well-designed exhibits have multilingual descriptions including English.

Accommodation in Toliara

Upmarket
Capricorne Ⓦ www.madagascar-resorts.com
Hyppocampo Ⓦ www.hyppocampo-tulear.com
Serena Ⓦ www.serenatulear.com
Victory Ⓦ www.hoteltulear-victory.com

Moderate
Longo Hotel Arcobaleno Ⓔ longo.hotel@yahoo.it
Manatane Ⓔ hotel.manatane@yahoo.fr
Sud Plazza Ⓔ sud_plaz@yahoo.fr

Budget
Chez Lalah Ⓣ 94 434 17
Refuge Ⓣ 94 423 28

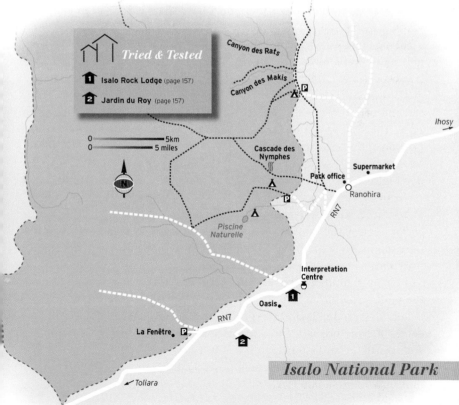

Digging for sapphires is done without machinery. (DA)

Ilakaka sapphire mines

Every other shop has the word 'saphir' above its doorway in this extraordinary sapphire boomtown. Ilakaka is no longer as lawless a place as it was after it first sprung up in 1998, and some tourists do now stop to visit the gem shops. A Swiss resident runs visits to the open mines allowing tourists to see first-hand the massive effort (and danger) involved in finding these tiny gems. As many as 200 men may work in a single pit, forming human chains to shovel the earth up the steep sides. Visits last about an hour and can be followed by a cutting and polishing demonstrations in the showroom if requested (Ⓦ www. colorlinemadagascar.blogspot.co.uk).

La Fenêtre

Not far from the Maison de l'Isalo Interpretation Centre is another popular site – perhaps too popular at times. A natural rock formation known as La Fenêtre provides a window to the setting sun. It is just off RN7 so no hiking is necessary, nor do you need a permit or guide.

(HR)

Isalo Rock Lodge
ⓦ www.isalorocklodge.com

RAINBOW
TOURS

This impressive 60-room hotel is located high up on the sandstone formations of the Isalo Massif. From the lodge, views over the surroundings are panoramic. The luxurious rooms, spa and fine restaurant have made this new lodge a deservedly popular choice among our clients. The restaurant, with pool bar, seats 100 guests and offers decadent cuisine that is a blend of European and Malagasy styles. Visitors to the park can explore the area up to a point using 4x4s, on horseback, or on foot.

Jardin du Roy
ⓦ www.lejardinduroy.com

IMAGINE
AFRICA

Situated on the southern boundary of the Isalo National Park, Jardin du Roy blends modern luxury with a Malagasy touch; each of the 25 rooms has air conditioning, en-suite facilities and its own veranda, and there is a pool set within the gardens. Known for its unique landscape of eroded sandstone formations, the incredible scenery of the neighbouring park is fantastic for hiking, and visitors can enjoy the rock pools and gorges, and explore the dramatic Canyon des Singes and Canyon des Rats.

Sakaraha highlights

Zombitse National Park

Zombitse is a stark example of the effects of deforestation. Years of continuous felling have turned the surrounding areas into an arid moonscape and what remains is an isolated pocket of forest, thankfully now protected. The 36,300ha park is an important example of a boundary zone between the western and southern domains of vegetation and so has a high level of biodiversity.

Zombitse is of major significance to birdwatchers as it offers the chance to glimpse one of Madagascar's rarest endemics, Appert's greenbul, which is confined to this forest. In addition to birds, you have

Sportive lemurs hide in tree holes by day. (DA)

a good chance of seeing Verreaux's sifakas, red-fronted brown lemurs, or a nocturnal Hubbard's sportive lemur peering out of its nest hole. The locally endemic Standing's day gecko is also easily found. There are four easy circuits, taking about 1–2½hrs each.

It takes just over an hour to reach the park from Isalo, or nearly three hours driving from Toliara, so serious birdwatchers should leave as early as possible in the morning to avoid the heat and catch the post-dawn bird activity.

Toliara highlights

Arboretum d'Antsokay
Ⓦ www.antsokayarboretum.org
This botanical garden should not be missed by anyone with an interest in the flora – and accompanying fauna – of the southwest. Around a thousand plant species are showcased, mostly endemic to the region, and many with medicinal qualities. English-speaking guides take you on a two-hour tour of the 7ha planted area of the 50ha arboretum where you will see around 100 species of *Euphorbia* and 60 species of *Kalanchoe*, as well as an abundance of birds and reptiles. Indeed, with the spiny forest fast disappearing, this is one of the best places in the region for birders. Try to arrive as early as possible to avoid the heat of the day, or stay overnight here in one their bungalows.

Marine Museum
Ⓣ Monday–Friday 08.00–11.30 & 14.30–17.30, Saturday 08.00–11.30
Marine enthusiasts should schedule a short visit to the Musée de la Mer near to Toliara port. The main attraction is the preserved coelacanths: seven have been caught in the region, of which three are on display here. The fascinating collection also includes shells, coral, whale teeth and bones, crustaceans and lots of other marine curiosities – as well as, rather inexplicably given that it is neither aquatic nor from Madagascar, a complete ostrich skeleton.

An island aflame

Each year, up to a third of the island of Madagascar is deliberately burned. That is a gigantic area more than twice as big as Portugal or the US state of Indiana. The purpose of this burning, known locally as *tavy*, is to encourage regrowth of fresh grasses for feeding zebu, or to prepare plots for conversion into rice paddies.

Carefully controlled slash-and-burn can be a sustainable – if controversial – form of forest management if practised on a rotation that leaves several fallow years for regrowth. But Madagascar's population is too large for *tavy* to be sustainable. Such is the need to feed zebu and grow rice that the majority of the island's forest has long been cleared for these purposes. After a few cycles of burning, the soil is exhausted of nutrients and the land is typically colonised by grassy scrub.

The fight for survival drives the Malagasy to seek these short-term gains; but long-term the picture is bleak. Vast tracts of Madagascar have been rendered unusable. Worse, the grasses do not have strong enough root systems to hold the earth together, so erosion and landslides are becoming an increasing problem with each passing wet season. There are also obvious risks of the fires spreading out of control beyond the intended area; one such fire burned 6,000ha of Isalo National Park a couple of years ago.

Although deeply ingrained in the Malagasy traditional culture, *tavy* is in fact illegal. But you only have to see the scale on which it is practised to realise that the law is not – and perhaps cannot be – enforced.

South Malagasy Arts and Traditions Museum (Cedratom)

⏱ Monday–Friday 07.30–11.30 & 14.30–17.30; Saturday 07.30–11.30

This museum run by the university in Toliara has some remarkable cultural and historical exhibits – mainly from the Mahafaly tribe – including replica tombs, a Mikea mask (genuine masks are rare in Madagascar) with real human teeth, and some Sakalava erotic tomb sculptures.

A Mahafaly tomb (DA)

In Conversation with...

How does your expert knowledge help you provide travellers with unique experiences?

We have climbed mountains, forged rivers, trekked across plains, canoed rapids, dined by starlight and trudged through rainforests. We have travelled by foot, horse, helicopter, yacht and plane to bring the very best of Africa to our clients. And we have loved every minute of it.

Pulse Africa is staffed by a handpicked group of 'travellers' who experience each and every product before recommending it. We have been travelling to Madagascar for over 15 years and always look forward to the next trip, knowing we will discover something new and exciting every time.

Over the years, Pulse Africa has established close ties and reliable relationships with suppliers on the ground, who share the same level of professionalism and enthusiasm as we do. As a result, we offer seamless, trouble-free trips leaving our clients to enjoy their holiday to the maximum.

While we aim to give clients a very personal service drawing from the experience we have built up over the years, we also thoroughly enjoy sharing our adventures, magical finds and travel tips with them. For us, although the silver service and white-gloved butlers have a role to play, the real luxury is that of experiencing the magnificence of a destination in an exclusive manner, often in some of the remotest parts of Madagascar.

With a 50% client referral rate, we must be doing something right.

What makes a Pulse Africa trip so special?

It is about our attention to detail which has come from years of experience and constant travelling to the destinations concerned. It is about creating the correct expectations and then fulfilling them. At Pulse Africa, we pride ourselves on our ability to understand our clients' holiday wishes and to match them with the destinations, lodges and guides that are best suited to each individual. We often say 'it is about putting the right people in the right place'.

It is also about sharing the hidden gems we have discovered on our travels, and in Madagascar these are plentiful. In fact one is spoilt for choice. For us, it is often about getting off the beaten track as the road less travelled yields many delights. In remote areas where tourists are a rare sight, guests will be greeted by happy, inquisitive children and a warm smile.

Pulse Africa

What should one consider when planning a trip to Madagascar?

Travellers are no longer observers of the world; they want to experience the destination, and for us there is no better way to do this than to travel by road with a qualified guide. Apart from learning about the many fascinating aspects of Madagascar, one is more likely to wander through a local market, sample delicious local cuisine, interact with the people or even play soccer with the children.

Madagascar is a third world country where many roads are in disrepair, air travel is hampered by slow airport procedures and distances are vast. Often less is more and while it is important to experience the diversity of the island it needs to be done with as little 'waiting around in airports time' as possible. So proper prior planning is essential. As they say: the journey is the destination.

 Pulse Africa specialises in tailor-made personalised holidays to southern Africa, east Africa and the Indian Ocean islands. With over 20 years' experience, and thousands of miles under their belt, they are well equipped to turn your holiday dreams into a reality. They are based in South Africa with representation in UK, USA and Europe. We spoke to Nicci Lenferna, director of the company.

ⓣ +27 (0)11 325 2290   ⓕ +27 (0)11 325 2226
ⓔ info@pulseafrica.com   ⓦ www.pulseafrica.com

Ifaty

Ifaty offers sand, sea and snorkelling – the perfect place to relax after many days spent motoring down the RN7. There are several seafront hotels with bungalows strung out over several kilometres of coastline. Diving is one of the main attractions (it can usually be arranged with or via your hotel) but there are some excellent inland reserves that even non-naturalists will enjoy and horse-riding is on offer too. A small information centre created by voluntourism NGO ReefDoctor (Ⓦ www.reefdoctor.org) educates tourists, locals and schoolchildren about the area's threatened land and marine environments.

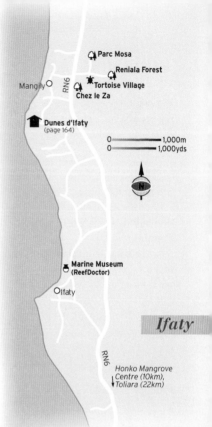

Parc Mosa
Reniala Forest
Mangily ○   Tortoise Village
RN6   Chez le Za
Dunes d'Ifaty
(page 164)

0 ⟼ 1,000m
0 ⟼ 1,000yds

N

Marine Museum
(ReefDoctor)
○ Ifaty

Ifaty

RN6

Honko Mangrove
Centre (10km),
↓ Toliara (22km)

There are many baobabs in Reniala Forest. (DA)

Ifaty highlights

Reniala Forest
ⓦ www.reniala.jimdo.com ⊘ summer 08.00–18.00, winter 07.30–17.30
This outstanding reserve protects 45ha of spiny forest, especially recommended for those interested in birds and flora. An early-morning visit more or less guarantees long-tailed ground-rollers and sub-desert mesites. Guides, who live at the reserve and can be arranged on arrival, are excellent at locating these two species and are also knowledgeable about the area's unique plant life. In addition to birds there are around a thousand *Adansonia rubrostipa* baobabs, many octopus trees and lots of *Euphorbia*. There is a one-hour and a two-hour trail. Night walks are also possible.

Practicalities

Ifaty is only 27km north up the coastal road from Toliara, but it is a poor track with deep sand in places. Depending the type of vehicle you are travelling in, the journey takes between 30 minutes and two hours. There are no banks, post offices, shops or similar infrastructure at Ifaty, so be sure to change enough cash before leaving Toliara.

Scuba diving centres are based at the following hotels in the Ifaty area: Bamboo Club, Dunes, Hôtel de la Plage, Ifaty Beach Club, Lakana Vezo, Mora Mora, Nautilus, and Vovotelo.

Accommodation at Ifaty

For full details of tour operator-recommended accommodation, see page 164.

Upmarket
Hôtel de la Plage ⓦ www.hotelplage-tulear.com
Nautilus ⓦ www.nautilusmada.mg
Paradisier ⓦ www.paradisier.net

Moderate
Bamboo Club ⓦ www.bamboo-club.com
Ifaty Beach Club ⓦ www.ifaty.com
Lakana Vezo ⓦ www.madagascar-resorts.com
Mora Mora ⓣ 94 915 39
Vovotelo ⓔ hotelvovotelo@simicro.mg

Long-tailed ground-roller (DA)

Tortoise Village

Ⓦ www.villagetortues.com ✪ daily 09.00–17.00

Tortoise Village was set up by a group of conservation organisations for the protection of the two southwestern species: spider and radiated tortoises. Both are seriously threatened by illegal trade (for pets abroad) and hunting (by locals for food). Around 1,200 are resident including some confiscated by customs. Set in 7ha of spiny forest with small baobabs, with a further 7ha of fenced areas, the guided tour will show you the tortoises and explain the efforts to conserve them. Allow an hour for a visit; you may see other reptiles, birds and brown lemurs.

(DA)

Honko Mangrove Information Centre

Ⓦ www.honko.org

This new mangrove conservation and education centre is midway between Toliara and Ifaty. It was set up by a Belgian NGO to restore nearby mangroves and teach locals to use them sustainably. Trained guides lead visitors along a 400m elevated boardwalk to experience the mangrove habitat and a hide enables close viewing of birdlife. They also organise cultural visits to the village of Ambondrolava in the company of a guide who will give you an insight into local daily life.

Tried & Tested

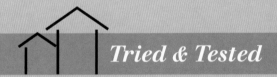

Les Dunes d'Ifaty
Ⓦ www.lesdunesdifaty.com

RAINBOW TOURS

This is the area's most popular hotel with its 19 spacious villas and 22 standard and deluxe rooms. Situated near to Mangily village, Les Dunes offers excellent hospitality, has an attractive swimming pool, and is on the edge of a large lagoon where snorkelling is good. Visitors come primarily to see the remarkable  unprotected spiny forest nearby. The large restaurant offers excellent seafood dishes, as well as traditional Malagasy and French cuisine. Activities on offer include snorkelling, diving, quad biking and horse-riding.

Anakao

Anakao is a pretty little Vezo fishing village with colourful boats drawn up on the sands. Hotels catering for all budgets have opened in recent years so it now competes with Ifaty for beaches and opportunities for snorkelling, diving and birdwatching. Reptile enthusiasts will also enjoy exploring the spiny forest here.

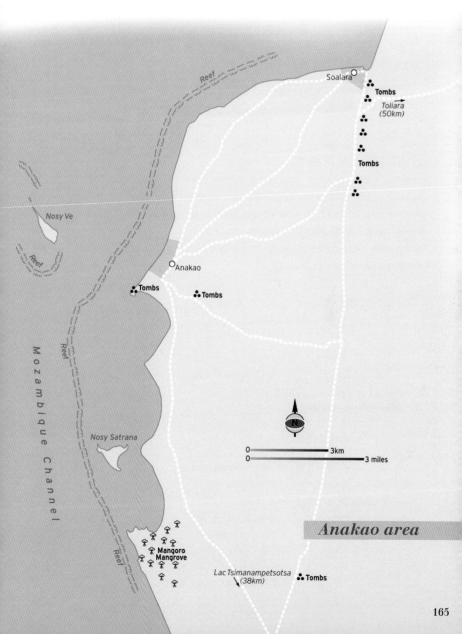

(DA)

Practicalities

Anakao is accessible from Toliara via a very tough 56km dirt road, or much more easily by boat. All the hotels provide a transfer service. Like at Ifaty, there are no money exchange facilities. Fresh water is a problem too; only a few hotels have running water. And if seafood is not your thing, your dining options in Anakao will be very limited.

Accommodation in Anakao

Upmarket
Anakao Ocean Lodge Ⓦ www.anakao-madagascar.com
Chez Diego Ⓔ laltraluna@hotmail.it
Lalandaka Ⓦ www.lalandaka.com
Prince Anakao Ⓦ www.hotelprinceanakao.com

Moderate
Longo Vezo Ⓦ www.longovezo.org
Peter Pan Ⓦ www.peterpanhotel.com
Safari Vezo Ⓦ www.safarivezo.com
Soalaza Ⓔ lacombe-christian@voila.fr

Budget
Chez Emile Ⓔ emile@compagniedusud.com
Trano Mena Ⓔ lalbatros_8@yahoo.fr

Anakao highlights

A day spent exploring on foot is rewarding. Take the track behind the village heading south. On the outskirts of Anakao you will find some interesting **tombs** (one has a satellite dish on the roof to provide eternal entertainment for the ancestors) and will then come to a small peninsula with a couple more tombs. It is still possible to find fragments of subfossil eggshell from the long-extinct elephant bird here, but please keep your collecting instincts under control so that others can enjoy this extraordinary glimpse of the past. It is illegal to take these eggshells out of the country. Birders would be well advised to take an early-morning walk on one of the tracks through the spiny forest, setting off shortly before sunrise.

Lying 4km off Anakao, the island of **Nosy Ve** with its tranquil white beaches is home to the world's southernmost breeding colony of red-tailed tropic-birds. They breed year-round so you can be sure of seeing them at their nest sites under bushes at the southern end of the island, as well as flying overhead.

Only day visits are possible as there are no buildings on the island and camping is forbidden. Bring plenty of sun protection; there is a shortage of shade in which to shelter from the searing sun.

Further south, **Nosy Satrana** is a small peaceful island closer to the shore. In fact you can walk out to it on a sandbar at low tide. It offers excellent diving and good snorkelling, but is rather rockier than Nosy Ve and has no tropic-birds.

Tsimanampetsotsa National Park

A shallow soda lake – 15km long by 2km at its widest point – is the focus for this terrific national park. The large limestone plateau here has some of the most striking spiny forest vegetation in Madagascar, with countless locally endemic species. The lake is renowned for its waterfowl, notably flamingos, and other rare endemic birds including the Madagascar plover. There are some quite extraordinary baobabs, pachypodiums, and a magnificent banyan tree with its aerial roots hugging the side of a cliff face. The park sits on a large underground aquifer that runs north, evidenced by the numerous sinkholes and caves. In the sacred cave of Mitoho, a rare endemic species of blind fish is easily seen.

Lying about 50km south of Anakao down a very bad road, a visit is only just manageable as a day trip. It would be far better to stay a night, either camping or in the moderate accommodation at nearby Ambola. There is no public transport so it is necessary to arrange your visit as an excursion from Anakao or Toliara.

Taolagnaro (Fort Dauphin) and surrounds 170

7 Taolagnaro and Surrounds

The southeast region offers some tremendous opportunities for wildlife-viewing to suit all budgets and levels of energy. Most famous by far is Berenty Reserve, where the resident troops of ring-tailed lemurs have been the stars of countless television documentaries worldwide. But equally worthy of attention – and rather less demanding on the pocket – are Andohahela National Park (rainforest, spiny forest and transition forest), Ifotaka Community Forest (gallery forest and spiny forest) and Mandena Conservation Zone (littoral forest and wetlands). The base for exploring the region is the laid-back coastal town of Taolagnaro, still popularly known by its French colonial name of Fort Dauphin. It is one of the most beautifully located of all popular destinations in Madagascar. Built on a small peninsula, it is bordered on three sides by beaches and breakers and backed by high green mountains which dwindle into spiny forest to the west.

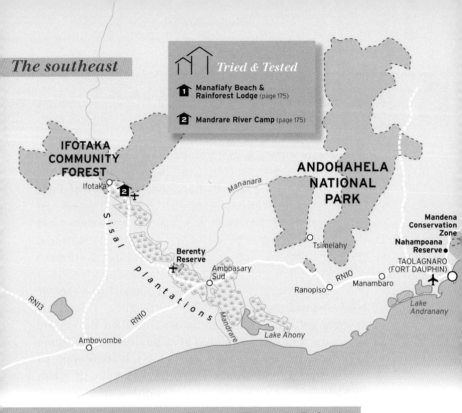

Tried & Tested

1 Manafiafy Beach & Rainforest Lodge (page 175)

2 Mandrare River Camp (page 175)

IFOTAKA COMMUNITY FOREST

Ifotaka

Sisal Plantations

RN13

RN10

Ambovombe

Mananara

Berenty Reserve

Amboasary Sud

Mandrare

Lake Anony

Ranopiso

ANDOHAHELA NATIONAL PARK

Tsimelahy

RN10

Manambaro

Mandena Conservation Zone

Nahampoana Reserve

TAOLAGNARO (FORT DAUPHIN)

Lake Andranany

Taolagnaro (Fort Dauphin) and surrounds

In recent years, Taolagnaro has experienced an unprecedented influx of new residents, mainly as a result of a controversial ilmenite (titanium ore) mine (see page 173). On the one hand this has created much employment and accelerated development of local infrastructure, but on the other it has also led to some serious social and economic issues for the poorer local residents.

The upside for tourism is that there are now plenty of international-standard hotels in Taolagnaro itself, but beyond the town good accommodation in the region is still limited to a small handful of lodges. See page 175 for those recommended by tour operators.

Highlights in and around Taolagnaro

Taolagnaro has several **beaches** and some of the most superb coastline in the Indian Ocean for surfing. The easy-to-reach Libanona Beach is great for swimming, snorkelling and **watersports**. Monseigneur Beach and Baie des Galions are also recommended, with watersports instructors and gear for hire from Ankoba Sports at the latter (⑩ www.ankoba.com).

On the northeastern peninsula of the town, dating from 1643, is **Fort Flacourt** (⏱ Tuesday–Saturday 08.00–11.00 & 14.30–17.30). It is now a working military compound so a guide is obligatory for a tour. Inside, at the **Musée de l'Anosy**, there are exhibits of old maps, photographs, uniforms and other cultural artefacts.

On the town's southern peninsula, **Libanona Ecology Centre** (⏱ Monday–Friday 08.00–12.00 & 14.30–17.30) is a beautiful site set up by a group of local ecologists as a regional training centre for environmental science and conservation. It is an inspiring place open to visitors.

Pic St Louis

There is a good hiking trail to the summit of this mountain, which dominates Taolagnaro's skyline. The hike (1½–2hrs each way) can be demanding and the trail is not always clearly marked, so if you are not up for an adventure by scaling several peaks it is recommended to take a local guide! The reward is some excellent panoramic views – as far as Ste Luce Bay on a clear day.

Nahampoana Reserve

Ⓦ www.nahampoana.com

This is an easily accessible zoo-cum-reserve and botanical garden owned by a local tour operator. The 67ha park is just 7km (15 minutes' drive) from Taolagnaro on the way to Ste Luce Bay. Although some species are from other parts of Madagascar, it provides several tame lemurs, reptiles and an interesting array of regional vegetation. Allow a full day for a visit or stay in one of their en-suite rooms.

Pic St Louis (LB)

Practicalities

The southeast of Madagascar is effectively an island within an island. It is impossible to reach this region overland unless you have an adventurous spirit and plenty of time to spare, so most tourists fly into Taolagnaro – either from Tana or Toliara. A few of the most upmarket lodges have their own airstrips so that their clients can be transferred directly by light aircraft, cutting out hours of bumping along the rather poor roads of the region.

Taolagnaro is a fairly developed town with a small supermarket, a post office and several banks with ATMs. There is a helpful local tourist office on Rue Realy Abel (ⓔ officetourismeftu@moov.mg ⏰ Monday–Friday 08.30–12.00 & 14.30–18.00). The cost of living here has become higher than in most other regions as a result of the new mine.

Accommodation in Taolagnaro

Upmarket
Azura ⓦ www.hotel-azura.com
Croix du Sud, Dauphin & Galion ⓦ www.madagascar-resorts.com
Kaleta ⓦ www.kaletahotel-fortdauphin.com
Libanona Beach View ⓔ libanonabeachview@fortnet.net

Moderate
Panorama ⓔ hotelpanorama_lamarina@yahoo.fr
Soavy ⓔ deriazi@yahoo.fr

Budget
Chez Jacqueline ⓣ 92 900 73
Mahavoky ⓣ 92 902 32; 92 914 15

Accommodation further afield

For full details of tour operator-recommended accommodation, see page 175.

Upmarket
Berenty ⓦ www.madagascar-resorts.com

Budget and camping
Ifotaka Community Bungalows ⓔ ferguson.barry@gmail.com
Camping is possible at Mandena, Andohahela and Ifotaka.

At the centre of QMM's controversial titanium mine is a floating mineral separation plant connected to a dredger. (ED)

Mandena Conservation Zone

This protected reserve was established by QMM, the partnership between Rio Tinto and the Malagasy government which runs the new mine. Mandena protects 230ha of rare littoral forest in the region that is the centre of the mining project and is now mainly community-managed. It includes 160ha of the least-degraded fragments of forest and 60ha of wetlands.

The reserve has been thoughtfully conceived to give tourists as much variety as possible. It is primarily a botanical experience, but there are six species of lemur and many birds and reptiles too. There is an easy circuit which takes three to four hours as well as a boat trip. Sited 10km from Taolagnaro, it makes a convenient full-day excursion.

Highlights further afield

Andohahela National Park

This national park opened to tourists in 1998, and much thought has gone into the blend of low-key facilities and the involvement of locals. The reserve spans rainforest, spiny forest and transition forest and thus is of major importance and interest. A visit to most areas of the park requires a 4x4 and camping gear.

The rainforest area has a trail system and campsites, plus all the rainforest requisites: waterfalls, orchids and lemurs. It is also popular with birders who come here looking for the rare red-tailed newtonia. The spiny forest zone is hot and shadeless but wonderful for wildlife, birding and botany. Even if you were to see no animals, the chance

Ste Luce Bay (LB)

to walk through untouched spiny forest gives you a glimpse of how extraordinary this land must have seemed to the first Europeans. Apart from the unique trees and plants, if you're lucky you could see sifakas, tenrecs, reptiles, and plenty of birds endemic to the south, such as the running coua and sickle-billed vanga. The scenery in the transition forest is wonderful, with flora including the locally endemic triangle palm, elephant's ear plants and pachypodiums.

Ste Luce Bay

Some 65km (three hours' drive) northeast of Taolagnaro is the beautiful and historically interesting bay where the French colonists of 1638 first landed. There is a superb beach, an ecolodge (see opposite) and a protected area of humid coastal forest here under the same ownership as Berenty.

Ifotaka Community Forest

This admirable project 110km from Taolagnaro began in 2001, following a government initiative encouraging communities to manage their own natural resources. The local Antandroy people allow woodcutting for fuel, building and cattle grazing in certain parts of the protected area, while preserving sacred and environmentally important areas for ecotourism. All the characteristic animals of the south (including Verreaux's sifakas and ring-tailed lemurs) can be seen here. It is usually very hot and dry, but the wildlife makes it worthwhile, most especially for birders. A variety of treks can also be organised in the area. There are some very basic huts for the budget traveller as well as luxury 'safari tents' for those seeking greater comfort (see Mandara River Camp opposite).

White-browed owl (DA)

Tried & Tested

Manafiafy Beach & Rainforest Lodge
Ⓦ www.manafiafy.com

Set on a sheltered, forest-fringed bay, Manafiafy is a new six-bungalow lodge offering barefoot luxury in a tranquil setting. Entirely powered by solar energy, the lodge also offers sumptuous meals cooked with fresh ingredients that include seafood barbecues on the beach. Take in the magnificent views of the sheltered bay from your private deck, or climb the observation tower to watch whales. Boat trips, snorkelling and picnicked walks into the forest to spot birds and lemurs are also on offer.

Mandrare River Camp
Ⓦ www.madaclassic.com

Mandrare has just six private en-suite tents, each enjoying breathtaking views over the Mandrare River. The remote location allows you to explore the untouched natural wonders of this part of the world and the food, accommodation and service on offer mean you get to experience it all in comfort. We particularly love the variety of activities available, which include exploring the spiny forest in search of lemurs and other wildlife endemic to this area, birding in the wetlands and learning about the local Antandroy culture.

Berenty Reserve

This is the key destination of many package tours and most visitors love it. The reserve lies some 87km to the west of Taolagnaro amid a vast sisal plantation, and the drive there is part of the experience; your guide will stop to show you interesting tombs, villages and plants along the route.

The joy of Berenty is its broad flat forest trails that allow safe wandering on your own, including nocturnal jaunts. Brown lemurs, ringtails and sifakas are all guaranteed sightings. The ringtails have an air of swaggering arrogance, are as at home on the ground as in trees, and are photogenic with their waving striped tails. Attractive though they are, they cannot compete with the Verreaux's sifakas for soft-toy cuddliness. Unlike ringtails, they rarely come down to the ground, but when they do they move with a comical and entertaining sideways 'dance'.

Birding is good too, especially at dawn. A guided dusk visit to the area of spiny forest is a must – not only for the mouse lemurs but also the surreal, magical experience of those weird giant octopus trees in silhouette. And don't miss the splendid **Museum of the Antandroy**, with its excellent ethnological displays illustrating the traditional practices of the Antandroy people.

On the downside, Berenty is very pricey by comparison with other lodges in Madagascar, given that the accommodation is rather simple (although comfortable). Note that you cannot turn up without a booking or with your own transport, and camping is not permitted, so there is no way to visit on a budget.

The catch-22 of sisal

The first export of this crop from Madagascar was 42 tonnes in 1922. By 1938, this had reached 2,537 tonnes. Some 20 years later, the sisal plantations of the de Heaulme family (owners of Berenty Reserve) covered 16,000ha and, by the mid-1990s, 30,000ha of endemic spiny forest (over 100 square miles) had been cleared to make way for the crop, with plantations under the ownership of six different companies. The de Heaulme plantation alone employs 15,000 people who cut 300,000 leaves per day.

Demand for sisal has continued to increase, with exports reaching 5,000 tonnes in 2005, putting more spiny forest at risk. Why? Because we 'green' consumers in the EU are demanding biodegradable packaging. And what is the best biodegradable substance? Sisal!

What makes Madagascar a compelling destination to explore?

Being cut off from Africa by the Indian Ocean, Madagascar's endemic and rich flora and fauna have evolved independently making it the Galápagos of Africa. Almost every one of nature's colourful creatures that you discover will be completely unique to the island. A paradise for adventure and discovery, yet still virtually undiscovered!

What is the best way to discover Madagascar's secret treasures?

Make the most of your time by discovering Madagascar with the people who know it best! At Nomad, we have local experts who are passionate, experienced and knowledgeable and will look after you from start to finish. We will ensure that your itinerary shows you the best that Madagascar has on offer. Travel with a company that is large enough to count on but small enough to care.

What would be your top tip for travelling in Madagascar?

Madagascar is perfect for special interest travel. Consider what you'd like to get out of your holiday and then speak to us about the best time of year to visit and the ultimate destination for your specific interest. We'll keep you enthralled throughout!

Nomad Africa Adventure Tours, a well-respected tour operator since 1997, runs camping and accommodated experiential and adventure tours through southern and east Africa, as well as some exotic destinations. They respect every one of their travellers and want to show them the 'ultimate African experience'. This takes passion, experience and a deep understanding of this wonderful and unique continent. We spoke to founder Alex Rutherford.

① +27 (0)21 845 7400 Ⓔ marketing@nomadtours.co.za
Ⓦ www.nomadtours.co.za

8 The North and Islands

The north of Madagascar is characterised by its variety. With the Tsaratanana Massif bringing more rain to the Nosy Be area than is normal for the west coast, and the pocket of dry climate around Antsiranana (Diego Suarez), the weather can alter dramatically within short distances. Antsiranana is situated on a peninsula in a huge natural harbour, and surrounded by numerous sandy bays including a couple now popular with kitesurfers. To the south are two of the country's finest protected areas: Montagne d'Ambre is an isolated patch of rainforest and the first national park; while Ankarana protects dry deciduous forest, *tsingy* formations and extensive caves. Both harbour an outstanding array of wildlife. Stretching down the northwest coast is a string of idyllic tropical paradise islands, many occupied by exclusive lodges. Here is the jewel in Madagascar's underwater crown, with world-class dive sites at the Mitsio and Radama islands.

Antsiranana and the bays

Forgivingly named after 16th-century Portuguese explorer Diogo Soares who arrived and proceeded to murder and rape the inhabitants or sell them into slavery, Diego Suarez – or Antsiranana in Malagasy – is a town with an eventful history. It played an important but largely forgotten role in World War II, which you can read about on page 183.

The port's isolation behind its mountain barrier and its long association with non-Malagasy races have given it an unusually cosmopolitan population and lots of colour: there are Arabs, European-descended Creoles, Indians, Chinese and Comorans.

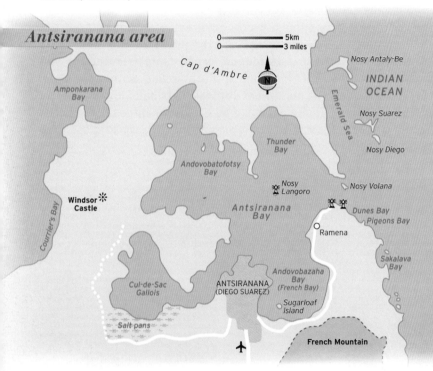

Antsiranana area

0 — 5km
0 — 3 miles

Cap d'Ambre

Nosy Antaly-Be

INDIAN OCEAN

Amponkarana Bay

Emerald Sea

Nosy Suarez

Nosy Diego

Thunder Bay

Andovobatofotsy Bay

Nosy Langoro

Nosy Volana

Windsor Castle

Antsiranana Bay

Dunes Bay

Pigeons Bay

Ramena

Courrier's Bay

Sakalava Bay

Cul-de-Sac Gallois

Andovobazaha Bay (French Bay)

ANTSIRANANA (DIEGO SUAREZ)

Sugarloaf Island

Salt pans

French Mountain

Highlights in and around Antsiranana

War cemeteries

The **British War Cemetery** on the outskirts of town is a sad insight into Anglo-Malagasy history: rows of graves of the British troops killed in the battle for Diego Suarez in 1942, and the larger numbers who died from disease during the occupation of the port. Impeccably maintained by the Commonwealth War Graves Commission, this is a peaceful and moving place. The **French War Cemetery** is also nearby.

Practicalities

The road connection between Tana and Antsiranana is now reasonably good, but it is a journey of around 1,200km with relatively few tourist sites *en route*, so those with limited time may prefer to fly. There are flights to and from Tana most days as well as weekly connections with some other northern towns.

The town has several banks with ATMs, a post office, and a couple of internet cafés. The well-organised regional tourist office is located at the intersection of Rue Colbert and Rue Flacourt (Ⓦ www.office-tourisme-diego-suarez.com Ⓒ Monday–Friday 08.00–12.00 & 15.00–18.00, Saturday 08.00–12.00) and they also run an information kiosk in Place Foch.

Accommodation in Antsiranana

Upmarket
Allamanda Ⓦ www.allamanda-hotel.com
Colbert Ⓦ www.hlcdiego.com
Grand Hotel Ⓦ www.grand-hotel-diego.com

Moderate
Hotel Firdoss Ⓦ www.hotelfirdoss.com
Paradis du Nord Ⓦ www.leparadisdunord-diego.com

Budget
Orchidée Ⓣ 82 210 65

Accommodation east of Antsiranana

Upmarket
Babaomby Island Lodge (Emerald Sea) Ⓦ www.babaomby.com
King's Lodge & Panorama (Andovobazaha Bay) Ⓦ www.kingdelapiste.de
La Note Bleue Park (Andovobazaha Bay) Ⓦ www.diego-hotel.com
Meva Plage (Andovobazaha Bay) Ⓦ www.mevaplagehotel.com
Royal Sakalava (Sakalava Bay) Ⓦ www.royalsakalava.com
Sakalava Lodge (Sakalava Bay) Ⓦ www.sakalava.com

Moderate
Jungle Park (Andovobazaha Bay) Ⓦ www.jungle-park-nature.com
Le 5 Trop Près (Ramena) Ⓦ www.normada.com/5trop
Casa en Falafy (Ramena) Ⓦ www.case-en-falafy.com

Andovobazaha Bay and French Mountain

Just to the east of town is Andovobazaha Bay with the prominent **Sugarloaf Island** standing at its centre, overlooked by half a dozen hotels perched around the sweeping shoreline. Behind the bay is French Mountain, which gets its name from the memorial to the French and Malagasy killed during the Allied invasion in 1942. Now officially a protected area, there is a trail which takes you up past several baobabs (two different species) to a cave with excellent views across the bay. Go early in the morning for the best birdwatching (and to avoid the heat of the day). If you are lucky you may also spot Sandford's brown lemurs, snakes and chameleons.

Ramena peninsula

At the opposite end of Andovobazaha Bay from Antsiranana, the beach resort of **Ramena** provides a pleasant alternative to staying in town. It is about 18km from the centre and 45 minutes' drive from the airport. There is a relaxed atmosphere in this friendly fishing village, but daily life centres around the boat-strewn beach so it is not always peaceful.

You can find tranquillity at the bays further round the headland. These are walkable from Ramena, but take your passport as you have to cross a military zone for which a permit must be obtained at the gatehouse. Follow the surfaced road from Ramena past the barracks then along

Ramena lighthouse (FD)

The Battle of Diego Suarez

Madagascar's geographical location gave it immense strategic importance at the time of World War II. Since 1885, the French had had a great naval base here, and it was evident that whoever held Diego Suarez (as Antsiranana was then known) controlled the western Indian Ocean. As the authorities were Vichy French, Britain recognised the need to occupy the island before it was handed over to her enemies. So, in the spring of 1942, Britain mounted Operation Ironclad, its first ever large-scale combined land, sea and air operation, to capture Diego Suarez as the initial step in occupying the whole island.

British ships after the assault on Diego Suarez (IWM)

A force of some 13,000 troops with tanks and artillery, supported by 46 warships and transport vessels and 101 aircraft of the Fleet Air Arm, assembled before dawn on 5 May 1942. Wary of the heavily defended narrow harbour entrance, the British decided to land on the west coast and march to Diego Suarez from the landward side. An intense battle for possession of the town began. The breakthrough came the following evening when a British destroyer charged through the harbour entrance under the guns of the French batteries and landed a body of 50 Marines onto the quay. This tiny force stormed through the town, successfully capturing the main barracks and the artillery headquarters. Overall, the fighting resulted in more than 1,000 casualties.

Britain's vital maritime route to the east had been secured – but only in the nick of time. Barely three weeks after the capture, a Japanese submarine flotilla arrived and launched a daring night raid that sank a British ship. But with the island's main naval base in British hands, it was expected that the French Governor General would bow to the inevitable and relinquish control of the whole island. However, he held out for exactly six months and one day before surrendering. The significance of this was that French troops involved in a campaign lasting longer than six months were entitled to a medal and an increased pension! After a brief period of British military administration, the island was handed over to General de Gaulle's Free French movement.

Which of your tours would you recommend for a first-time visitor to Madagascar?

RAMARTOUR Madagascar recommends a tour geared to discovering the diversity of Madagascar's nature while also experiencing Malagasy life and culture. We specialise in tailor-made tours, and our flexible team will build a suitable customised itinerary for anyone wishing to travel in Madagascar; our slogan is – Let us guide you!

What would you recommend for those seeking adventure and exploration?

Travelling anywhere in Madagascar is already adventurous – a world apart from our visitors' normal lives. But for those wanting a little more excitement, the Manambolo and Tsiribihina river trips allow visitors to get in deep into Madagascar's beautiful biodiversity. There are also hikes in remote settings such as the rainforest of Masoala National Park or the Andringitra mountains. Contact us for more suggestions.

What kind of involvement do your tours have with local Malagasy communities?

RAMARTOUR Madagascar is a local tour operator known for its flexibility and dynamism, which comes from its leader Jonah Ramampionona, previously a tour guide working around the entire island. His spirit of creating a job for everyone and his active co-operation with development NGOs are proof that RAMARTOUR Madagascar is truly involved in community-level development.

RAMARTOUR Madagascar is a family-run business with an emphasis on value for money and the human touch. The company, led by Jonah Ramampionona (Malagasy) and Wendy van Tilburg (Dutch), is a young and dynamic team offering an intimate customer experience and ready to make your trip unforgettable. We spoke to Jonah Ramampionona.

Ⓣ +261 (0)32 02 133 68/+261 (0)33 14 978 81
Ⓔ info@ramartour.com Ⓦ www.ramartour.com

an open stretch to the hillside. The track passes some ruined buildings and there is a signpost to the lighthouse. Continue along the track and the view opens up seaward as you approach **Dunes Bay**. The bay itself is overlooked by an old gun emplacement, in front of which there is a small island accessible from the beach. The whole area is excellent for wildlife, especially the pools, and you can continue your walk around the coast to **Pigeons Bay**.

A few kilometres further south is **Sakalava Bay**, accessible by road from Ramena (14km). On the 5km-long beach are two smart lodges (see page 181) with a windsurfing and kitesurfing school.

Emerald Sea

To the north, on the opposite side of the harbour mouth, is a lagoon known as the **Emerald Sea**. These turquoise waters and beautiful beach are reachable only by boat from Ramena or Antsiranana. The shallow water is perfect for swimming and snorkelling – and windsurfing and kitesurfing are also available. It is close enough for a day trip or you could stay in the 'safari tents' of the lodge there (see page 181).

Windsor Castle and beyond

A few hours' drive due west from Antsiranana, past extensive salt pans, the 390m-high monolith of **Windsor Castle** is steep-sided and flat-topped, so made a perfect lookout point during times of war; the views from there are superb. It was fortified by the French, occupied by the Vichy forces, and liberated by the British. A ruined staircase still runs to the top but it is a hot, shadeless climb so take plenty of water and sun protection.

Beyond Windsor Castle is an area of rugged beauty and the fine beach of **Courrier's Bay**, where the invading fleet of Operation Ironclad landed in 1942. Here is the starting

A *Pachypodium* stands near Windsor Castle with Courrier's Bay behind. (DA)

point for a number of hiking, fishing, climbing and diving activities, as well as visits to **Nosy Hara** – a protected group of small islets where the rare Madagascar fish eagle is easily seen.

South of Antsiranana

It takes less than an hour to reach Montagne d'Ambre from Antsiranana, so it can be done as a day trip, although a longer stay in the area is highly recommended. Ankarana is also just reachable as a day trip, but as the journey takes 2½ hours each way that does not leave a lot of time for exploring unless you are prepared to make a very early start. On the way to Ankarana, the Red Tsingy and a sacred crocodile lake make interesting stop-offs for those not in a hurry.

Highlights south of Antsiranana

Fontenay Nature Park

Ⓦ www.lefontenay-madagascar.com

At Joffreville, some 4km from Montagne d'Ambre National Park, this 300ha forested reserve is open to all but is free of charge only to guests of the hotel Domaine de Fontenay (see page 189). The well-maintained trail system takes you past bubbling streams and waterfalls to spectacular views over the distant bays of Antsiranana. Sanford's brown lemurs are often sighted, and sometimes also crowned lemurs too if the lychee and mango trees are in fruit (December–February). The park is good for reptiles, and birders will find that some of the Montagne d'Ambre bird species are easier to sight here because of the more open canopy. On guided night walks (possible during the summer months from September to April), one can often find mouse lemurs, greater dwarf lemurs, and leaf-tailed geckoes.

Practicalities

Joffreville (the base for visiting Montagne d'Ambre National Park) is 23km from Antsiranana, and Mahamasina (the main entry point for Ankarana National Park) is 108km. They are both villages with little in the way of infrastructure except for their hotels. There are no banks in the 240km section between Ankarafantsika and Ambanja.

The two further gateways to Ankarana are on the west side of the park and accessible only by 4x4 (one of them cannot be reached at all during the rainy season). The extra time and effort of reaching this side is rewarded with the most spectacular caves and *tsingy* formations.

Accommodation near Montagne d'Ambre

For full details of tour operator-recommended accommodation, see page 189.

Moderate
Auberge Sakay Tany ⊤ 032 04 281 22

Budget and camping
The national park has a campsite and a simple hut with bunk beds.

Accommodation near Ankarana

For full details of tour operator-recommended accommodation, see page 193.

Upmarket
Ankarana Lodge ⓦ www.ankarana-lodge.com

Budget
Goulam Lodge Ⓔ goulamguide_ds@yahoo.fr

Montagne d'Ambre National Park

This 18,500ha national park was created in 1958, the French colonial government recognising the unique nature of the volcanic massif and its splendid montane rainforest. The massif ranges in altitude from 850m to 1,475m and has its own microclimate with rainfall similar to the eastern region. It is one of the most visitor-friendly of Madagascar's protected areas, with broad trails, fascinating flora and fauna, a comfortable climate and excellent guides. In the dry season vehicles can drive right into the main picnic area, making it suitable even for travellers with restricted walking ability. The park has over 30km of paths, many of which are quite flat and easy. Three waterfalls provide the focal points for day visitors.

Bird's nest ferns are a prominent rainforest feature. (DA)

The park is as exciting for its plants as for its animals. All visitors are impressed by the tree ferns and the huge, epiphytic bird's nest ferns which grow on trees. The distinctive screw pines are also common and you can see the Madagascar cycad. Huge strangler figs add to the spectacle.

Most visitors want to see lemurs, and two diurnal species have become habituated: Sanford's brown lemurs and crowned lemurs. Another mammal often seen is the ring-tailed mongoose, and if you are really lucky you could see a fossa or its relative the falanouc. At eye level you may spot some large chameleons, and a good guide should be able to find some of the minuscule *Brookesia* chameleons too. Plus there are many frogs, pill millipedes, butterflies and other invertebrates. Even non-birders will be fascinated by the numerous species here: the Madagascar crested ibis is striking enough to impress anybody, as is the Madagascar paradise flycatcher with its long, trailing tail feathers. The locally endemic Amber Mountain rock thrush is tame and ubiquitous, but the jackpot is one of Madagascar's most beautiful birds: the pitta-like ground-roller.

Domaine de Fontenay
Ⓦ www.lefontenay-madagascar.com

Built in 1902, this old country residence provides the perfect base for visiting Montagne d'Ambre National Park as well as the hotel's own 300-hectare private reserve, Fontenay Nature Park. The eight spacious rooms and one suite are all decorated in colonial style and each contains a large bath in which to unwind after a day's trekking. The hotel also has expert guides who can take you to the Red Tsingy, Antsiranana (Diego Suarez) and its three bays, and then all around Montagne d'Ambre National Park.

The Litchi Tree
Ⓦ www.thelitchitree.com

Formerly the home of Colonel Joffre, the building has been lovingly renovated into a small boutique hotel close to the national park entrance. The hallway has been converted into the restaurant which serves continental and Malagasy dishes. There are five spacious rooms, each with an en-suite bathroom (with shower). Nothing is too much trouble for the owner, Hervé, who goes all out to ensure guests have a wonderful time. The tasteful decor and relaxed ambience make this the preferred choice for visitors to Montagne d'Ambre.

Nature Lodge
Ⓦ www.naturelodge-ambre.com

Situated just south of the charming village of Joffreville, Nature Lodge provides an ideal base from which to explore the surrounding Montagne d'Ambre National Park. The 12 simple yet spacious thatched chalets have private decks overlooking the bay and the mountains. In the communal areas, an attractively designed bar and restaurant offers warm, friendly service and delicious meals cooked with a good selection of fresh ingredients and seafood. The guided birdwatching is excellent – as are the evening cocktails that round off the day.

189

Red Tsingy

About an hour south of Antsiranana are these spectacular geological features. Like the true *tsingy* of Ankarana and Bemaraha, the Red Tsingy are erosion phenomena, but are formed from laterite rather than limestone, giving them a striking orange-red hue and a rather more rounded Dali-esque appearance then their duller spiky cousins. Some 46km along the main road, you take a 17km track which is only passable by 4x4 (and not accessible at all for much of the wet season, December–March).

(FD)

The legends of Lake Antanavo

Some 75km south of Antsiranana is a sacred lake that, like the Red Tsingy, is down a track (4km) that is impassable in the rainy season. The lake itself is not particularly scenic, but its crocodilian inhabitants and the tales surrounding them are what draw visitors. On certain days the crocs are fed, greatly increasing your chance of seeing one.

The story is that once upon a time the village of Anivorano was situated amid semi-desert and a thirsty traveller arrived asking for a drink. When his request was refused he warned the villagers that they would soon have more water than they could cope with. No sooner had he left than the earth opened, water gushed out, and the mean locals and their houses were inundated. The crocodiles which now inhabit the lake are considered to be ancestors of the drowned villagers, supposedly wearing jewellery belonging to their previous selves. The biggest and most important one wore a bracelet.

Some say that around 20 years ago a big croc came up into the rice fields and was killed by a mob of young locals. But when they saw that it was the revered bracelet-wearing one, the worried villagers gave him a proper burial in the cemetery. Then one by one all those who had been involved in the killing mysteriously died.

Ankarana National Park

An area of *tsingy* (limestone karst pinnacles) and forest, the Ankarana Massif – a plateau measuring some 5km by 20km – is penetrated by numerous caves and canyons. Some of the largest caves have collapsed, forming isolated pockets of river-fed forest with their own perfectly protected flora and fauna. Dry deciduous forest grows around the periphery and into the wider canyons. Many other caves are home to large colonies of bats. Dramatic geological features are not the sole attraction; Sanford's brown

lemurs and crowned lemurs are here, as are several nocturnal lemur species, myriad reptiles and frogs, and birds including the white-breasted mesite, hook-billed vanga and crested coua.

There are three gateways to the national park, all quite distant from one another. The choice depends on the season, what you are most interested in seeing, how much time you have, whether you have a 4x4 at your disposal and the level of accommodation required. Discuss the options with your tour operator to be sure you will get the best out of your visit.

Crested coua (FD)

(DA)

Tried & Tested

Iharana Bush Camp
Ⓦ www.tinyurl.com/iharana

About 16km from the town of Ambilobe, Iharana Bush Camp has eight bungalows with en-suite showers. Their design reflects a unique crossover between traditional Malagasy and African styles. Bathrooms and bedrooms are on separate levels (with no banister on the stairs so take a torch). From the terraces, sunsets are marvellous and views of the fortress-like Ankarana West are truly stunning. The kitchen and restaurant create the atmosphere of a bush camp with excellent food that is mostly locally sourced.

Relais de l'Ankarana
Ⓦ www.relais-ankarana.e-monsite.com

Located just outside Ankarana National Park, this simple hotel overlooks vast savannahs and the small restaurant offers tasty food to go with the great panoramic views. The Ankarana reserve is home to ten species of lemurs and 92 species of birds, as well as chameleons, baobabs and pachypodiums. The English and French speaking guides know the park and its community intimately. They are the perfect people to introduce you to the stunning set of underground rivers, canyons, rainforests, caves and of course the *tsingy*.

In Conversation with...

How does your experience as a company help you provide a special service?

We have the most experienced Madagascar team of any UK-based operator. I have been visiting the country since 1992, and co-wrote and contributed to various Madagascar books. My colleague Rachel Dobb lived there for nine months, travelling extensively. Both of us are also involved with various NGOs and inspiring initiatives, including Association Mitsinjo at Andasibe, Missouri Botanical Gardens, Durrell Wildlife Conservation Trust and BirdLife International. Rainbow Tours

has also long supported Madagascar Development Fund projects. Our ground handler is one of the most highly rated in the country (and the only inbound operator to be run by a Malagasy woman and without a European partner). Continual excellent feedback about their guides and drivers from our clients says it all. With our deep involvement in Madagascar we are able to impart knowledge to clients in order to help them to delve beneath the surface of this extraordinarily complex country, giving them more value for their time and money.

Are any of your tours particularly good for wildlife spotting? What might you see?

All of our Madagascar tours – whether for individuals or small groups – allow visitors the opportunity to see some of the island's beguiling and compellingly unique wildlife. First-time visitors should try to get to at least one site in each of the three chief floristic zones: rainforest (eg: Andasibe-Mantadia), sub-arid south (eg: Isalo or Berenty) and seasonally dry deciduous forest. Each of these ecotypes has its own locally endemic assemblage of plants and animals, so all are totally different. Our 'Lemurs of Madagascar' sample itinerary for individual travellers, which can be done almost year-round, follows this principle. A bonus at Andasibe-Mantadia and Berenty is that you can take night walks.

Rainbow Tours

RAINBOW TOURS

What do you believe makes Madagascar special?

Madagascar is in a class of its own – it has elements of Asia and Africa, yet is neither. Whenever I visit, I am always reminded of Hilary Bradt's description of the 'basic gentleness' of the Malagasy people. I love learning about the endlessly layered and intricate culture of what is one of the last large, habitable landmasses to have been settled by people. And of course there is

the fantastically varied scenery, including all sorts of weird and wonderful geological formations, achingly beautiful rainforests, bizarre plants in the drier areas, and – to top it all – the wildlife. Many Malagasy animals belong to groups which have long since died out on the continents, and visitors have the opportunity to see up close some of the world's rarest wildlife, such as critically endangered silky sifakas in Marojejy or equally rare Madagascar fish eagles at Anjajavy or Ankarafantsika. And then there are the bizarre: the aye-aye, leaf-tailed geckos, sunbird-asities, giraffe-necked weevils and hissing cockroaches. It is one of the last places where a substantial number of animals new to science are being described all the time.

Could you share your top Madagascar travel tips with us?

As with many under-developed tropical countries, it is essential to visit with an open mind. Lower your expectations, and you lower the risk of disappointment; things in Madagascar are generally quite 'low key'. Know that you are visiting a destination where the infrastructure is modest, and where often a degree of flexibility and humour is required when things don't

work strictly to plan. Be prepared for the lowlights, which include extreme poverty and some severe environmental degradation. Study your guidebook and tour operator's travel guidelines well before you go. And expect the unexpected: while you might not find some of the species you set out to see, you will encounter a delightful array of surprises wherever you venture.

Rainbow's expertise has earned them four *Best Tour Operator of the Year* awards in the last nine years. With honesty, enthusiasm and in-depth first-hand experience, they work closely with Malagasy ground operators and support inspiring local initiatives. We spoke to Derek Schuurman.

① +44 (0)20 7666 1252 ⓔ info@rainbowtours.co.uk
ⓦ www.rainbowtours.co.uk

Islands of the northwest

Dozens of islands are dotted along the northwestern coastline, a region blessed with an almost perfect climate for much of the year. By far the largest of these is Nosy Be (the name means 'big island'), where tourism developed decades before it did on the mainland. Consequently the area is now much more expensive than the rest of Madagascar and hotels are much more plentiful too.

But it can be worth it: not only are there many wonderful beaches, but there are opportunities throughout the region for swimming, snorkelling, scuba diving, kayaking, fishing, sailing, windsurfing, kitesurfing and several other watersports. In the right season you may see whales, dolphins, turtles, manta rays and whale sharks. Some of the islands have protected forests with walking trails, where wildlife such as lemurs and chameleons may be seen. A handful of the most exclusive lodges have a whole island to themselves, affording you true desert-island tranquillity.

Highlights around Nosy Be

Nosy Be and nearby islands

True to its name, **Nosy Be** is not a small island; it takes about two hours to drive a full circuit of the main 'ring road'. Broadly speaking, the island is quite developed and busy in the southern part, becoming progressively more calm and remote towards the north. Most of the hotels are along the western beachfront, and the airport is on the eastern side of the island.

On the far southeastern peninsula is the nature reserve of **Lokobe**. It is not open to the public but there is a buffer zone where forest walks are allowed. Sportive lemurs, black lemurs, ground boas and chameleons are all often seen on guided walks. You can also make an excursion to the interior of the island to visit its highest point. **Mont Passot** is 326m high and has a series of deep-blue crater lakes.

Many tourists opt to stay on one of the two satellite islands that has accommodation. **Nosy Komba** is a popular choice. *Komba* means 'lemur' and it is the black lemurs here that bring in the visitors. Over the years the villagers have gradually learned how to make a dollar or two from these day trippers and now a huge array of locally produced handicrafts is on sale here. Some of the lemurs are fully habituated to jumping on tourists' shoulders to pose for a photo in return for a mouthful of banana. The best and most peaceful beaches are at the southern end of Nosy Komba. The other choice is **Nosy Sakatia**, a 4km-long island, just 750m off the west coast of Nosy Be. Much of the island is denuded but there is a sacred hill which doubles as a nature reserve. This is a favourite place to stay for those keen on deep sea fishing and scuba diving; and a spearfishing and freediving centre has recently opened there (Ⓦ www.orcasakatia.co.za).

Islands of the northwest

0 ———— 20km
0 ———— 20 miles

Nosy Lava
Nosy Ankarea
The Mitsio Islands
Grande Mitsio
Les Quatre Frères
2 Nosy Tsarabanjina

Mozambique

Channel

Nosy Be
Befotaka Bay
Mahazandry Bay
Fasène Airport
Nosy Sakatia **5**
Nosy Faly

Ambaro Bay

HELL-VILLE (Andoany)
Nosy Ankazoberavina **1**
Russian Bay
Nosy Tanikely
6 Nosy Komba

Kakambana Bay
Nosy Iranja **4**
3
Ampasindava Bay

The Radama Islands
Nosy Kalakajoro
Rafaralahy Bay
Nosy Berafia (Nosy Ovy)
Nosy Antanimora
Sahamalaza Bay
Nosy Valiha
Ramanetaka Bay
Radama Peninsula

Nosy Saba

Tried & Tested

1 Ankazoberavina Ecolodge (page 202)

2 Constance Lodge Tsarabanjina (page 202)

3 Eden Lodge (page 202)

4 Iranja Lodge (page 203)

5 Sakatia Lodge (page 203)

6 Tsara Komba Lodge (page 203)

Practicalities

There are two routes to the islands of the northwest: you can cross by boat from Ankify on the mainland, or you can fly into the airport on the main island of Nosy Be. If you are staying at one of the small island resorts then you will transfer from Nosy Be (or Ankify) by boat. If you are staying on Nosy Be itself, then in most cases you can transfer to your accommodation by road. The airport is well connected with daily flights from Tana, plus some domestic connections to other towns and even a few direct international flights from Paris and Milan.

Travellers interested in exploring the whole area, including the Radama and Mitsio archipelagos, should consider a yacht charter, which may be combined with fishing or diving excursions (see ⓦ www.madagascat.co.za).

The only banks are in Hell-Ville on Nosy Be, where you will also find cybercafés, airline offices and a couple of supermarkets. There is a very helpful tourist office there too (ⓦ www.nosybe-tourisme.mg ⊕ Monday-Friday 08.00-12.00 & 15.00-18.00, weekend 08.00-12.00).

Accommodation

For details of tour operator-recommended accommodation, see pages 202-3.

Upmarket
Amarina (Nosy Be) ⓦ www.amarinahotel.com
Ankify Lodge (Ankify) ⓦ www.ledauphinbleu.eu
Baobab (Ankify) ⓔ baobabankify@yahoo.fr
Heure Bleue (Nosy Be) ⓦ www.heurebleue.com
Jardin Vanille (Nosy Komba) ⓦ www.jardinvanille.com
Loharano Hotel (Nosy Be) ⓦ www.loharanohotel.com
Mahafaly Lodge (Nosy Komba) ⓔ guyramanantsoa@moov.mg
Orangea Village (Nosy Be) ⓦ www.orangea-nosybe.com
Sakatia Towers (Nosy Sakatia) ⓦ www.sakatiatowers.com
Vanila (Nosy Be) ⓦ www.vanila-hotel.com

Moderate
Chez Eugénie (Nosy Be) ⓦ www.chez-eugenie.com
Chez Yolande (Nosy Komba) ⓦ www.hotel-nosykomba.com

Budget
Rahim's (Nosy Be) ⓣ 86 927 54

The tiny island of **Nosy Tanikely** (this is another no-nonsense name: *tanikely* means literally 'small land') is the centre of a marine reserve which offers the best snorkelling within the immediate vicinity of Nosy Be. It is popular and can get overcrowded, but it is a beautiful little island with an amazing variety of marine life: coral, starfish, anemones, turtles, lobsters and every colour and shape of fish. On shore there is a trail up to a century-old lighthouse, with lemurs, bats and white-tailed tropic-birds to be seen on the way.

Turtles are often seen around Nosy Tanikely. (RD)

Islands southwest of Nosy Be

Nosy Ankazoberavina (meaning 'island with big-leaved trees') is a 14ha paradise situated 26km from Nosy Be. The forest here is home to flying foxes, chameleons and a few lemurs, and there are mangroves and a beautiful palm-lined beach on the northern side. The area is a marine reserve and turtles come to the island to lay their eggs.

Some 25km further southwest, **Nosy Iranja** is actually a pair of small islands connected by a sandbar (walkable at low tide), one of which is an important breeding reserve for both hawksbill and green turtles. The northern island is home to a charming old lighthouse designed by Gustave Eiffel.

Both of these islands are potentially reachable from Nosy Be as a day trip (it takes about 1½ hours to get to Nosy Iranja) and both of them have an ecolodge so you could stay a few nights. See the tour operator reviews on pages 202–3 for full details.

Often seen on dives, lionfish are well known for their ornate beauty and venomous spines. (JWA)

Radama Islands highlights

The Radama Islands, which lie 90km to the southwest of Nosy Be (and thus are only really accessible by yacht) harbour some of the best diving sites in Madagascar. They are set in a breathtaking coastline of bays backed by high mountains. Most of these high sandstone islands are steep-sided above and below the water and covered with scrub, grass and trees. Sharp eroded rock formations, however, render the remaining forest rather difficult to explore.

Nosy Kalakajoro features dense, impenetrable forest on the south side. There are good beaches and snorkelling is worthwhile. **Nosy Berafia** (or Nosy Ovy, 'potato island') is the largest of the Radamas, but the environmental degradation is terrible. Nearly all the trees have been cut and goats have completed the destruction of its flora. **Nosy Antanimora**, with its broad sandy beaches and turquoise water, lives up to its name which translates loosely as 'land of relaxation'. The fourth member of the group, **Nosy Valiha**, is privately owned.

Respect for nature

Madagascar's coastal environments comprise some of the most ecologically sensitive areas of the country. Be aware of the effect your presence and activities have on local habitats and ensure you dispose of litter appropriately. Swimmers, snorkellers and divers should avoid all physical contact with corals and other marine life. Divers must also take care to avoid damaging reefs by maintaining good buoyancy control to avoid accidental contact or stirring up sediment. You should also refrain from collecting (or buying) shells.

Mitsio Islands highlights

A number of yacht charters offer multi-day excursions to the Mitsio archipelago some 50km northeast of Nosy Be. This is the Maldives of Madagascar, with world-class diving, perfect beaches and an exclusive island resort. Manta rays can often be seen in this area.

Nosy Tsarabanjina (meaning 'good-looking') is a small but incredibly beautiful island with a luxury lodge (see page 202). The red, grey and black volcanic rocks, rising quite high at its centre, have a mass of lush, green vegetation clinging to them, including baobabs and pachypodiums. But its real glory is the pure white beaches of coarse sand, along which laps crystal-clear ocean. Turtles and rays rest near the beaches.

Four imposing lumps of silver basalt rising 51–88m from the sea are known as **Les Quatre Frères** ('the four brothers'). Two of them are home to hundreds of nesting seabirds, including brown boobies, frigate birds and white-tailed tropic-birds; and a pair of Madagascar fish eagles nests on one. The sides drop vertically to about 20–30m, and they are popular dive sites.

The largest island, **Grande Mitsio**, is populated by local Malagasy who survive on their denuded island through farming, cattle and goats. Huge basalt columns are prominent features on the northern and western extremities. There is a good beach at **Nosy Lava**, an elongated reef covered in vegetation. It is the northernmost island in the archipelago and home to another pair of fish eagles.

Volcanic formations on Grande Mitsio (DA)

Constance Lodge Tsarabanjina
Ⓦ http://tsarabanjina.constancehotels.com

Located in the Mitsio Archipelago, Tsarabanjina is fringed by white sandy beaches with extraordinary birds, lush vegetation and encircled with stunning, wildlife-rich coral reefs. The 25 unique thatched rosewood bungalows are located on both of the island's gorgeous main beaches, North and South, each with a private terrace facing the ocean. You can choose to snorkel directly from the beach, enjoy some of the best diving in Madagascar or simply make use of the complimentary windsurfers, canoes and catamarans.

Ecolodge Ankazoberavina
Ⓦ www.ankazoberavina.it

On its own forested and reef-ringed island, this ecolodge has eight spacious wooden bungalows. Each has a large bedroom, en-suite bathroom with hot water, electricity and private veranda. There is space on the mezzanine for two extra twin beds for families with young children. The village has a generator but guests are asked to use flashlights at night since turtles regularly come ashore to lay eggs. (Each bungalow is just 20m from the sea, on the edge of dense woodland.) The restaurant deck also overlooks the sea.

Eden Lodge
Ⓦ www.edenlodge.net/en

One of our favourites; combining luxury with the natural surroundings of Madagascar, this is the only entirely solar-powered hotel in the world! Half an hour from Nosy Be, and only accessible by boat, these eight lavishly appointed beachside apartments all open on to private terraces. The wildlife here comes to the guests; lemurs and parrots frequently lounge in the trees planted around the lodge, steps away from the comfort of your bungalow. Days here are spent on white, crystalline sand and nights scanning the forest for lemurs.

Iranja Lodge
Ⓦ www.iranjalodge.co.za

If this incredible pair of islands, linked by a sandbar at low tide, was in the Seychelles you'd have to be a lottery winner to stay here. However Iranja Lodge, set within its own 13 hectares of land, is much more accessible. Some of the 29 rooms have private terraces and are particularly suited to romantic breaks, while others sleep up to six to cater for families. There are plenty of watersports to keep anyone who wants activities busy, and turtles, dolphins and whales can all been seen nearby at the right time of the year.

Sakatia Lodge
Ⓦ wwww.sakatia.co.za

RAINBOW TOURS

One of the most sought-after accommodations in the Nosy Be archipelago, Sakatia Lodge is situated at the edge of a sacred hill and nature reserve on the island of Nosy Sakatia. The lodge has eight en-suite ocean-view bungalows and a larger family villa. General manager Jacques Vieira always ensures his visitors have a memorable stay. The food is excellent, and Sakatia Lodge has a well-equipped dive centre making it one of the very best locations for those wanting to explore the underwater world off northwest Madagascar.

Tsara Komba Lodge
Ⓦ www.tsarakomba.com/uk

Tsara Komba is a beautiful lodge set above an idyllic beach. There are eight thatched bungalows dotted around tropical gardens on the hillside. The sea views from the large verandas are stunning and best enjoyed with a glass of Tsara Komba's famous coconut rum punch. Food in the restaurant is excellent with fresh fish caught by local fisherman who land their pirogues on the beach. The lodge has close ties with the local community and has funded clean water supplies, healthcare and school equipment for nearby villages.

9 The Remote West

Vast areas of Madagascar's western region are impenetrable by all but the most tenacious explorers. But two western coastal towns – Morondava and Mahajanga – *are* accessible by road and plane, and act as gateways to a number of exciting destinations. The west offers a mostly dry climate, deciduous forest (with some excellent reserves to protect it), and endless sandy beaches with shallow lagoons. This is the region in which to see the best examples of baobabs, and in particular the famous Baobab Avenue. It is also the principal place to find one of Madagascar's extraordinary natural wonders: *tsingy* limestone pinnacles. Adventure-seekers will be tempted by the river trips that involve a few days canoeing or boating through some of the country's remotest areas *en route* to the west coast. In the northwest, miles from anywhere, is a trio of luxurious fly-in resorts, perfect for spending a few days unwinding after a packed itinerary exploring the rest of the country.

Mahajanga and the northwest

The northwest

Grottes
d'Anjohibe

Betsiboka Estuary

MAHAJANGA
(Majunga)

Katsepy

Mahajamba

Ambohitrombikely
Fort

RN4

Marovoay

Ankarafantsika
National Park

RN6

Ambondromamy

0 ━━━━ 50km
0 ━━━━ 25 miles

The two western regions of Mahajanga (Majunga) and Morondava are not connected by direct roads, so you cannot travel between the two without returning to Tana. This section deals with what you can see and do around Mahajanga; for the Morondava area turn to page 214. The province's easily accessible hotspots such as Ankarafantsika National Park and the fly-in resorts contrast with the barely accessible region to the southwest.

Highlights in and around Mahajanga

Mahajanga is a hot but breezy town with a large Indian population. A wide boulevard follows the sea along the western part of town, terminating near a lighthouse. Halfway along is the fattest tree in the country: the **Mahajanga baobab**. It is thought to have been planted by Arab traders around 700 years ago as it is an African baobab, a species not found naturally in Madagascar. A university-run museum, **Mozea Akiba** (☉ Tuesday–Friday 09.00–11.00 & 15.00–17.00, weekend 15.00–17.00), has displays showing the history of the region, as well as an exhibition of palaeontology and ethnology.

To the north of Mahajanga is a small sacred lake on a site once owned by Madagascar's first president, Philibert Tsiranana. Aside from the lake, which is home to crocodiles, **Mangatsa** has a restaurant, mangroves, baobabs, mango and coconut plantations, and you may see sifakas. The 16km drive there takes about half an hour. Another half an hour further in this direction is the seafront resort hotel of **Antsanitia** (see page 207). The famous **Anjohibe caves** are 82km (four hours' drive) northeast of Mahajanga and accessible only in the dry season by 4x4. There are two places to visit: the caves themselves and a natural swimming pool atop a waterfall. The caves are full of stalactites and stalagmites (and bats), and have several kilometres of passages, which are thought to have once been used as a place of sacrifice. There are six less well known **caves at Belobaka**, about 20 minutes south from Mahajanga.

Practicalities

Mahajanga is 560km from Tana on a good road, which takes around nine hours. Daily flights connect the same two places, and there are weekly flights between Mahajanga and some other towns.

It is a large port town with many hotels, banks, cybercafés and a supermarket. At the time of writing the regional tourist office, ORTM, has a temporary office at the airport but no premises in the town (Ⓦ www.majunga.org).

Accommodation in Mahajanga

Upmarket
Badamier Ⓦ www.hotelmajunga-lebadamier.com
Coco Lodge Ⓦ www.coco-lodge.com
Sunny Motel Ⓦ www.sunnymada.com
Tropicana Ⓦ www.hotel-majunga.com

Moderate
New Continental Ⓣ 62 225 70
Ravinala Ⓔ ravinalahotel@moov.mg

Budget
Kanto Ⓣ 62 229 78

Accommodation further afield

For full details of tour operator-recommended accommodation, see page 211.

Upmarket
Antsanatia (an hour north of Mahajanga) Ⓦ www.antsanitia.com
Lodge des Terres Blanches Ⓦ www.lodgeterresblanches.com
Maison de Marovasa-Be Ⓦ www.marovasabe.com

Moderate
Gîte d'Ampijoroa (Ankarafantsika)
Ⓔ ankarafantsika@gmail.com

Camping
Camping is possible at the entrance to Ankarafantsika National Park.

Green pigeons (FV)

The first is a sacred place where people come to make wishes, but the other five are more spectacular for stalactites and stalagmites. It is said a fence and gate were once erected to manage the tourism, but the resident spirits objected to this arrangement and sent lightning which struck and destroyed the barrier. Some 20km southeast of town is the impressive **Fort Ambohitrombikely** with excellent views. It was built on the highest point in the region in 1824 by King Radama I.

Ankarafantsika National Park

This is a super national park; it's easy to get to, thrilling to visit with abundant wildlife, and has clear, level or stepped paths which make hiking a pleasure. With accommodation available nearby, this is a must for naturalists. The park straddles RN4 about 120km (two hours' drive) from Mahajanga. The most-visited part is on the southwestern side of the road, with Lake Ravelobe to the north – but the reserve covers over 130,000ha stretching far beyond the area usually visited by tourists.

Ankarafantsika protects typical dry, deciduous forest with sparse understorey and lots of lianas. There are 130 bird species (with highlights like the Van Dam's vanga, Madagascar fish eagle and white-breasted mesite), eight easily seen lemur species and reptiles galore. Wildlife-viewing in Ankarafantsika starts as soon as you arrive. Right beside the parking area is a tree that Coquerel's sifakas use as a dormitory. On your walks you may also see mongoose lemurs, western woolly lemurs and sportive lemurs; and this is the only place where you might see the golden-brown mouse lemur. If you're keen to see crocodiles they may be sighted in Lake Ravelobe year round, but the best months are July to October when the water level is lowest.

The park is also home to the **Angonoka Tortoise Programme** operated by the Durrell Wildlife Conservation Trust. This project is successfully captive-breeding the world's rarest tortoise – the ploughshare (see page 55) – for reintroduction to their original habitat. The site is not officially visitable but you can view the tortoises through a fence.

Madagascar
bee-eater (FV)

Some of the Coquerel's sifaka at Ankarafantsika are habituated. (DA)

Baobabs on the shoreline at Moramba Bay (DA)

Anjajavy and other fly-in resort highlights

If you are looking to get away from it all, then it is difficult to think of a better place to do that than at one of the three resorts on the section of coastline between Mahajanga and Nosy Be. See pages 207 and 211 for their contact details. Access to the lodges is by light aircraft from Mahajanga or Tana.

Lodge des Terres Blanches really does qualify for the cliché 'best kept secret' (at least from English-speaking tourists) since it sees far fewer visitors than the other two. By comparison, the accommodation here is simple but comfortable. The six double bungalows sit next to a gorgeous white beach fringed with forest. It is a popular resort for sport-fishermen, and the two boats are largely used for fishing trips. However, you can arrange to be taken to some beautiful coves along the coast, to baobab-arrayed islands, or to an area of *tsingy*.

La Maison de Marovasa-Be has three suites and six luxury rooms, all with en-suite bathrooms and balconies. The location is, perhaps, not as attractive as that of the other two lodges, and its forest has suffered from slash-and-burn agriculture (*tavy*). However, the hotel itself is beautifully thought-out and the owners are involved with a local NGO working to benefit local communities, including a reforestation programme in which visitors can participate.

Anjajavy is about as good as you can get in Madagascar. This is not just a luxury seaside hotel: in addition to its comfortable villas it protects 450ha of Madagascar's dwindling dry deciduous forest. In some places this grows right on the *tsingy* limestone.

Wildlife viewing here is effortless, including Coquerel's sifakas, brown lemurs, mouse lemurs and sportive lemurs. Birds include flocks of bright green grey-headed love-birds, sickle-billed vangas, crested ibises, crested couas and vasa parrots, to name just a few. You may also see ground boas, hognose snakes and plenty of chameleons and beautiful butterflies, as well as botanical wonders including lots of baobabs and an undescribed species of cycad tree.

There's a couple of caves too, with spectacular stalactites and stalagmites (and bats), and one with the skulls of an extinct giant lemur species embedded in the rocks. Then there are the coral reefs, *tsingy*, pristine beaches and extensive mangroves. It is an equally wonderful spot for relaxation, with a good beach, lovely swimming pool and 'oasis' garden.

Sickle-billed vanga (FV)

Tried & Tested

Anjajavy
Ⓦ www.anjajavy.com

We think Anjajavy is one of the most comfortable boutique hotels in Madagascar: 25 luxury rosewood villas set along the Mozambique Channel offer not only stunning white sandy beaches to relax on, but also some amazing walks to discover more of Madagascar's flora and fauna. Free activities include windsurfing, mountain biking or use of their catamarans and they also organise some fantastic big game and fly fishing excursions. You could, of course, just relax in the hammock on your veranda after a swim in the pool.

What makes a trip to Madagascar exciting?

Madagascar is the fourth biggest island in the world and one of its very best culture and nature destinations. Indeed, 80% of its plant and animal species cannot be found elsewhere on this blue planet; it is known for its outstanding wildlife discovery. Airtours won the National Tourism Board's tour operator award, organised by Conservation International and Madagascar National Parks in collaboration with Responsible Travel in October 2009, because of the authenticity of its product in the Zahamena Corridor, bearing in mind the respect of the natural environment. This is the reason why Airtours was set up: to give you a special look of what authenticity means (our motto is 'Madagascar at the heart of authenticity'). We are thrilled to offer you an unforgettable discovery, filled with excitement, as we take you all over Madagascar. If you are fond of discovery and wildlife, allow us to take you on a thrilling and adventurous journey in the beautiful country of Madagascar, making the means and resources available to guarantee you a nice stay and countless memories.

Which of your tours would you recommend for a first-time visitor?

Madagascar is rich in the biodiversity which tourists seek. For the first-time visitor we would say the RN7 Deep South Tour is a must (especially if they can only stay 10 days). On the way to the south, they will discover lots of towns, cultures, and many different landscapes including terraced rice fields. The further you go, the more you will discover nature's richness: the rainforest, Ranomafana National Park, zebus, spiny forest, bays and more. Apart from this, you will never forget the warm welcome of the Malagasy people and the smiles of the children wherever you go. Moreover we take into account travellers' own interests to help fulfil their desire, such as birdwatching (over 200 bird species can be found in Madagascar and half of those are endemic), succulents, orchids or scuba diving.

What would you recommend for travellers seeking adventure and exploration?

To make your visit most profitable, we recommend you come for at least 10 to 15 days. But be aware that you will not be able to explore the whole of this beautiful country in one visit. Madagascar is for those who have a passion for wildlife and, whether by yourself or in a group, the country offers a large range of activities and adventure affordable for all as we tailor-make your trip so that you can make the most of your time in Madagascar. You will get more out of your trip if you choose to travel with a qualified travel agency that can meet your expectations.

What makes your trips to Madagascar special?

Madagascar Airtours offers you a large range of eco-oriented products, bringing a touch of exoticism to your tropical experience. Our devoted, dynamic and highly qualified staff guarantee an international standard and memorable stay. They will take you to the national parks with experienced tour guides, visiting the world-famous heritage.

The country's motto is 'Madagascar naturally', motivating people to protect endangered species. If you come to Madagascar, you will be invited to participate in preserving these species and the environment. Scientists from *National Geographic*, coming to Madagascar through Madagascar Airtours, come back with friends and relatives not for work purposes but for the beauty of the country.

Founded in 1968, Madagascar Airtours has been among the pioneers of travel agencies and tour operators for over 40 years. Being representative of American Express in Madagascar, it ensures the security and safety of your stay and offers you an adventure of authenticity throughout Madagascar and its isles. We spoke to managing director Olivia Madhow Rasoamanarivo.

ⓣ +261 20 22 241 92　ⓔ airtours@madagascar-airtours.com
ⓦ www.madagascar-airtours.com

Independently owned and operated by Madagascar Airtours.

Morondava and the west

The Morondava area was the centre of the Sakalava kingdom, and their tombs bear witness to their power and creativity. Today it is the centre of a prosperous rice-growing area – and has successfully introduced ostrich farming to Madagascar! For tourists it is best known as a seaside resort with a laid-back atmosphere. Morondava is the southern gateway to many of the attractions of the western region and is the centre for visiting the western deciduous forest, the famous baobabs, and the Tsingy de Bemaraha National Park.

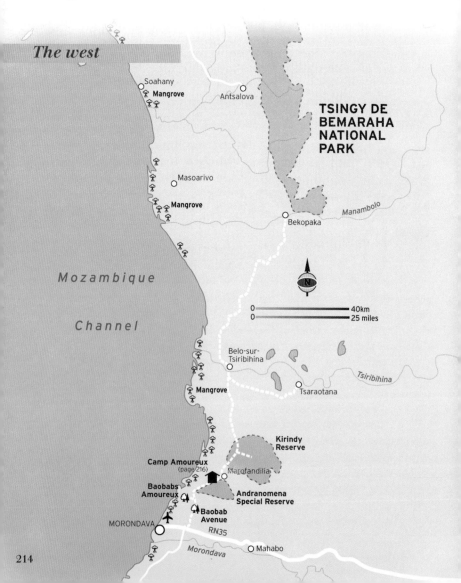

The west

Soahany
Mangrove
Antsalova

TSINGY DE BEMARAHA NATIONAL PARK

Masoarivo

Mangrove

Manambolo

Bekopaka

Mozambique

Channel

0 ——— 40km
0 ——— 25 miles

Belo-sur-Tsiribihina

Tsiribihina

Mangrove

Tsaraotana

Kirindy Reserve

Camp Amoureux
(page 216)

Marofandilia

Baobabs Amoureux

Andranomena Special Reserve

Baobab Avenue

MORONDAVA

RN35

Morondava

Mahabo

Practicalities

Morondava is 701km from Tana and served by a decaying road that typically takes 15 hours, so many tourists opt to fly. The town is served by regular flights from Tana. Most of the best hotels are situated on the peninsula, a district known as Nosy Kely.

In the centre of town there is a bank with an ATM and at least one cybercafé. The regional tourist office does not have visitable premises, but you can contact them online via Ⓦ www.baobab-madagascar.org.

Accommodation in Morondava

Upmarket
Chez Maggie Ⓦ www.chezmaggie.com
Palissandre Côte Ouest Ⓦ www.palissandrecote-ouest.com
Renala Ⓦ www.renala.net

Moderate
Bougainvilliers Ⓔ bol_nd@yahoo.fr
Mantalys (near airport) Ⓔ hotelmantalys@yahoo.fr
Philaos Ⓣ 95 520 81

Budget
Cheval de Mer Ⓣ 032 04 703 91
Zoom Ⓣ 95 920 59

Accommodation at Bemaraha

Upmarket
Olympe du Bemaraha Ⓦ www.olympedubemaraha-madagascar.com
Orchidée du Bemaraha Ⓦ www.orchideedubemaraha.com
Relais de Tsingy Ⓦ www.tsingy-de-bemaraha.com
Tsingy Lodge Ⓦ www.tsingy-lodge.com

Moderate
Camp Croco Ⓦ www.madcameleon.com

Budget
Auberge de Tsingy Ⓔ mbeach@blueline.mg

Highlights in and around Morondava

Baobab Avenue

ⓦ www.alleedesbaobabs.org

This cluster of towering Grandidier's baobabs is one of Madagascar's most famous views. In 2008, Baobab Avenue (together with about 300 baobabs in the immediate area) became an officially protected Natural Monument. The best light for photography is just before sunset (it brings out the red hue in the bark) but sunrise is almost as good, and you're much more likely to have the place to yourself. An organisation called Fomba (Friends of Madagascar's Baobabs) has recently constructed a canopy walkway so that you can watch the sun setting over the Avenue from the boughs of a neighbouring baobab. The site is 18km (40 minutes' drive) from Morondava.

Some 7km beyond the Avenue are the **Baobabs Amoureux** ('baobab lovers'), so called because they are a romantically intertwined pair. Nearby, **Andranomena Special Reserve** protects 6,420ha of dense dry deciduous forest including three species of baobab.

If you are continuing on to Kirindy, do make time to stop at the village of Marofandilia on the way. In this inspiring village there is an art boutique where you can buy excellent woodcarvings. It began as a Peace Corps project and is now a thriving independent business.

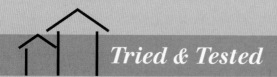

Tried & Tested

Camp Amoureux
ⓦ www.tinyurl.com/campamoureux

RAINBOW TOURS

At long last, some good accommodation for those who want to explore Kirindy! In the forest near Marofandilia, 44km from Morondava and close to the Baobab Avenue, this well-tended camp has seven tented bungalows, with en-suite shower and toilet. Each is on a solid platform and can be set up as a double or a twin  room. The restaurant seats 20 guests and serves good, locally sourced fare, a speciality being *poulet au coco* (coconut chicken). There is good wildlife viewing around the area both by day and by night.

Red-tailed sportive lemur (FV)

Kirindy Reserve

This is one of the most rewarding natural areas in Madagascar. Until a few years ago its sole purpose was the sustainable harvesting of trees, but despite this selective logging, the wildlife here is abundant. It is one of the few places where you may see the giant jumping rat and the narrow-striped mongoose, and is also the best place by far to see the fossa – the island's largest carnivore. Birds include the rare white-breasted mesite, crested ibis, vasa parrots, harrier-hawks, kingfishers, sunbirds and vangas. Some 50 reptiles and 15 amphibians are also found in the reserve.

A night walk here is a must. One nocturnal local endemic is the tiny Madame Berthe's mouse lemur. Weighing just 30g, it is the world's smallest primate. Kirindy is also home to many tenrecs and bats.

The best time to visit is November or December. At this time of year you can watch collared iguanas seeking out open sandy spots to lay their clutches of eggs, while hognose snakes eagerly sniff out these freshly laid snacks, unearthing them with their snouts and swallowing the eggs whole.

Kirindy is about 65km (2½ hours' drive) northeast of Morondava. There are basic huts for overnight stays, or you can find more comfortable accommodation approximately 20km back towards the Baobab Avenue at Camp Amoureux (see box opposite).

Tsingy de Bemaraha National Park

Protecting Madagascar's largest area of *tsingy*, this national park is one of the wonders of Madagascar and has rightly been recognised as a UNESCO World Heritage Site. The scenery rivals anything in the country and it is a treasure trove for botanists. At 152,000ha it is also one of Madagascar's most extensive protected areas.

The awe-inspiring grey forest of rock pinnacles is matched by the care with which walkways have been constructed to allow visitors to see this place in safety. Steps, boardwalks, steel ladders, cable ropes, and suspension bridges form a pathway allowing tourists to explore the *tsingy*. Amid all this grey are splashes of green from the pachypodiums

and other strange succulents which find footholds in the crevices. And there's plenty of wildlife too, including Decken's sifakas, red-fronted brown lemurs, chameleons and collared iguanas.

Access is impossible for much of the rainy season so you need to plan a visit between April/May and November/December. The base village of Bekopaka is 187km from Morondava, which takes 10 hours in a 4x4. (An alternative route to Bemaraha is along the Manambolo River; see page 221.) With the time and effort needed to get there, you should spend at least three days so you can experience several walking circuits. These differ greatly in difficulty but those with the most dramatic views are demanding and require a good level of fitness.

Bemaraha is home to the largest and most impressive *tsingy* formations in the country. (FL)

In Conversation with...
Zà Tours

What are the main reasons to choose Zà Tours as your ground handler in Madagascar?

There is so much to see and to enjoy in Madagascar and tourists need to find an efficient tour company to meet their high expectations. They are right to choose Zà Tours for the following reasons: every client is treated as a VIP and our professional staff are hugely motivated to provide good value services. Our company has been in the business for almost 15 years now and enjoys an excellent track record during that period.

Zà Tours offers a vast range of wildlife opportunities; can you recommend some areas?

Madagascar's claim to fame is undoubtedly wildlife. Our rainforest is home to most of our species. In Andasibe you can see the indri (largest living lemur), the emerald green Parson's chameleon and trees festooned with bird's nest ferns and orchids, to name just a few. Ranomafana and Masoala are worth mentioning too. The unique skyward spiny bush in the south shelters the 'dancing lemur' sifaka and the iconic ring-tailed lemur – Berenty is arguably the best place to view them. And Kirindy forest is the place to see the puma-like fossa, reptiles and invertebrates. Scientists have identified over 12,000 invertebrate species here, including the comet moth (the world's biggest moth) and giraffe beetle (so called because of the male's long neck).

Have you any words for our readers before they decide to come to Madagascar?

Zà Tours is an expert in tailor-made travels throughout Madagascar. Do tell us your interests and wishes and we will do the rest to satisfy them. We are ready to take up the challenge: make this unusual destination an outstanding one. With us, clients are in the most capable hands.

Named after the famous statuesque zà baobab, one of Madagascar's best-known treasures, Zà Tours is an Antananarivo-based tour operator. They specialise in customised itineraries for groups and individuals and cater for all interests. Their experienced staff are fluent in English and will take good care of your reservations, transfers and excursions. We spoke to Nivo Ravelojaona.

ⓣ +261 20 22 424 22   ⓔ zatour@iris.mg
Ⓦ www.zatours-madagascar.com

River trip highlights

River trips offer an excellent way to access remote areas of Madagascar, but are only for the intrepid. Combining a river journey with standard overland, biking or trekking programmes can make an ideal adventure holiday. Two of the most popular are floats on the lazy western rivers Tsiribihina and Manambolo.

The banks of the Tsiribihina (PYB)

Descending the **Tsiribihina** involves a three- to five-day trip, starting in Miandrivazo. This is the most popular river journey and most people love it for the wildlife seen from the boat (mainly birdlife) as well as the glimpses of rural life on the riverbanks. The **Manambolo** takes a similar amount of time and begins at Ankavandra. This is a spectacular journey through the untouched homeland of the Sakalava people as well as Tsingy de Bemaraha National Park. The chances of seeing the area's special wildlife, such as Decken's sifakas and Madagascar fish eagles, are high.

Vazimba

Vazimba is the name given to the earliest inhabitants of Madagascar, highland pastoralists who were displaced or absorbed by later immigrants. Once thought to be pre-Indonesian aboriginals from Africa, it is now generally accepted that they were survivors of the earliest Austronesian immigrants who were pushed to the west by later arrivals. It is this region where the last of them are thought to have lived, and many families living around these parts claim distant Vazimba ancestry.

Nowadays, popular belief maintains that they may not have been human at all, but rather a sort of malevolent spirit. Some say they were a pygmy tribe, but legends vary from region to region and their tombs are now places of pilgrimage where sacrifices are made for favours and cures. It is *fady* (taboo) to step over such a tomb, or to bring pork or garlic into the vicinity. Vazimba are also thought of as ancestral guardians of the soil, haunting certain springs and rocks where offerings may be made.

10 Eastern Adventure

Madagascar's dramatic and rain-drenched east coast is notoriously both rewarding and challenging. In July 1817, British military officer and missionary James Hastie wrote in his diary: 'If this is the good season for travelling this country, I assert it is impossible to proceed in the bad.' Nowadays little has changed: many areas are cut off in the wet season and even in the dry season it is difficult to travel between the half dozen eastern regions covered in this chapter without taking to the air. But these areas are worth the effort. A relaxing boat trip along the Pangalanes Canal, overnighting at one of its lake resorts, is an increasingly popular route to the east-coast port of Toamasina. Further north are the spectacular rainforests of Masoala and Marojejy. Exotic crops - such as vanilla, cloves, coffee and pepper - bring a taste of exoticism to the east. And offshore is Ile Sainte Marie, a cliché of a tropical island with endless deserted beaches overhung by coconut palms.

South of Mananjary

The main reason tourists come to the coastal region south of Mananjary is for the railway journey down from Fianarantsoa to Manakara. Most then return directly to Fianarantsoa by road, but a few take the opportunity to explore the little-visited towns along this section of coastline. It is possible to get as far south as Vangaindrano on a good road. To continue beyond that to Taolagnaro requires at least two days, an adventurous spirit and a good off-road vehicle.

(SF)

Practicalities

The train from Fianarantsoa to Manakara takes eight to ten hours, leaving at 06.45 on alternate days and returning the following day. Many tour operators are reluctant to incorporate this railway journey into their tours because frequent schedule changes, delays and breakdowns can play havoc with a tight itinerary, so if you want to take the train you would be wise to include a disposable day into your plan to avoid risking disruption to your trip.

The road journey between Manakara and Fianarantsoa takes about six hours and passes through Ranomafana (see page 142). Manakara is a small town but it has banks and an internet café. Similar facilities are also to be found in Mananjary, Farafangana and Vangaindrano – as well as basic to moderate accommodation – if you decide to explore this section of coastline.

Accommodation in Manakara

Moderate
Ampilao Beach Ⓔ ampilaobeach.hotel@yahoo.fr
Antemoro Ⓣ 032 43 705 33
Flamboyants Ⓣ 032 52 459 51
Vanille Ⓔ hotellavanillemanakara@yahoo.fr

Budget
Delices d'Orient Ⓣ 72 217 34

The legend of Darafify

Many, many years ago, when Madagascar was still young, the land was surrounded by fresh water. One day a giant named Darafify came striding down the eastern shoreline, carrying a bag of salt over one shoulder. He paused for a rest. A fisherman paddling his pirogue saw what he thought were two enormous trees standing on the edge of the water. These were a pair of splendid trees with fine, straight trunks – just the thing for a new pirogue, he mused. So he set to work cutting the nearest one down with his axe. Feeling a sudden agonising blow to his ankle, Darafify let out a roar of pain and dropped his bag of salt in the water. And that is how the sea came to be salty.

Highlights south of Mananjary

Mananjary and Manakara are rather sleepy seaside towns. The former is known for its *sambatra* – mass circumcision ceremonies performed every seven years (the next is around October 2014). The seafront at Manakara is beautiful, with colonial buildings and shady trees, although swimming here is not advisable. Near to Farafangana is a special reserve called Manombo, which is home to the extremely rare grey-headed lemur, but tourist infrastructure is minimal.

More than a dozen varieties of banana are grown in this region. (DA)

FCE Railway to Manakara

The Fianarantsoa–Côte Est (FCE) railway runs for 163km between Fianarantsoa and Manakara. Constructed between 1926 and 1936, it passes over 67 bridges, through 48 tunnels, and even crosses the runway at Manakara airport. Many of the rails once formed part of a track in Alsace, but were seized from the Germans after World War I, and were eventually shipped to Madagascar by the French. It makes lengthy stops at 18 stations *en route* to take on locally grown fruit and other produce. The lives of some 100,000 people along the line depend on the FCE to bring supplies in and to send their goods to market. So it was a tragedy when, in 2000, cyclones caused almost 300 landslides that buried the track – and took months to clear. Locals came to understand that it was due to deforestation and poor farming methods that the mudslides had been so severe, and so new agricultural practices were quickly adopted. Now vetiver grass is planted between crops on slopes along the track to protect against washouts. A nice booklet describing the history of the FCE is available from the ticket office.

This railway line has a dramatic history: between 5,000 and 10,000 men are thought to have lost their lives in its construction. (DA)

In Conversation with...
Cortez Travel & Expeditions

What is your favourite itinerary?

Having criss-crossed Madagascar for the past 25 years and experienced so many of the unique wonders in each area, my favourite itinerary is one that I will design for you to meet your expectations and best suited to your interests, whether it be primates, avifauna, reptiles and amphibians, whales, orchids, palms, succulents, spices, photography, culture, special celebrations, or all of the above.

What do you believe makes travel in Madagascar special?

A forgotten land as far as tourism is concerned, Madagascar is still, fortunately, the way the world used to be. The unique fauna and flora are usually the prime reasons to undertake a journey to the 'Red Island' but what most travellers take home are indelible memories of being genuinely welcomed by a gentle people, beautiful children, and spectacular scenery.

Are there new possibilities for 'beyond the beaten path' experiences?

For die-hard adventurers, Madagascar has a great deal to offer: honeymoon at Le Petit Relais in the rainforest of the Masoala, teeming with exceptional wildlife and a true forest hideaway; explore Marojejy with its awesome, rugged terrain and the rare white silky sifaka; or climb Pic Boby in Andringitra, second highest mountain in Madagascar – all designated UNESCO World Heritage Sites.

Designing and promoting travel to Madagascar in a sensitive way is the focus of Cortez, rated Top Travel Specialist by Condé Nast. With Monique Rodriguez in Madagascar and Susan Herbst in California, their in-depth and up-to-date knowledge of this challenging destination allows them to 'tell it like it is' so travellers come away with fascinating, unforgettable memories. We spoke to Susan Herbst.

Ⓣ +1 858 755 5136   Ⓔ info@cortez-usa.com
Ⓦ www.cortez-usa.com

227

Pangalanes Canal and Toamasina (Tamatave)

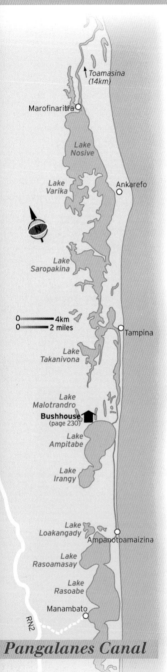

Toamasina (14km)

Marofinaritra

Lake Nosive

Lake Varika

Ankarefo

Lake Saropakina

0 ——— 4km
0 ——— 2 miles

Tampina

Lake Takanivona

Lake Malotrandro
Bushhouse
(page 230)

Lake Ampitabe

Lake Irangy

Lake Loakangady

Ampanotoamaizina

Lake Rasoamasay

Lake Rasoabe

Manambato

RN2

Pangalanes Canal

Pangalanes highlights

The Pangalanes Canal is a series of lakes that was linked by artificial canals in French colonial times for commercial use, a quiet inland waterway being preferable to an often stormy sea. The waterways fell into disuse, but in the 1980s a grand project to rehabilitate them was carried out. Silted canals were dredged, new warehouses built and a fleet of modern tug barge units purchased to operate a cargo service. That may once have worked, but now the warehouses and quaysides are empty and the tug barge units gone. The canal is still much used by local fishermen for transporting their goods in pirogues and for fishing. It once ran 665km from Toamasina to Vangaindrano, but some sections are no longer navigable. The northern section, as far south as Manambato, has been developed for tourism with lakeside bungalows and private nature reserves.

Manambato, a picturesque lakeside resort reached from RN2 via a 7km dirt road, is the main access point for boat trips up the canal to Lake Ampitabe and onward to Toamasina. There are white sand beaches at Manambato and some fairly basic lakeshore hotels. There is also accommodation at the northern end of Lake Rasoamasay. But the tourist focus of the Pangalanes Canal is at Lake Ampitabe, which is a very peaceful spot with broad white beaches and clean water for swimming. There is also a private nature reserve with several introduced species of lemur and, at a nearby lake, thousands of insect-eating pitcher plants.

Practicalities

Toamasina (Tamatave) can be reached from Tana by air (daily flights) or overland. The direct road route passes by the rainforest at Andasibe (see page 123) and takes about seven hours. A popular alternative to the final quarter of this road journey is to take a boat along the Pangalanes Canal from Manambato. There are hotels at Lake Ampitabe and one at Lake Rasoamasay, so most people stay at least one night *en route*, but you could get from Manambato to Toamasina in under three hours by non-stop motor launch.

Toamasina is a large town with several banks, reliable cybercafés and two good supermarkets. The regional tourist information office is based at 83 Boulevard Joffre (Ⓦ www.tamatave-tourisme.com).

Beyond Toamasina, the road gets worse the further north you go. It is possible to get as far as the village of Soanierana-Ivongo (from where ferries cross to Ile Sainte Marie) in less than four hours, but thereafter the road becomes virtually impassable. There is little to see along this stretch and most tourists heading on to Ile Sainte Marie from Toamasina prefer to fly between the two.

Accommodation on the Pangalanes Canal

For full details of tour operator-recommended accommodation, see page 230.

Upmarket
Palmarium (Lake Ampitabe) Ⓦ www.palmarium.biz

Moderate
Ony Hotel (Lake Rasoamasay) Ⓦ http://onyhotel.free.fr
Pangalanes Hotel (Lake Ampitabe) ① 53 334 03

Accommodation in Toamasina

Upmarket
Calypso Ⓦ www.hotelcalypso.mg
Neptune Ⓦ www.hotel-neptune-tamatave.com

Moderate
Joffre Ⓔ hotel.joffre@moov.mg
Labourdonnais Ⓦ www.labourdonnais-hotel-tamatave.com

Bushhouse
ⓦ www.bushhouse-madagascar.com

The journey to Bushhouse by speedboat along the lake system of the Pangalanes Canal is all part of the adventure of staying here. The simple ten-room lodge enjoys a fantastic view across Lake Ampitabe to the sand dunes with the Indian Ocean beyond. Although you're in a remote area there are lots of things to do, including visiting the nearby Palmarium wildlife reserve, with its various species of lemur, walking along the lakeshore to see the insect-eating pitcher plants, or making a visit to the local village.

Highlights in and around Toamasina

The large town of Toamasina – still popularly known by its colonial name of Tamatave – has always had an air of shabby elegance with some fine palm-lined boulevards and once-impressive colonial houses. Every few years a cyclone hits, and it spends some time in a new state of shabbiness before rebuilding. It is a spirited, bustling city with a good variety of bars, snack bars and restaurants.

Toamasina's main boulevard (DA)

HELP Madagascar

Ⓦ www.helpmg.org Ⓔ kbrmad@gmail.com

If you have some spare time in Toamasina, pay a visit to this inspiring charity run by Kim and Colin Radford. They help disadvantaged youngsters with health, schooling and other necessities. Each year, HELP assists at least 200 children and young adults to attend school, many of whom are enrolled in intensive catch-up classes designed to help orphans, dropouts and illiterate teens reintegrate into school. The course includes free school supplies, a daily hot lunch, and medical assistance. HELP also sponsors young adults on vocational training programmes such as carpentry, metalwork and sewing.

The tranquil lake at Ivoloina (DA)

Ivoloina Park

Ⓦ www.seemadagascar.com ⊕ 09.00–17.00

This began life more than two decades ago as a rather grand botanical garden but is now a 282ha forest with numerous walking trails, a lake and conservation education centre. There is a small zoo area with both free-ranging and captive lemurs (including an aye-aye) as well as radiated tortoises, tomato frogs, tenrecs, parrots and chameleons. The park is funded and run by the Madagascar Fauna Group, a consortium of some 30 zoos from around the world with a special interest in Madagascar.

A visit here is rewarding both for what you see and what the organisation is doing in terms of educating the local population about conservation. You can explore the forest on a network of trails of varying difficulty, which include wildlife interpretation boards, or take a pirogue trip on the lake. An abundance of birds, reptiles and lemurs can be seen from the trails and guides are not obligatory except for big groups. Ivoloina is 12km (30 minutes' drive) north of Toamasina.

In Conversation with...

What makes your trips to Madagascar special?

We have been sourcing the best destinations, untouched areas and most special secret locations in Madagascar for the last six years. We have significant background in hosting and guiding in southern Africa and we have extended our expertise to the 'Island Continent'.

Everyone who has been on safari on the African mainland wants to get to Madagascar, not to be subjected to shopping, beaches and cities, but rather to see the country's incredible flora and fauna. Extraordinary Expeditions is the first tour operator focusing on nature travellers and enthusiasts. We know the destinations, the best guides in the country (some of whom have had training in South Africa) and have superb ground staff in the major centres for ease of logistics and flow. Conrad Hennig, the MD of Extraordinary Expeditions, studied zoology and has worked for superb safari companies all over the world (Wilderness Safaris, Quark Expeditions and Natural Habitat Adventures) so knows the ins and outs of what is needed to really make Madagascar a stand-out destination for discerning visitors.

Which of your tours would you recommend for a first-time visitor?

There are numerous focuses for first-time visitors. The incredible untouched forest at Andasibe-Mantadia, the wondrous spiny desert near Mandrare (at Ifotaka near Fort Dauphin) and the superb diving off the islands north of Nosy Be are probably ample for first time visitors. However, specific recommendations will be made only when time of year, interests and budget are considered. We have plenty of experience with regards to making traveller-specific recommendations.

What would you recommend for travellers who want to take a more adventurous approach to exploring?

There are around 100 species of lemur in Madagascar, and some are so rare and so localised it takes quite some effort to find them! Species such as the Devil's (or Perrier's) sifaka, Madame Berthe's mouse lemur (smallest primate in the world), and the ultimate Malagasy predator the fossa can be found; you just need proper people to help plan itineraries and guides who know where to find the rarities and make it all come together. This is where Extraordinary Expeditions can help! Some of the world's most untouched coral reefs are also found around the 200+ islands off Madagascar, and we have intimate knowledge of where to find truly pristine reefs.

For visitors to the Island Continent, what will the biggest surprises be?

Madagascar is such an island of contrasts. One of the biggest surprises is when you are just about to land: look out and you will think you are over Asia – rice paddies everywhere! I love the French influence on the country's gastronomy; prepare to experience some sensational food (in decent restaurants), great preserves, salads, vegetables and especially desserts! With cacao, vanilla and every fruit known to the world growing in profusion in Madagascar, the food is what takes most by surprise. There are some awesome restaurants in Tana, Toamasina and even off the beaten track (like Isalo and Morondava) and we pride ourselves in their recommendation.

The other surprise in particular with regard to visitors who have been on an African safari is that there is nothing dangerous at all. You are able to walk around with a flashlight at night without dangerous animals following you! It is a total delight being so safe in the forests, especially for kids.

Extraordinary Expeditions is a small, specialist operator focusing on providing the ultimate in nature-centric and creative travel arrangements. Madagascar for the uninitiated can be a very trying destination, but they ensure that a traveller's time is maximised in the various natural wonders that the Island Continent offers, and minimised in the cities and in travel. We spoke to founder and CEO Conrad Hennig.

Ⓣ +27 (0)11 706 5959 Ⓔ conrad@ex-ex.co.za
Ⓦ www.ex-ex.co.za

Northeastern rainforests

The northeast region is home to some of the largest and most impressive rainforests in Madagascar, protected by the national parks of Masoala and Marojejy, which were recently designated a UNESCO World Heritage Site in Danger. Nestled in Antongil Bay, Maroantsetra is the gateway town for Masoala as well as the wonderful island special reserve of Nosy Mangabe. Some 100km to the north of Masoala is the town of Sambava, from where Marojejy National Park may be accessed.

Highlights around Antongil Bay

Aye-Aye Island

The small village of Mananara sees few visitors despite the fact that it is the only place where one is very likely to see an aye-aye in the wild.

Aye-Aye Island is a privately owned river island of about 10ha with a few resident aye-ayes as well as white-fronted brown lemurs. Normally

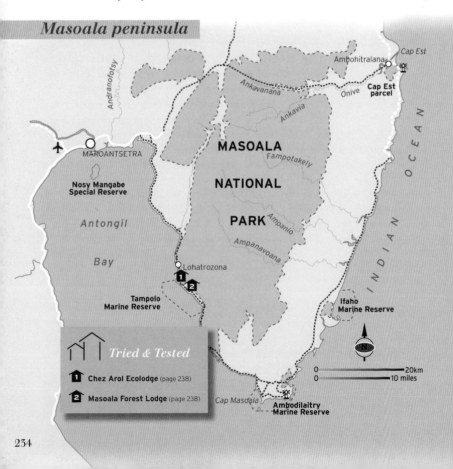

Masoala peninsula

Cap Est
Ambohitralana
Cap Est parcel
Andranofotsy
Ankavanana
Onive
Ankavia
MAROANTSETRA
MASOALA
Fampotakely
Nosy Mangabe
Special Reserve
NATIONAL
Antongil
PARK
Ampanio
Ampanavoana
Bay
Lohatrozona
Tampolo
Marine Reserve
Ifaho
Marine Reserve
Tried & Tested
1 Chez Arol Ecolodge (page 238)
2 Masoala Forest Lodge (page 238)
Cap Masoala
Ambodilaitry
Marine Reserve

O C E A N
I N D I A N

0 — 20km
0 — 10 miles

Practicalities

Aye-Aye island is just outside Mananara, a town at the southern end of Antongil Bay. It has a small airport but there are not always regular flights. The town has mobile phone coverage but no internet access. The one small bank has no ATM (getting cash can take hours) and only takes MasterCard, not Visa.

At Maroantsetra, the gateway town for Masoala, the bank situation is the same and the town is similarly isolated, although flights are much more regular. It has internet cafés and a small supermarket. There is good accommodation at the edge of Masoala National Park but on the island special reserve of Nosy Mangabe camping is the only option if you want to stay overnight. Access to both places is by boat from Maroantsetra, where there are also good hotels.

Sambava has the closest airport for Marojejy National Park, with flights from Tana and Antsiranana. There are plenty of hotels there, several banks and a couple of cybercafés. From Sambava, it is 60km to the park.

Accommodation at Maroantsetra and Masoala

For full details of tour operator-recommended accommodation, see page 238.

Upmarket
Masoala Resort (Maroantsetra) Ⓦ www.masoalaresort.com
Relais du Masoala (Maroantsetra) Ⓦ www.madagascar-lodge.com
Tampolodge (Masoala) Ⓦ www.tampolodge.com

Moderate
Hippocampe (Maroantsetra) Ⓦ www.madahippocampe.com

Camping
There are national park campsites both at Masoala and on Nosy Mangabe.

Accommodation at Sambava and Marojejy

Moderate
Mimi Hotel (Sambava) Ⓦ http://mimi-hotel.marojejy.com
Orchidea Beach II (Sambava) Ⓔ orchideabeach2@moov.mg

Camping
There are three campsites within Marojejy National Park Ⓦ www.marojejy.com

The idyllic bay of Nosy Mangabe (DA)

aye-ayes live high in the rainforest canopy and have large territories. On Aye-Aye Island, however, their range is restricted by the island's small size and the trees are much lower and less dense, so they are comparatively easy to see.

Visits to the island take only an hour or so in the evening and you are not guaranteed to see an aye-aye, but an overnight stay (either camping or in the simple cabin with bunks) makes a sighting more likely than not. Unfortunately Mananara is frequently dropped from Air Madagascar's schedules so access to the area is not always possible.

Masoala National Park

Despite difficulty of access and dodgy weather, this is perhaps the leading destination for ecotourists who want to see Madagascar's most important natural habitat in terms of biodiversity – the eastern rainforest, exemplified by Nosy Mangabe and the Masoala Peninsula. These places require fitness and fortitude but the rewards for nature-lovers are great. Fitness is needed for the hills and mud which are an aspect of all the reserves, and fortitude because this is the

Short-legged ground-roller (FV)

wettest place in Madagascar, with annual

rainfall exceeding 500cm. The driest months tend to be November and December.

Unless you're up for some serious trekking, this 230,000ha park can be reached from Maroantsetra only by boat (1½–2 hours). Despite an ongoing problem with illegal logging, there are still large expanses of virgin forest along with stunning beaches of golden sand dotted with eroded rocks. Some parts of the peninsula, seen on a sunny day, can arguably be described as the most beautiful in Madagascar. The wildlife is equally stunning. You will need to work for it, but nevertheless the opportunity to see red ruffed lemur in its only habitat, helmet and Bernier's vangas, scaly ground-roller and other rare endemic birds plus a host of reptiles and invertebrates is not to be missed.

Nosy Mangabe Special Reserve

In fine weather the island of Nosy Mangabe in Antongil Bay is superb. Accessible by boat (30 minutes) from Maroantsetra, this special reserve has beautiful sandy coves, marvellous trees with huge buttress roots and also strangler figs. And it is bursting with wildlife. You will almost certainly see white-fronted brown lemurs, black-and-white ruffed lemurs, green-backed mantella frogs, stump-tailed chameleons and various snakes and birds. Day trips are possible but if you camp here then a night walk is a must: weird and wonderful leaf-tailed geckoes are another guaranteed sighting and, if you are very lucky, you may see aye-ayes.

There is a glorious sandy beach along a bay where you can swim – perhaps even in the company of dolphins and turtles. Forest trails of varying difficulty take you to the island's summit (332m), an old lighthouse, and the Plage des Hollandais where fascinating 17th-century Dutch inscriptions are carved on the rocks. For wildlife, the half-day summit circuit is particularly recommended.

Tried & Tested

Chez Arol Ecolodge
ⓦ http://arollodge.free.fr

With arguably the best location for naturalists visiting Masoala National Park, being close to the rainforest trails of Lohatrozona, this small, eco-friendly owner-run lodge has eight simple bungalows, of which most have en-suite facilities. Chez Arol Ecolodge's combination of attentive staff, excellent food (including bread and cakes baked freshly each day) and prime location on the edge of both rainforest and ocean make it a great choice. The lodge supports a local school as well as protection of a nearby marine reserve.

Masoala Forest Lodge
ⓦ www.masoalaforestlodge.com

Only accessible on foot or by boat, five simple but comfortable thatched tents constructed from local materials make up the extraordinary Masoala Forest camp. Nestling in a primary rainforest setting, just above endless stretches of perfect beaches, it offers comfort in an otherwise inaccessible area. Meals are cooked using fresh, organic ingredients and served communally in a traditional longhouse. The spectacular setting means you won't be short of something to do; we recommend exploring the islands and reefs by kayak.

Female white-fronted brown lemur on Nosy Mangabe (DA)

Highlights near Sambava

This is the centre of the vanilla- and coconut-growing region, and an important area for cloves and coffee production. Sambava has a good beach and a dramatic sea often with huge waves.

Marojejy National Park

Ⓦ www.marojejy.com

Declared a national park in 1998, Marojejy is one of Madagascar's most exciting wilderness areas, in what is perhaps the most remote pristine rainforest remaining. You need to be reasonably fit – and able to tolerate the heat – to enjoy it fully, but there are few other areas in Madagascar to compare for awesome splendour and the feeling of ultimate wilderness. Imposing mountains and craggy cliffs are surrounded by lush rainforests full of wildlife. This is the best place in Madagascar to see the gorgeous silky sifaka, one of the five rarest primates in the world, and the helmet vanga. There are panther chameleons, rufous-headed ground-rollers, yellow-bellied sunbird-asities, leaf-tailed geckos, frogs galore, huge millipedes, wonderful spiders and – be warned – lots of leeches!

The park only has sufficient infrastructure to accept small groups. There is just one path to the top of the mountain, with three 'camps' at different altitudes. Each camp comprises simple cabins with bunk beds and a shared shower and flush toilet. The first camp (reached after a 4½hr walk) is at an elevation of 425m and Marojejy's summit is 2,132m; you need proper hiking boots, a walking pole and warm clothing. You also need good weather, but if you are in luck then the view from the top is awesome and the feeling of space unmatched. The best times to visit are April to May and September to December when there is less rain.

Lined leaf-tailed gecko (FV)

The Marojejy Massif is rugged, mountainous and remote. (FV)

Illegal logging of precious woods

The partial political vacuum that has existed since Madagascar's 2009 coup has been exploited by loggers plundering protected areas for precious wood. The majority of this illegal activity has taken place in Masoala and Marojejy. In just the first few months, at least 100,000 slow-growing rosewood and ebony trees worth hundreds of millions of dollars were felled. The logs, mostly destined to be shipped to China for furniture-making, begin their journey to the ports by being floated down rivers, but the density of the wood is such that every tree needs to be strapped to half a dozen lighter-weight species to prevent it from sinking. Further trees are cut just so the loggers can get access to the precious timber. Consequently total losses to Madagascar's forests may exceed a million trees a year.

International efforts by conservationists to halt the logging have achieved some impressive successes, especially in lobbying shipping companies to refuse the cargo, but with the Chinese mafia now involved and corrupt officials at all levels implicated in the trade, the challenge of stemming the flow before it is too late is becoming ever greater.

In Conversation with...

Explain your enthusiasm for Madagascar to someone who thinks they might want to go there.

Madagascar is a fabulous country, with an incredible variety of habitats and wildlife – the bit most people are drawn in by. It has a fascinating cultural aspect too – something you only really discover when you visit – and scenically there are so many different stunning views it is quite breathtaking.

That said, visitors do need to be aware that travel there can be chaotic and I probably put off as many people as I encourage. Last-minute schedule changes, long distances to travel over poor roads, and properties often simpler than the overall cost of the holiday might reflect, are all part of the charm, but not for everyone. I try to spell out the good bits as well as the bad bits and let people decide if it sounds exciting or too much like *'I'm a Celebrity'*.

You're making me wonder why anyone would go! Does it all have to be 'adventure travel'?

It definitely doesn't. With a well-planned itinerary – not biting off too much of this huge island – and a good guide alongside you, it's possible to see some incredible things, well off the obvious tourist trail, and come home with lots of life-long memories.

We make sure that even the journeys between places are part of the fun, using private vehicles, boats and planes where appropriate, to allow people to enjoy the getting there almost as much as being somewhere. And there are some top-end lodges and camps, so even if you've had a couple of nights in a relatively simple property, you can then stay somewhere with beautiful rooms and superb food.

Madagascar has many must-see places; have you got a top three set of recommendations for your clients?

Not really, since it all depends on their preferences. Some people want to hike, so we'll recommend national parks where you can get a good few miles in, whereas others have specific animals they want to see, which dictates the areas or parks they visit.

We don't arrange trips departing on particular days or big group trips, and there aren't any set itineraries to work from, so we really can have a conversation and understand from our clients what they want from their trip, giving ideas of what's possible throughout. It's a narrowing down process, but with a bit of time and effort at the planning stage, we're confident that we can put together the perfect itinerary.

Aardvark is a company that arranges a lot of family holidays; is Madagascar suitable for families?

Definitely. Although much of the flora and fauna is subtle, children tend to love bugs and reptiles, and as there aren't dangerous animals it's possible to explore on foot and have a lot of freedom around the lodges and camps. There are also lots of activities available for the whole family, from watersports at the beach locations, to horseriding near Isalo. For families or couples looking for somewhere really different, it's a wonderful island and somewhere we love helping to plan exciting trips to.

With offices in the UK and USA, Aardvark Safaris work with their clients to tailor-make their dream Madagascar holiday. With over 20 years' experience, they've slept in the beds, eaten the meals and walked with the guides. You can be confident that they have the knowledge and expertise to ensure all your holiday wishes are fulfilled. We spoke to co-founder Richard Smith.

℡ +44 (0)1980 849160 (UK); +1 888 776 0888 (US)
✉ mail@aardvarksafaris.com (UK); info@aardvarksafaris.com (US)
🌐 www.aardvarksafaris.co.uk (UK); www.aardvarksafaris.com (US)

Libertalia and the pirates of Madagascar

From the late 17th century, Madagascar developed into a stronghold for pirates. Countless unfortunate sailors became shipwrecked and stranded on the island and many were left with little option but to turn to piracy. A Welshman (David Williams), some Englishmen (Thomas White, Henry 'John' Every and William Kidd) and an American (Thomas Tew) were just some of the famous names among a Madagascar pirate population which, in its heyday, numbered nearly one thousand. Their main base was Ile Sainte Marie, just off the east coast of Madagascar, and Antongil Bay to the north.

The pirates intercepted and plundered merchant ships as they crossed through the Indian Ocean, helping themselves to their cargoes of silks, spices, jewels and coins. With little motivation to risk their lives, the low-paid crew of these merchant ships rarely put up a fight – and the bands of pirates regularly recruited new members from among these seamen. They also targeted pilgrim ships, for they knew that the wealthy Muslims aboard would normally be carrying items of great value to Mecca. Merchants in Réunion, Africa and India happily fenced the pirates' loot.

Legend has it that **Libertalia**, a utopian pirate society, sprung up in Madagascar around this time under the leadership of Frenchman Captain James Misson. The degree of truth in the story has long been the subject of debate (some claim it was entirely fabricated by Daniel Defoe) but it is said that the pirates renounced their nationalities in favour of calling themselves Liberi and adopting a form of communal rule with all possessions held in common and all decisions put to the vote. They were anarchists who waged war against states and lawmakers, attacking their ships, sparing prisoners and freeing slaves.

If you want to discover more on the subject, then be sure to visit the **Museum of Pirates**, set up in central Antananarivo by Swiss-owned Madagascar tour operator PRIORI (Ⓦ www.piratenmuseum.ch).

Captain William Kidd purportedly lost half his crew to Libertalia in 1697.

Ile Sainte Marie

Ile Sainte Marie is a stunning tropical island with plenty of beautiful beaches, bays protected from sharks by coral reefs, hills covered with luxuriant vegetation, and a relative absence of unsightly tourist development. Some 50km long and 7km at its widest point, this is a popular end-of-trip destination for a few days of relaxation. Most of the beach hotels are ranged along the west coast, with only a few in the east. Several more are on Ile aux Nattes to the south.

History

The island of Sainte Marie was named by European sailors when it became the major hideout of pirates in the Indian Ocean. From the 1680s to around 1720 these pirates dominated the seas surrounding Africa.

Later a Frenchman, Jean-Onésime Filet ('La Bigorne'), was shipwrecked on Sainte Marie while escaping the wrath of a jealous husband in Réunion. La Bigorne turned his amorous attentions with remarkable success to Princess Bety, who was the daughter of King Ratsimilaho. Upon their marriage the happy couple received Ile Sainte Marie as a gift from the king, and the island was in turn presented to the mother country by La Bigorne and his wife. Thus France gained its first piece of Madagascar in 1750.

245

Practicalities

There are flights every day from Tana and Toamasina to Ile Sainte Marie. It is also possible to get there by ferry (see page 229). Taxis are easily found on the island in the main town (Ambodifotatra) or at the airport, or can be summoned by any hotel reception. To go north of Lonkintsy the road is bad and you need a 4x4 or motorbike. Many hotels have bikes, scooters, motorbikes and/or quads for hire. Do not be put off by some hotels' proximity to the airport as there are only a couple of planes per day. There are banks and an ATM in Ambodifotatra as well as some cybercafés.

Access to the small island of Ile aux Nattes is by pirogue ferry from the southern tip of Ile Sainte Marie, near to the airport. There are no banks or internet cafés on Ile aux Nattes, nor are there any roads, so you will need to walk everywhere – but the island is small enough to circumnavigate on foot in three hours.

The weather here is changeable. At any time of year expect some days of rain and wind interspersed with calm sunny weather. The best months for a visit tend to be June and mid-August to December, but good weather is possible anytime.

Accommodation

For full details of tour operator-recommended accommodation, see page 248.

Upmarket
Baboo Village (Ile aux Nattes) ⓦ www.baboo-village.com
Le Libertalia ⓦ www.lelibertalia.com
Maningory (Ile aux Nattes) ⓦ www.maningoryhotel.com
Masoandro Lodge ⓦ www.hsm.mg
Petite Traversée (Ile aux Nattes) ⓦ www.madxperience.com
Soanambo Hotel ⓦ www.hsm.mg
Vanivola ⓦ www.vanivola.com

Moderate
Baleine ⓦ www.hotel-la-baleine.com
Chez Sika (Ile aux Nattes) ⓦ www.chezsica.com
Mora Mora ⓦ www.moramora.info

Budget
Bar de la Marine (Ile aux Nattes) ⓦ www.bardelamarine.com
Mangoustan ⓔ mangoustanhotel@yahoo.fr

Ile Sainte Marie highlights

Ile Sainte Marie is the best place in Madagascar for **whale-watching**. July to September is the prime time to see them but you could be lucky in June or October. You can watch them from any of the beachfront hotels or take a boat excursion. For a really hands-on experience, stay at Princesse Bora where you'll get the chance to assist whale researchers.

The shallows around Sainte Marie are ideal for **snorkelling and diving**. Most of the coral reefs are in good condition and the water is usually clear, although some of the huge table corals have been broken off by fish traps. The best snorkelling sites are near Atafana and La Crique, and also the west side of Ile aux Nattes.

There are some interesting sights around Ambodifotatra. Most famous is the **pirates' cemetery** just after the bay bridge south of town. This is quite an impressive place, with gravestones dating from the 1830s, including one carved with a classic skull and crossbones.

At the far northeast, beyond the end of the road, is a **natural pool** with a waterfall, enormous basalt rocks and beautiful beach. Also in the area is Albrand Lighthouse, dating from colonial times.

Near the village of Vohilava in the south of the island, **Parc Endemika** is a small park-cum-zoo which cares primarily for rescued animals, mainly confiscated or unwanted pet lemurs, as well as some reptile species including tortoises, chameleons and snakes.

The pirates' cemetery on Ile Sainte Marie (FV)

Ile aux Nattes

To many visitors this pristine little island off the southern tip of Sainte Marie is even better than the main island. Being car-free it is much more peaceful. Day trippers can cross the narrow channel by pirogue and those who want to stay overnight at one of Ile aux Nattes' many hotels may choose for the pirogue to take them directly to their chosen accommodation. The best beaches are in the north of the island: calm, shallow, crystal-clear water, with soft white sand overhung by picture-postcard palms.

The circumference of the island is 8km, and it possible to walk all the way round at low tide. There is much to see during a short walking tour, including the island's unique and amazing orchid, *Eulophiella roempleriana*, known popularly as *l'orchidée rose*. It is 2m high with deep pink flowers. A small trip to the interior of the island is recommended. Aniribe village at the centre is pure unspoiled Madagascar.

Head south from there up to the old lighthouse; at the junction in the path 200m before the lighthouse, stop to visit Espace Vert – a small shop selling cloves, lemongrass, honey, vanilla, cinnamon and other local spices. Ralai, the owner, loves to practise his English and if you ask he will proudly show you the English grammar book he has written in Malagasy.

Tried & Tested

Princesse Bora Lodge & Spa
Ⓦ www.princessebora.com

RAINBOW TOURS

This is Ile Ste Marie's best accommodation. Twenty lovely en-suite villas are set amid a coconut grove beside a long white lagoon-front beach. A dedicated and professional team ensures top-notch service. Each villa has a suspended double bed, living area, private facilities with separate toilet and a sea-view veranda. Some also have double basins, AC and a mezzanine for up to two children. There are also five glass-fronted executive beach villas. The lodge has a spa and a newly opened in-house scuba diving centre.

Whale-watching

Every year humpback whales migrating from their summer feeding-grounds in Antarctica arrive in the waters off Madagascar between July and September to mate, give birth and nurture their young. Whales migrate because there is more food available in the nutrient-rich polar regions than in tropical waters, but their calves have insufficient blubber to protect them from colder water. It takes six weeks for the whales to make the 5,000km journey from Antarctica, during which they lose up to a third of their bodyweight.

The majority of the whales head for the protected, shallow waters of Antongil Bay but many can be observed either in transit or lingering between Ile Sainte Marie and the mainland, often in very close viewing distance of the shore.

Humpbacks are undoubtedly one of the most entertaining whales because of their exuberant displays of breaching (jumping), lobtailing (tail-slapping) and pec-slapping (flipper-slapping). Males competing for females often indulge in forceful displays of head-lunging and slapping to create surges and explosions of water to intimidate their rivals. But the behaviour it is most renowned for is its singing. The male produces one of the most complex, constantly evolving songs in the animal kingdom using sounds spanning the highest and lowest frequencies audible to the human ear. Many whale-watching boats are now equipped with hydrophones to enable visitors to listen in on the performance.

Appendix 1

Malagasy language

If you are on an organised tour, most guides and receptionists you encounter will speak reasonable English. It is less common for other staff such as drivers, porters, and waiters to know much English, and certainly most locals you meet will not. Everyone can speak French, but even if you are also fluent in French it is polite to learn a few words of the local lingo. It never fails to impress the Malagasy if you make an effort with their language, and it is amazing how much of a conversation you can have with just half a dozen words!

Pronunciation

The Malagasy alphabet is the same as in English, but with C, Q, U, W and X omitted. Most of the letters are pronounced the same as their English counterparts. But the letter 'o' is always long, so *fody* is pronounced 'foody'. The letter 's' varies regionally and may sound like English 's' or 'sh'. The letter 'j' sounds like 'dz'.

Malagasy words always end in a vowel, and that vowel is typically almost silent. The word *salama* therefore normally sounds more like 'salam', but there is some regional/contextual variation in this and neither pronunciation is strictly wrong.

Polite words and greetings

If you learn just four Malagasy words, then choose these:

azafady	please; excuse me
misaotra	thank you
manao ahoana	hello
veloma	goodbye

The preferred greeting varies regionally, but *manao ahoana* will be understood wherever you go. Others you might encounter are *salama*, *akory*, and *mbola tsara*.

Whenever Malagasy people meet, they ask 'what news?' Regardless of the circumstances the accepted response is always 'no news'. This is similar to a formal English greeting; when we ask 'how are you?'

we expect a reply like 'I'm fine' even if the person is not fine. A more natural way of translating 'what news? no news' into English might be 'what's happening? nothing much'.

Inona no vaovao?	What news?
Tsy misy (vaovao)	There's no (news)

Useful little words

For extra courtesy (especially if speaking to someone older) add *tompoko*. If you say *azafady tompoko* that is like saying 'excuse me, sir'. Here are some more frequently encountered words:

tsara	good
ratsy	bad
be	big; very; lots
kely	small

Expanding your vocabulary

A really effective way of learning useful new words is to ask your Malagasy guides about the meaning of local place names. Most towns begin with *Am-*, *An-* or *Ant-* as this simply indicates a place. The rest of the name is often descriptive. Antsirabe is *ant-sira-be*: a place with lots of salt (*sira*). Analakely is *an-ala-kely*: a place with a small forest (*ala*). Some words often found in place names are:

ala	forest
arivo	thousand
fotsy (-potsy)	white
hazo	tree
mafana	hot
mainty (mainti-)	black
manga	blue; mango
maro	many
nosy (nosi-)	island
rano (-drano)	water
sira	salt
soa	beautiful; good
tanana	town
tany (tani-)	land
tsy (tsi-)	not; none
vato (-bato)	stone
vohitra (vohi-; -bohi-)	hill; mountain

Conversational phrases

Iza no anaranao?	What's your name?
Ny anarako...	My name is...
Mandra pihaona	See you again
Tsara mandry	Goodnight
Tsy azoko	I don't understand
Tsy haiko	I don't know
Ombay lalana	Pardon (may I pass)
Andao andeha	Let's go
Ho ela velona!	Cheers!
Aiza...?	Where is...?
Lavitra ve izany?	Is it far?
Misy ve...?	Is there any...?
Mila... aho	I want...
Mitady... aho	I'm looking for...
Misy toerana hatoriana ve?	Is there a place to sleep?
Vita ve?	Is it ready?
Te hividy sakafo aho	I would like to buy some food
Ohatrinona?	How much is it?
Lafo be!	Too expensive!
Tsy lasa!	No way!
Tsy misy	I have nothing
Fa tsy mila	I don't need it
Mandehana!	Go away!
Noana aho	I'm hungry
Mangetaheta aho	I'm thirsty
Vizaka aho	I'm tired
Mba ampio aho!	Please help me!

Numbers

iray; iraika	1
roa	2
telo	3
efatra	4
dimy	5
enina	6
fito	7
valo	8
sivy	9
folo	10
zato	100
arivo	1,000

Menu reader

rano	water
ronono	milk
dite	tea
kafe	coffee
labiera	beer
divay	wine
sakafo; hanina	food; meal
vary	rice
laoka	accompaniment to the rice
hena	meat
(hen')akoho	chicken
(hena)kisoa	pig; pork
(hen')omby	zebu; beef
gana; ganagana	duck
trondro	fish
atody	egg
ovy	potato
tsaramaso	beans
voatabia	tomato
salady	salad
mananasy	pineapple
akondro	banana
sira	salt
siramamy	sugar (literally 'sweet salt')
dibera	butter
lasaosy	sauce
sakay	hot chilli sauce
lasary	condiment of lemon/mango/papaya
ravitoto	pork with shredded cassava leaves
romazava	beef stew
ro-patsa	beef and potato stew with dried shrimp
sambo	samosa
koba	rice ground with peanuts and banana
mofo	bread
mofo gasy	sweet rice doughnut
ramanonaka	savoury rice doughnut
menakely	doughnut ring
mofo akondro	banana fritter
mofo bageda	sweet potato fritter

Note: In Malagasy, a noun's plural form is the same as the singular.

Appendix 2

Selected reading

This appendix gives an overview of the English-language literature on the subject of Madagascar. Most of these books cannot easily be purchased in Madagascar as there are very few bookshops there. (And those books which are available often cost considerably more than in Europe or the US.) Virtually all of the books listed in this appendix can be found on Amazon or ordered via high-street bookshops. You can also obtain most of them, as well as many more specialist works not mentioned here, from ⓦ www.madabook.com.

Other Madagascar titles from Bradt

In addition to this guidebook from Bradt Travel Guides' *Highlights* series, there is also a Madagascar guidebook in Bradt's standard series by the same authors. The key difference is that, while the present book is aimed at travellers on tailor-made or group tours, the standard *Bradt Guide to Madagascar* includes extensive contact details and information for backpackers and other independent travellers wishing to arrange their accommodation, transport and park visits themselves.

Madagascar Wildlife: A Visitor's Guide from Bradt's *Wildlife* series makes an ideal companion to either guidebook for travellers interested in the flora and fauna. This full-colour book by Nick Garbutt, Hilary Bradt and Derek Schuurman covers the island's wildlife in much greater detail than is possible in the natural history chapter of this book, and includes advice on the best places to spot the most sought-after species. Much revised since it was first published in 1996, it is now in its third edition.

From early 2013, Bradt's position as a leading publisher on Madagascar will be consolidated with the republication of *Madagascar: The Eighth Continent* by Peter Tyson. This is an engaging journey of discovery recounted by a journalist who followed the ground-breaking work of four scientists in Madagascar: a primatologist studying lemurs, an archaeologist trying to work out where the Malagasy people came from, a herpetologist discovering countless new reptile species, and a palaeoarchaeologist interested in understanding the recent extinction of all the country's large animals.

Wildlife

Two prominent primatologists have published books on Madagascar in the last few years. *Madagascar: the Forest of our Ancestors* by Patricia Wright (Biotope, 2010) is a gorgeously illustrated coffee-table book exploring the incredible diversity of Madagascar's rainforests, while *Lords and Lemurs* by Alison Jolly (Houghton Mifflin, 2004) focuses primarily on Berenty and the southeast region.

In 2011, the BBC Natural History Unit produced a stunning nature documentary, simply called *Madagascar*, in four one-hour parts. It is available on DVD and Blu-ray.

Lemurs and other mammals

The definitive field guide to lemurs is *Lemurs of Madagascar* by Russell Mittermeier et al (Conservation International, 3rd ed, 2010). It is extremely comprehensive, but weighing in at 1.4kg is not very portable. Thankfully Conservation International also produces some laminated pamphlets in their *Pocket Guide Series* illustrating each species and showing its distribution. A more general guide to the mammals, including tenrecs, bats, rodents and carnivores as well as lemurs, is *Mammals of Madagascar: A Complete Guide* by Nick Garbutt (A&C Black, 2007) in which photographs of almost all species appear.

Gerald Durrell's tale of visiting Madagascar to collect aye-ayes for Jersey Zoo, *The Aye-aye and I* (Harper Collins, 1992 and Summersdale, 2008) is an enjoyable read with plenty of humour.

Birds

There are two birding field guides by Ian Sinclair and Olivier Langrand. The first (*Birds of the Indian Ocean Islands*; Struik, 1999) is the most user friendly with excellent illustrations and maps but no photos. The other (*A Photographic Guide to the Birds of the Indian Ocean Islands*; Struik, 2006) has bilingual English/French text and photos instead of illustrations, but does not cover all species. There are also two more detailed hardback field guides but both are now out of print and harder to find: *Guide to the Birds of Madagascar* by Olivier Langrand (Yale, 1990) has illustrations and distribution maps, while *Birds of Madagascar* by Peter Morris and Frank Hawkins (Pica Press, 1999) has photos but no maps. The British Library released a CD featuring recordings of the calls of 127 species (*Bird Sounds of Madagascar* by Frank Hawkins and Richard Ranft, 2007). More difficult to find and considerably more expensive is the four-CD set *Oiseaux de Madagascar, Mayotte, Comores, Seychelles, Réunion, Maurice* by Pierre Huguet and Claude Chappuis (SEOF, 2003) which includes 327 species.

Frogs and reptiles

For herps, there is only one universally respected identification book: *Field Guide to the Amphibians and Reptiles of Madagascar* by Frank Glaw and Miguel Vences (self-published by the authors, 2007). This is another of those 'field' guides that is too big to be used practically in the field. At a little over 1.4kg, you might be better leaving it at home and identifying the species from your photographs after you get back.

Conservation International's *Pocket Guide Series* includes laminated identification pamphlets *Frogs of Madagascar: Genus Mantella* (2008) and *Turtles and Tortoises of Madagascar and Adjacent Indian Ocean Islands* (2008).

Botanical guides

The publishing arm of Royal Botanic Gardens, Kew, has produced a range of excellent (though fairly pricey) books on Malagasy flora, including: *Field Guide to the Orchids of Madagascar* by Phillip Cribb and Johan Hermans (2009), *Field Guide to the Palms of Madagascar* by John Dransfield et al (2006), *The Leguminosae of Madagascar* by David du Puy et al (2001), *Generic Tree Flora of Madagascar* by George E Schatz (2001) and *Atlas of the Vegetation of Madagascar* by Justin Moat and Paul Smith (2007).

Published in two large hardback volumes, *Succulent and Xerophytic Plants of Madagascar* by Werner Rauh (Strawberry Press, 1995/1998) is a great work clearly born of a passion for the plants of the dry south.

The Remarkable Baobab (Weidenfeld & Nicolson, 2004) by the author of the bestselling *Remarkable Trees of the World*, Thomas Pakenham, tells the engaging story of the *Adansonia* genus, six out of eight species of which live exclusively in Madagascar.

History, people and culture

Sir Mervyn Brown's *History of Madagascar* (Tunnacliffe, 1996) is the most accurate, comprehensive and readable of the histories, written by a former British ambassador to the country and Britain's foremost expert on the subject. A more recent work, *Madagascar: a Short History* by Solofo Randrianja and Stephen Ellis (Hurst, 2009) covers the years from the island's settlement up to 2002.

The fascinating and bizarre tale of the reign of Queen Ranavalona I – sometimes known as the Wicked Queen or Ranavalona the Cruel – is told in *Female Caligula: Ranavalona, the Mad Queen of Madagascar* by Keith Laidler (John Wiley, 2005). An equally absorbing historical account follows an archaeological team's search for evidence of the shipwrecked Englishman Robert Drury (see page 000): *In Search of the Red Slave* by Mike Parker Pearson and Karen Godden (Sutton Publishing, 2002) reads like a whodunit, but is equally interesting as a portrait of the Tandroy people. Drury's original 1729 book, which goes by the lengthy title of *Madagascar: or Robert Drury's Journal During Fifteen Years' Captivity on that Island*, is now available as a print-on-demand paperback from numerous reprint publishers.

For those interested in *fady* and other Malagasy cultural beliefs, the most detailed book is *Taboo: a Study of Malagasy Customs and Beliefs* (Oslo University Press/George Allen & Unwin, 1960) by Norwegian Lutheran missionary Jørgen Ruud. Copies of a more recent paperback reprint by Humanities Press can be found for sale in Tana.

Language

If you would like to learn a little Malagasy then Janie Rasoloson's *Malagasy-English/English-Malagasy Dictionary and Phrasebook* (Hippocrene, 2001) is a handy pocket gude. If you speak French, then a very compact and neatly presented alternative is the French–Malagasy phrasebook *Le Malgache de Poche* by Helena Ravoson Voahanginirina and Narivelo Rajaonarimanana (Assimil, 2004).

The downloadable audiobook *Rhythms Easy Malagasy* (EuroTalk, 2011) is a one-hour crash course from which you can learn some basic words. In a similar vein, *Learn Malagasy* (EuroTalk, 2008) is an interactive speaking and listening programme for PC/Mac aimed at teaching essential words and phrases to beginners.

Maps

Numerous cartographic publishers produce small-scale folded road maps of Madagascar, but detailed regional maps are almost impossible to find outside the country. For these you will need to visit FTM in Antananarivo or order from their website (Ⓦ www.ftm.mg) but be prepared for international delivery to take many weeks. Their main products include 1:500,000 maps (a set of 11 covers the whole country), 1:100,000 (set of 479) and 1:10,000 street plans of the main towns.

Cuisine

Mankafy Sakafo: Delicious Meals from Madagascar by Jill A Donenfeld (iUniverse, 2007) is perhaps the only English-language book of Malagasy recipes. In French there are *La Cuisine de Madagascar* (Editions Orphie G Doyen, 1992) and *Cuisine Malgache, Cuisine Creole* (Librairie de Madagascar, 1997), and in German *Essen Wie auf Madagascar* (Th Gut Verlag, 2006). For video recipes see Ⓦ www.youtube.com/lemurbaby.

Index

Index

First edition published July 2012
Bradt Travel Guides Ltd
IDC House, The Vale, Chalfont St Peter, Bucks SL9 9RZ, England
www.bradtguides.com
Published in the USA by The Globe Pequot Press Inc,
PO Box 480, Guilford, Connecticut 06437-0480

Text copyright © 2012 Daniel Austin and Hilary Bradt
Maps copyright © 2012 Bradt Travel Guides Ltd
Photographs copyright © 2012 Individual photographers (see below)
Project Managers: Daniel Austin and Anna Moores

ISBN: 978 1 84162 425 9

British Library Cataloguing in Publication Data
A catalogue record for this book is available from the British Library

Photographs
J W Alker/imagebroker/Alamy (JWA); Daniel Austin (DA); Pierre-Yves Babelon/Alamy (PYB/A); Pierre-Yves Babelon (PYB); Paul Bertner (PB); Didier Bier (DB); Sabena Jane Blackbird/Alamy (SJB); Laszlo Bolgar (LB); Janice Booth (JB); Fernanda C Gil Cardoso (FCGC); Emmanuel Dinh (ED); Reinhard Dirscherl/Alamy (RD); François Dorothé (FD); Leonora Enking (LE); Steve Evans (SE); Salym Fayad (SF); Augustine Fou (AF); Safiye Aybike Göcek (SAG); Vincent Grafhorst/Minden Pictures/FLPA (VG); Laurent Heroux (LH); John Hyde/Alaska Stock/Alamy (JH); Imperial War Museum (IWM); Michaël Jacobs (MJ); Harriet Joao (HJ); Frans Lanting Studio/Alamy (FL); Chad Lebo (CL); Karl Lehmann/LP Images/Alamy (KL); Madagascar Library (ML); Chris Mattison/FLPA (CM); Hannah McNeish (HM); NH53 (NH); Oledoe (OD); Massimo Pacifico/Tips Images/Tips Italia Srl a socio unico/Alamy (MP); Andry Pertignat (AP); Hery Zo Rakotondramanana (HZR); Haja Rasambainarivo (HR); Cyril Ruoso/Minden Pictures/FLPA (CR); Mark Scherz (MS); Tambako (TJ); Frank Vassen (FV); Chris Willis (CW)

Front cover (clockwise) Boy with bananas (DA); Grandidier's baobabs (VG); Panther chameleon (CM); Ring-tailed lemurs (CR)
Back cover Carved *aloalo* (DA); Diademed sifaka (DA)
Title page Eastern grey bamboo lemur (DA); Beach near Anjajavy (DA); Girls at Mahasoa (DA)
Page 29 images 1–4 (DA); image 5 (DB)
Part & chapter openers
Page 1: Hotel Ony bungalow (DA); Page 2: Boy with spear (SE); Page 3: 1555 map of Madagascar (ML); Page 25: Coquerel's sifaka (DA); Page 63: Silhouetted tourist (DA); Page 86: 'PK' milestone (DA); Page 87: Tour bus *en route* to Berenty (DA); Page 103: Panther chameleon (DA); Page 104: Jacaranda flower (HZR); Page 104: Taxis in Antananarivo (HZR); Page 105: *Rova* (queen's palace) (HZR); Page 129: Dirt road near Andringitra (SF); Page 168: Sifaka on octopus trees (MS); Page 169: Ring-tailed lemur (DA); Page 178: Madagascar giant day gecko (FD); Page 179: Turquoise waters of the northwest (FCGC); Page 204: *Furcifer lateralis* chameleon (DA); Page 205: Baobab Avenue (DA); Page 222: Leaf-tailed gecko (FV); Page 223: Pier on Ile Ste Marie (DA)

Maps David McCutcheon

Typeset and designed from the author's disc by
Nicola Erdpresser ® www.designcreateinnovate.co.uk

Production managed by Jellyfish Print Solutions; printed in India